Critical Perspectives on Canadian Theatre in English

General Editor Ric Knowles

2005

Aboriginal Drama and Theatre
ed. Rob Appleford
volume one
978-0-88754-792-8

African-Canadian Theatre
ed. Maureen Moynagh
volume two
978-0-88754-794-2

Judith Thompson
ed. Ric Knowles
volume three
978-0-88754-796-6

2006

Feminist Theatre and Performance
ed. Susan Bennett
volume four
978-0-88754-798-0

George F. Walker
ed. Harry Lane
volume five
978-0-88754-800-0

Theatre in British Columbia
ed. Ginny Ratsoy
volume six
978-0-88754-802-4

2007

Queer Theatre in Canada
ed. Rosalind Kerr
volume seven
978-0-88754-804-8

Environmental and Site-Specific Theatre
ed. Andrew Houston
volume eight
978-0-88754-806-2

Space and the Geographies of Theatre
ed. Michael McKinnie
volume nine
978-0-88754-808-6

2008

Sharon Pollock
ed. Sherrill Grace & Michelle La Flamme
volume ten
978-0-88754-751-5

Theatre in Alberta
ed. Anne Nothof
volume eleven
978-0-88754-753-9

Collective Creation, Collaboration and Devising
ed. Bruce Barton
volume twelve
978-0-88754-755-3

2009

Theatre Histories
ed. Alan Filewod
volume thirteen
978-0-88754-831-4

"Ethnic," Multicultural, and Intercultural Theatre
ed. Ric Knowles & Ingrid Mündel
volume fourteen
978-0-88754-832-1

Design and Scenography
ed. Natalie Rewa
volume fifteen
978-0-88754-833-8

2010

Theatre in Atlantic Canada
ed. Linda Burnett
volume sixteen
978-0-88754-890-1

Popular Political Theatre and Performance
ed. Julie Salverson
volume seventeen
978-0-88754-891-8

Canadian Shakespeare
ed. Susan Knutson
volume eighteen
978-0-88754-893-2

2011

Community Engaged Theatre and Performance
ed. Julie Salverson
volume nineteen
978-0-88754-932-8

Solo Performance
ed. Jenn Stephenson
volume twenty
978-0-88754-933-5

Theatre and Performance in Toronto
ed. Laura Levin
volume twenty-one
978-0-88754-934-2

PLAYWRIGHTS CANADA PRESS

Critical Perspectives on Canadian Theatre in English
volume three

Judith Thompson

Edited by Ric Knowles

Playwrights Canada Press
Toronto • Canada

First edition: May 2005

Playwrights Canada Press
202-269 Richmond Street West, Toronto, Ontario M5V 1X1
416-703-0013 • info@playwrightscanada.com • www.playwrightscanada.com

Cover image: Jin-me Yoon, *between departure and arrival*, 1996/1997. Partial installation view, Art Gallery of Ontario. Video projection, video montage on monitor, photographic mylar scroll, clocks with 3-D lettering, audio. Dimensions variable. Courtesy of the artist and Catriona Jeffries Gallery, Vancouver.
Production Editor/Cover Design: JLArt

Library and Archives Canada Cataloguing in Publication

Judith Thompson / edited by Ric Knowles.

(Critical perspectives on Canadian theatre in English ; v. 3)
Includes bibliographical references.
ISBN 978-0-88754-796-6

1. Thompson, Judith, 1954- --Criticism and interpretation.
I. Knowles, Ric

PS8589.H4883Z73 2005 C812'.54 C2005-902779-7

We acknowledge the financial support of the Canada Council for the Arts, the Ontario Arts Council (OAC), the Ontario Media Development Corporation, and the Government of Canada for our publishing activities.

Canada Council for the Arts Conseil des arts du Canada

ONTARIO ARTS COUNCIL
CONSEIL DES ARTS DE L'ONTARIO
an Ontario government agency
un organisme du gouvernement de l'Ontario

Canada

Ontario
Ontario Media Development Corporation

To

Christine

Table of Contents

General Editor's Preface

Critical Perspectives on Canadian Theatre in English sets out to make the best critical and scholarly work in the field readily available to teachers, students, and scholars of Canadian drama and theatre. In volumes organized by playwright, region, genre, theme, and cultural community, the series publishes the work of scholars and critics who have, since the so-called renaissance of Canadian theatre in the late 1960s and early 1970s, traced the coming-into-prominence of a vibrant theatrical community in English Canada.

Each volume in the series is edited and introduced by an expert in the field who has selected a representative sampling of the most important critical work on her or his subject since circa 1970, ordered chronologically according to the original dates of publication. Where appropriate, the volume editors have also commissioned new essays on their subjects. Each volume also provides a list of suggested further readings, and an introduction by the volume's editor.

It is my hope that this series, working together with complementary anthologies of plays published by Playwrights Canada Press, Talonbooks, and other Canadian drama publishers, will facilitate the teaching of Canadian drama and theatre in schools, colleges, and universities across the country for years to come. It is for this reason that the titles so far selected for the series—*Aboriginal Drama and Theatre, African-Canadian Theatre, Judith Thompson, George F. Walker, Theatre in British Columbia, Feminist Theatre and Performance, Space and the Geographies of Theatre, Environmental and Site Specific Theatre,* and *Queer Theatre*—are designed to work as companion volumes to a range of Canadian drama anthologies recently published or forthcoming from the country's major drama publishers that complement them: *Staging Coyote's Dream: An Anthology of First Nations Drama in English* (Playwrights Canada, 2003); the two volumes of *Testifyin': Contemporary African Canadian Drama* (Playwrights Canada, 2000, 2003); *Judith Thompson: Late 20th Century Plays* (Playwrights Canada, 2002); the various collections of plays by George F. Walker published by Talonbooks; *Playing the Pacific Province: An Anthology of British Columbia Plays, 1967-2000* (Playwrights Canada, 2001), and other projected volumes. I hope that with the combined availability of these anthologies and the volumes in this series, courses on a variety of aspects of Canadian drama and theatre will flourish in schools and universities within Canada and beyond its borders, and scholars new to the field will find accessible and comprehensive introductions to some of the field's most provocative and intriguing figures and issues.

Finally, the titles selected for *Critical Perspectives on Canadian Theatre in English* are designed to carve out both familiar and new areas of work. It is my intention that the series at once recognize the important critical heritage of scholarly work in the field and attempt to fill in its most significant gaps by highlighting important work from and about marginalized communities, work that has too often been neglected in courses on and criticism of Canadian drama and theatre. In its nationalist phase in the late 1960s and 70s, English-Canadian theatre criticism tended to neglect work by women, by First Nations peoples and people of colour, by Gay, Lesbian, Bi- or Trans-sexual artists, and by those working in politically, geographically, or aesthetically alternative spaces. While respecting, honouring, and representing important landmarks in Canadian postcolonial theatrical nationalism, *Critical Perspectives on Canadian Theatre in English* also sets out to serve as a corrective to its historical exclusions.

Ric Knowles

Acknowledgements

Scholarship is always collaborative, and never more so than in a project of this kind. I'd like, then, to thank all those who have written about the work of Judith Thompson over the years, those who have generously allowed their work to be included here, those others (including interviewers) whose work is not included in this volume but has informed all of our thinking, and those many reviewers who are only occasionally acknowledged in these pages but who have so often provided the first published responses to the plays on which subsequent scholarship has built.

I also wish to acknowledge the diligent work of two research assistants, Corrie Hodgson and Robyn Read, who have been invaluable in putting this volume together, and to thank Bruce Barton and his staff at *Theatre Research in Canada/Recherches théâtrales au Canada* for their generous co-operation on our venture of almost-simultaneous publication of two of the essays included here. Angela Rebeiro cannot be thanked too often for her constant, long-standing, and ongoing support of Canadian drama and theatre, and specifically here for going out on a limb with the series in which this is one of the first volumes. Finally, of course, I want to thank my colleague at the University of Guelph, Judith Thompson herself, for continuing to astonish us all.

All of the essays included here are published with permission of the copyright holder. George Toles's "'Cause You're the Only One I Want': The Anatomy of Love in the Plays of Judith Thompson," was first published in *Canadian Literature* 118 (Fall '88): 116-35; Robert Nunn's "Spatial Metaphor in the Plays of Judith Thompson" in *Theatre History in Canada/Histoire du théâtre au Canada* 10.1 (Spring 1989): 3-29; Julie Adam's "The Implicated Audience: Judith Thompson's Anti-Naturalism in *The Crackwalker*, *White Biting Dog*, *I Am Yours*, and *Lion in the Streets*" in *Women on the Canadian Stage: The Legacy of Hrotsvit*, ed. Rita Much (Winnipeg: Blizzard, 1992), 21-29; Jen Harvie's "Constructing Fictions of an Essential Reality *or* 'This Pickshur is Niiiice': Judith Thompson's *Lion in the Streets*," in *Theatre Research in Canada/Recherches théâtrales au Canada* 13. 1-2 (Spring/Fall 1992): 81-93; Sherrill Grace's "Going North on Judith Thompson's *Sled*," in *Essays in Theatre /Études théâtrales* 16.2 (May 1998): 153-64; Craig Stewart Walker's "Judith Thompson: Social Psychomachia," in *The Buried Astrolabe: Canadian Dramatic Imagination and Western Tradition* (Montreal and Kingston: McGill-Queen's UP, 2001), 394-411; Claudia Barnett's "Judith Thompson's Ghosts: The Revenants That Haunt the Plays," in *Canadian Theatre Review* 114 (Spring 2003): 33-37;

Penny Farfan's "Monstrous History: Judith Thompson's *Sled*" and Dalbir Singh's "Staging the Post-Colonial Monster in Judith Thompson's *Capture Me*" in *Canadian Theatre Review* 120 (Fall 2004): 46-49 and 43-45; and Robyn Read's "Who is the Stranger?: The Role of the Monstrous in Judith Thompson's *Capture Me*," and Laura Levin's "Environmental Affinities: Naturalism and the Porous Body," in *Theatre Research in Canada/Recherches théâtrales au Canada* 24.1-2 (Spring 2003 [first published in 2005]). Kim Solga's "Building an Ethical Architecture: Judith Thompson's *Habitat* and the Shape of Radical Humanism" was commissioned for this volume and is published here for the first time.

Introduction: Judith Thompson in Criticism

by Ric Knowles

It has been twenty-five years since Judith Thompson's first play, *The Crackwalker*, changed the face of Canadian Theatre. The play now appears in major international anthologies and receives major international productions, as do others of Thompson's corpus of—as this volume goes to press—eight full-length stage plays (*The Crackwalker, White Biting Dog, I Am Yours, Lion in the Streets, Sled, Perfect Pie, Habitat*, and *Capture Me*), and dozens of shorter works for the stage, screenplays, radio plays, and filmscripts.

It has been seventeen years since George Toles published the first major scholarly article on Thompson, "'Cause You're the Only One I Want": The Anatomy of Love in the Plays of Judith Thompson," reprinted here.[1] Toles's article initiated a minor scholarly industry on Judith Thompson, whose work, according to my own informal survey, has been the subject of more MA theses, PhD dissertations, scholarly chapters, articles, and interviews than that of any other Canadian playwright, with the possible and partial exceptions of Sharon Pollock and George F. Walker. Playwrights Canada Press will publish a collection of Thompson's own writings and interviews about her work in 2006, but for now, this book publishes what I take to be a representative sampling—by no means complete—of critical writings about her plays, covering what might be regarded as the dominant critical tradition on her work, together with some new and exciting initiatives by younger scholars that respond to new (and exciting) directions in Thompson's own work.

Toles's article, which remains one of the most influential pieces of writing about Thompson, focuses on *The Crackwalker, White Biting Dog* (which Toles felt at that time was her finest play), and *I Am Yours*. The article anticipates two major strands in subsequent criticism. Beginning with the observation that "perhaps the most distinctive, and consistent, quality of her characters is their lack of a public, social self that monitors and limits the exposure of the private self," and considering Thompson in the context of the Christian fiction of Flannery O'Connor and the ethical humanism of Paul Ricouer, Toles probes the unconscious of the plays' characters in ways that anticipate later psychoanalytic readings. At the same time, however, he explores the ineffable presence of what he calls the "'non-personal' reality of grace" in the plays:

> The characters dream of a structure secure enough to hold them in check, and, at a deeper level, of a power comparable to grace which will deliver them from the "thing" that possesses them.

"The formation of a soul, in Thompson's world," Toles argues, "depends on a moment of pristine clarity when one's whole being assents, for the first time knowing what ethical choice involves, either to good or to evil."

At the time he was writing Toles felt the need to argue for the quality of Thompson's work, concluding his article with the claim that "[s]he may well be Canada's best playwright." A year later, Robert Nunn opened his article, "Spatial Metaphor in the Plays of Judith Thompson," with a similar claim. Like Toles, he focused on the three then extant Thompson plays—*The Crackwalker*, *White Biting Dog*, and *I Am Yours*—and like Toles he approached the work through dream and the unconscious. But Nunn's starting point was the psychoanalytic work of Sigmund Freud and (especially) Jacques Lacan, and the ways in which Thompson's explorations of psychic space—consciousness and the unconscious, surface and depth, interior and exterior—have been metaphorically mapped onto both the social structure of the action and the stage settings for productions of the plays. His focus is on the cracks and fissures in the psychic and social surfaces, the eruptions that seep or explode through them, and the ways in which those fissures are invaded, penetrated, breached, and represented spatially on stage. Nunn's article has been the most frequently cited critical account of Thompson's work, its insights have been confirmed in a number of interviews with the playwright, and it serves as the background for later psycho-analytic critiques, particularly those by Cynthia Zimmerman and by Nunn himself in two important subsequent articles ("Strangers," "Crackwalking"). Nunn's article grounds virtually all of the essays published here, its richness feeding a variety of subsequent approaches, including approaches to many plays that had not been written at the time of its publication.

Julie Adam's 1992 essay, "The Implicated Audience: Judith Thompson's Anti-Naturalism in *The Crackwalker*, *White Biting Dog*, *I Am Yours* and *Lion in the Streets*," extends Nunn's work in a way that focuses neither on the psychoanalytical nor the social; rather it uses audience response criticism to frame its insights. Citing Nunn's analysis of spatial metaphors and the plays' "images of rupture and seepage," Adam argues that the plays also present a disturbing anti-naturalistic "seepage from stage into auditorium," an energy exchange between the audience and the performer that is central to the plays' theatricalism and that implicates the audience in the plays' action. Although she cites Brecht, and acknowledges Thompson's careful plotting of class and social positioning, Adam's focus is on the plays less as social or political commentary or intervention than as "universal" statements about human nature. She argues, for example, that "[t]he wars Mercy, Mack and Dee wage [in *I Am Yours*] are not class or gender wars, but wars against the abyss, their personal darkness that threatens to engulf them. The class war is just one concrete manifestation [...] of this more abstract and universal war." The argument is convincing, but it is perhaps telling that Adam does not include in this account the much more explicitly and necessarily class-based battles of Toi and his mother, the erstwhile Pegs, who have less leisure to consider any more abstract, personal abyss.

But the social dimension of Thompson's work, and specifically the social construction of identity, or "subjectivity," pointed to but not fully explored in Nunn's "Spatial Metaphors" article, has been the subject of a number of subsequent publications, including Jen Harvie's important 1992 essay, "Constructing Fictions of an Essential Reality, *Or* 'This Pickshur is Niiiice': Judith Thompson's *Lion in the Streets*," reprinted here, and much of my own work on Thompson (e.g. Knowles, "Achievement," "Dramaturgy"). Harvie's article, the first to focus on a single Judith Thompson play, was also the first major effort to grapple with Thompson's work through a feminist lens. Drawing on feminist "standpoint theory" and the work of Susan Bordo, Harvie argues that "*Lion in the Streets* constructs necessary but provisional fictions of reality"—that it recognizes the lived, very real material "realities" of gendered identities, while also recognizing that gender itself is constructed, a function of history rather than nature. "This allows," she argues, "that some concept of a static or essential reality may be helpful to a project of cultural emancipation, but also that such a concept should be considered provisional, and in that sense fictional, so that reality may furthermore be seen as not intractable but open to change." In a later, and equally important article not reprinted here, "(Im)Possibility: Fantasy and Judith Thompson's Drama," Harvie linked feminist with psychoanalytical readings of Thompson, directly taking into account for the first time the fundamental question of *desire* in Thompson's plays up to and including *Lion in the Streets*. Drawing on the psychoanalytic theory of Jean Laplanche and Jean-Bertrand Pontalis as applied in feminist and cultural criticism, Harvie argues in this 1996 essay that a complex awareness of the ambiguity of desire, of subjectivity as unfixed and shifting, of the individual's position at the border of the conscious and unconscious, and of fantasy's simultaneous articulation of unconscious desire and its simultaneous prohibition, illuminates not only the apparently divided subjectivity of Thompson's characters, but also the divided responses—the fantasies—of her audiences: "pleasure, in fantasy, lies in the setting out not in the having of objects," and the culmination of a fantasy/desire may rest in *choosing* to believe. In this argument Harvie not only extends the audience-response critique of Adam, but also addresses in a sophisticated way one of the central cruces in Thompson criticism: the question of to what extent, and for whom, Thompson's redemptive conclusions—her characters' or audiences' achievements of grace—can be taken at face value.

Not all feminist critiques have been favourably disposed to the cultural work performed by Thompson's plays. In a 1991 essay not reprinted here, "Who Speaks? Representations of Native Women in Some Canadian Plays," Susan Bennett cites the figure of Theresa in *The Crackwalker* as one among many representations of First Nations women in Canadian plays that she feels are appropriative. Sherrill Grace's 1998 essay, "Going North on Thompson's *Sled*," published here, the second full-length article on the play (following Robert Nunn's 1996 essay "Strangers to Ourselves: Judith Thompson's *Sled*," based on a pre-publication production draft), is concerned with the play's "discursive formation of 'North'," the North's place within Canadian culture, and the ways in which Canadianness is thereby gendered.[2] What, she asks, for the play and the culture, does "going North" *mean?* What does it mean in this play? One thing it means, it seems, is that Thompson has moved from searing, intricate explorations of individual psyches to carving out anatomies of the nation that are epic in scale, but fundamentally conservative—or culturally affirmative—in impact. "In *Sled*," Grace argues, Thompson "tries to create her image of Canada, from its assumed beginnings to its present precarious position as a nation at the end of the twentieth century"—however much that national vision, as Grace notes, revolves metonymically and metaphorically around Toronto. Grace argues that in *Sled* Thompson establishes a binary that "is gendered along the most conventional lines [...]: North = wilderness, mystery, otherness, and the feminine; South = civilization, familiar norms and social reality, and the masculine." She also argues that the south, "for all its negative aspects, remains the centre of the action," while the north [serves] as a function of the southern imaginary and as an obscure object of southern, urban desire for the Other, without which it cannot survive." Ultimately, she argues, the play reinscribes, almost in spite of itself, a binary logic, and "as a consequence, [Thompson's] attempt to empower women, and a part-Cree woman at that, reinscribes both the feminine and the native as the silent/silenced Other in a binary dominated by the kind of white, heterosexual masculinity critiqued in the play."

But not all feminists share Grace's perspective. In her afterword to the published script of *Sled*[3] Ann Wilson engages the play's representation of gendered violence, female subjectivity, and "the [gendered] problem of spectatorship" viewed from a different angle than in Julie Adam's article, and finds in the play an "exploration of men 'crowding' around women and the resulting negation of the female voice, the desires which it speaks and the fraught negotiation of the female subject to live in the face of this negation" (127).[3] Penny Farfan, in a recent (2004) article reprinted here that draws on the work of Freud and Cathy Caruth, engages with the violence tackled by Wilson, the "epic vision of contemporary Canada" to which Grace points, and in particular to the psychoanalytic theory deployed by Robert Nunn in his three articles on Thompson, but she focuses most specifically on "the history that has shaped" the contemporary condition, "the violent displacements that have constituted Canada's history of conquest, colonization, immigration, and assimilation." These displacements resurface in the play as a "return of the repressed," evoking, though not explicitly, the psychoanalytic postcolonial criticism of Franz Fanon. "In Thompson's postcolonial history play," Farfan argues, *pace* Sherrill Grace, "the Canadian wilderness is not the land itself but the traumatized psyches of the people who occupy a landscape marked by a violent history of conquest, displacement, rupture, and loss."

> In bringing to the stage the repressed past traumas that continue to shape present experience within a settler-invader nation such as Canada, Thompson contributes to the ongoing postcolonial project of challenging hegemonic representations of history.

Farfan's essay first appeared in the same issue of *Canadian Theatre Review* as Dalbir Singh's "Staging the Post-Colonial Monster in Judith Thompson's *Capture Me*," reprinted here, which looks at Thompson's most recent play as this volume goes to press, the darkly disturbing "stalker" play, *Capture Me*. Like

Farfan, Singh reads the play through a postcolonialist lens, but in this case he reverses the anticipated "othering" of the marginalized subject, and finds monstrosity in the figure of the dominant white male, who is "othered" by the play's discourses of subjection. Singh's essay is one of two recent articles on *Capture Me* by young scholars—students of Thompson—who worked with her on the Tarragon Theatre workshop of the play and its premiere production. The other, Robyn Read's 2005 essay, "Who is the Stranger? The Role of the Monstrous in Judith Thompson's *Capture Me*," also included here, draws on Margrit Shildrick's *Embodying the Monster: Encounters with the Vulnerable Self*, to reflect on the monstrous in the play, not as other, but as "a mirror of humanity." She analyses the permeable borders, interdependencies and relationships among three figures in the play—the monster, the foreign figure, and the mother—citing Thompson's own assertion that *Capture Me* is "about becoming what we most fear." Tracing the links between acting, writing, teaching, and transmogrification into the realm of the monstrous—all of which involve "the moment when each of us transcends our human-ness"—Read explores the ways in which *Capture Me* poses difficult questions about society's "Othering" of the monstrous rather than understanding it as, for better and for worse, a necessary part of being human.

Marc Maufort, in a chapter (not reprinted here) from his book *Transgressive Itineraries: Postcolonial Hybridizations of Dramatic Realism*, taking a broad view of Thompson's *oeuvre* up to and including *Sled*, also focuses on the Other inside the self (the subsection of the book in which this selection appears is entitled "Staging Otherness"). But Maufort calls this Otherness, in an apparently non-postcolonialist, modernist articulation, "man's [sic] self-alientation […] his innate Otherness" (28), and he argues that the characters' confrontations with their selves as Other are achieved through magic realism's conflation of several realms of experience. Using European critic Jeanne Delbaere's categories, he traces a shift in Thompson's reliance on magic realism from the "psychic," through the "grotesque," to (in *Sled*) the "mythic."

In her 2003 essay reprinted here, "Judith Thompson's Ghosts: The Revenants That Haunt the Plays," Claudia Barnett, takes as her examples *The Crackwalker*, *Lion in the Streets*, *Perfect Pie*, and *Sled*. Like Maufort, she deals with the ways in which Thompson's plays exceed realism, in her case focussing on their ghosts. Drawing on the work of Judith Butler and (especially) Peggy Phelan, Barnett traces the connections between ghosts and theatre, between corporeality and the incorporeal, between reality and memory, between life and death. Thompson's ghosts, she notes, "try to improve the lives of the living—not only the living characters within the plays, but also the live audiences who observe them." She argues that Isobel in *Lion in the Streets*, Annie Delaney in *Sled*, and Marie/Francesca in *Perfect Pie*, revenants all, achieve a material reality through their impact on the living, even as all dramatic characters achieve material reality through their impact on their audiences. And the lesson each of them teaches—"the lesson taught by all of Thompson's ghosts"—is, in Isobel's words, the last words in *Lion in the Streets*, to "take your life. I want you all to have your life."

The most extensive treatment of Thompson's *oeuvre* to date—too extensive to reproduce here in its entirety—is Craig Walker's long chapter, "Judith Thompson: Social Psychomachia," in his book *The Buried Astrolabe: Canadian Dramatic Imagination and Western Tradition*, where Thompson is considered, together with James Reaney, Michael Cook, Sharon Pollock, Michel Tremblay, and George F. Walker, to be one of "six of the country's most important contemporary playwrights" (vii). The portion of Walker's chapter reprinted here focuses primarily on work by Thompson that has otherwise received little critical attention: the radio and stage versions of *Tornado*; the radio plays *White Sand* and *Stop Talking Like That*; the short, monologue version of *Perfect Pie* and its later, full-length, four-character development for the stage; *Off the 401*, written to be performed as part of the multi-authored *Stolen Lands* and published in *Canadian Theatre Review*'s special issue on Thompson; and finally, the full-length *Sled*, Thompson's most recent play at the time of Walker's writing. In this selection and throughout his discussion of Thompson and her fellow Canadian playwrights Walker is concerned with continuities between the work and "Western tradition," understood broadly and variably to include post-enlightenment philosophy, psychoanalysis, theology, art, literature, and and the history of ideas, but occasionally coalescing into what he calls "the best of European culture" (6). He concludes his discussion of *Sled*, his chapter on Thompson, and his entire volume with a consideration of the eschatology of *Sled*, which in its workshop draft was entitled *Last Things* ("a reference to the four last things comprised by eschatological thought: death, judgment, heaven, and hell"):

> The confrontation of these last things occurs within each of us as we go, through an encounter with the inner life. And to transcend the barrier between our conscious selves and these four last things hidden deep within marks the first step towards transcending the barriers between us and our fellow human beings.

Walker's deeply humanist conclusion to his argument is based on his own, and what he considers to be Thompson's indebtedness to the Western liberal humanist tradition. The last two essays in this volume, less comfortable perhaps with the taken-for-granteds of Walker's "us" and with the legacies of that tradition, nevertheless share Walker's concern with overcoming barriers between people(s). Both of these essays concern themselves with locating Thompson's work within recent efforts to extend, problematize, and radicalize liberal humanism, shifting their analyses into the realm of what is coming to be known as a "radical" or "ethical humanism" that tries to de-centre Europe, its cultural assumptions, and its patriarchal and colonizing histories.

Laura Levin's recent (2005) essay, "Environmental Affinities: Naturalism and the Porous Body," argues that Thompson's plays extend and radicalize the naturalist aesthetic that is usually either associated with or explicitly dissociated from Thompson. This is accomplished in part, she argues, through the use of visual form in ways that link naturalism with surrealism in the reconnecting of human with environment, figure with ground. Levin's article can be read in part, once again, as an outgrowth of Robert Nunn's work on spatial metaphor, which she cites. But she also extends that work by drawing out the gendered and classed implications of spatial relationship in the plays and arguing that "Thompson presents the interpolation of self into setting as politically and ethically enabling":

> Ultimately, it is this intrinsic spatial dependency that serves as a basis for the radical ethics opened up by Thompson's work. This environmental relation is not predicated upon individualistic self-delineation and Cartesian self-possession. Rather, following the explorations of naturalist and surrealist artists, it embraces the possibilities of breaking down divisions between body and external world. Using a dramatic form that often pits the individual in antagonistic relation to its environment, Thompson re-figures the naturalist character as a being that is sensuously linked to the bodies of its neighbors.

Kim Solga's "Building an Ethical Architecture: Judith Thompson's *Habitat* and the Shape of Radical Humanism" was commissioned for this volume, and is the first full-length article on Thompson's somewhat anomalous play, *Habitat.* The play is anomalous in part because it is the first of Thompson's plays since *The Crackwalker* not to have received its premiere production at Toronto's Tarragon Theatre, having been commissioned by that city's flagship "Regional" theatre, Canadian Stage. It is also anomalous in functioning more directly than any of Thompson's other work as an "issue play"—the issue being the Not-In-My-Backyard syndrome in relation, in this case, to the establishment of a halfway house for troubled youth in the upscale "Mapleview Lanes," a fictional neighborhood that might be understood to represent the habitats of many of Canadian Stage's suburban patrons.

Like Levin, Solga locates *Habitat* within a new "radical ethics" project, but while Levin demonstrates the ways in which Thompson destabilizes figure-ground relationships in order to extend and radicalize naturalism, Solga focuses on a dissatisfaction with subject-object relations in order to extend and radicalize humanism itself. She begins with the play's title, arguing that "[u]nlike a house or even a 'home,' both of which imply security-in-exclusivity framed by closed doors and mediated by private capital, a habitat is a profoundly inclusive, ethical architecture." Where Levin draws on the discourses of contemporary visual arts and finds an enabling intersection of human and environment in Thompson's work, Solga extends the discourses of psychoanalysis and post-structuralism, drawing on the "female ethicists" Luce Irigaray, Kelly Oliver and (like Robyn Read) Margrit Shildrick. She finds an "*intercorporeal architecture*" in *Habitat,* which, like Levin's "interpellation of self into setting," gestures toward a newly ethical, spatialized type of intersubjectivity at work in the play, one that is reliant on touch rather than the objectifications of (scopophilic) vision.

Solga, like Levin and so many other Thompson scholars, draws on Robert Nunn's analysis of spatial metaphor, but she argues that in *Habitat* Thompson goes beyond metaphor: "Framed by a literal land battle—for the shape of a community, for a place for its outcasts—the play poses in real space and real time many of the questions that are latent in Thompson's earlier works: how are we supposed to come to feel, not just *for* one another but *with* one another? (How do we transform condescending sympathy into a genuine encounter with our others, recognized in their proper alterity?)" She argues, ultimately and hopefully, for *Habitat*'s insistence "that an intimate yet respectful physical connection with others is not only possible but essential if we are to build a true habitat – a genuine community"—and that "the air between bodies is not a distance to be revered or to be eliminated; it is exactly what gives us life."

In many ways the ethical, or radical humanist readings provided by Robyn Read, Laura Levin and Kim Solga, together with the postcolonialist and psychoanalytical readings provided by Dalbir Singh and Penny Farfan, return the reader, through the expanding and multiplying lenses of poststructuralist and postmodernist indeterminism, feminism and postcolonialism, to a reconsideration of the profoundly Christian and traditionalist humanism of George Toles, with which this volume began. It is a journey worth taking, in both directions.

Notes

1 This introduction will not provide parenthetical citations or Works Cited listings for essays published in this volume. Other citations, here and throughout the volume, will use MLA style.

2 For an alternative reading of *Sled*'s relationship to history, the nation, and the north considered through the lens of cultural memory, see Tompkins 10-11.

3 Here and throughout this volume references to *Sled* and to Wilson's essay are to the first Playwrights Canada printing of the play, in which Wilson's essay appeared as an Afterword. In subsequent printings her essay served as an Introduction, altering pagination throughout the volume.

4 See also Wilson's discussion of *Lion in the Streets* in her 1995 essay, "The Culture of Abuse." For a very different, cultural-feminist reading, in this case of *White Biting Dog*, see Rudakoff 118-20.

Works Cited

Bennett, Susan. "Who Speaks? Representations of Native Women in Some Canadian Plays." *Canadian Journal of Drama and Theatre* 1.2 (1991): 13-25.

Harvie, Jennifer. "(Im)Possibility: Fantasy and Judith Thompson's Drama." *On-stage and Off-stage: English Canadian Drama in Discourse.* Ed. Albert-Reiner Glaap and Rolf Althof. St John's, Nfld: Breakwater, 1996. 240-56.

Knowles, Ric[hard Paul]. "The Achievement of Grace." *Brick* 41 (Summer 1991): 33-36.

———. "The Dramaturgy of the Perverse." *Theatre Research International* 17.3 (Fall 1992): 226-35.

Maufort, Marc. *Transgressive Itineraries.* New York: Peter Lang, 2003. 27-41.

Nunn, Robert. "Crackwalking: Judith Thompson's Marginal Characters." *Siting the Other: Revisions of Marginality in Australian and English-Canadian Drama.* Ed. Marc Maufort. New York: Peter Lang, 2001. 311-23.

———. "Strangers to Ourselves: Judith Thompson's *Sled.*" *Canadian Theatre Review* 89 (Winter 1996): 29-32.

Rudakoff, Judith. "Under the Goddess's Cloak: recalling the Wild, Engendering the Power." *Women on the Canadian Stage: The Legacy of Hrotsvit.* Ed. Rita Much. Winnipeg: Blizzard Press, 1992. 115-30.

Tompkins, Joanne. "Canadian Theatre and Memorializing." *Canadian Theatre Review* 115 (Summer 2003): 5-11.

Walker, Craig Stewart. *The Buried Astrolabe: Canadian Dramatic Imagination and Western Tradition.* Montreal: Queen's UP, 2001. 355-411.

Wilson, Ann. "'Crowding Round Her': Violence and Female Subjectivity." Afterword. Judith Thompson. *Sled.* Toronto: Playwrights Canada, 1997. 125-30.

———. "The Culture of Abuse in *Under the Skin, This is for you, Anna,* and *Lion in the Streets.*" *Contemporary Issues in Canadian Drama.* Ed. Per Brask. Winnipeg: Blizzard, 1995. 160-70.

Zimmerman, Cynthia. "Judith Thompson: Voices in the Dark." *Playwriting Women: Female Voices in English Canada.* Toronto: Simon & Pierre, 1994. 176-209.

"Cause You're the Only One I Want": The Anatomy of Love in the Plays of Judith Thompson

by George Toles

DEE. Lionel, have some more brandy.
(to Mack) What are you thinking?
MACK. I was thinking... about my father having his heart attack at the top of the stairs... sorry, but it's true, that's what I was thinking, I mean seeing in my brain.
MERCY. He had it at the top of the stairs?
MACK. Yeah. The dog was at the bottom of the stairs and, she went berserk, you know, she was... the mother was in the kitchen, talking on the phone to the aunt, and she... the dog wouldn't let her near him, she wouldn't let the ambulance attendants... they had to... shoot her with one of those sleeping potions, then she had a stroke two days later. You'd go into the house and there was my mother passed out on the couch with a bottle of scotch and this paralyzed dog.... She still can't bark without slurring, really! She's got this slurred bark like when stroke victims talk outa the side of their mouth? *(does bark)*
DEE. She's a sweet dog. Golden Labrador.

—Judith Thompson, *I Am Yours*[1]

In a Judith Thompson play, the question "What are you thinking?" is never an occasion for reticence. Perhaps the most distinctive, and consistent, quality of her characters is their lack of a public, social self that monitors and limits the exposure of the private self. Thompson often establishes, as in the scene from which I've quoted, a familiar social context (friends gathered for after dinner conversation) whose proprieties are generally understood, and then shows one character after another doing violence to decorum as images from their unconscious force their way into speech. Mercy, one of the central characters in *I Am Yours* (1987), asks near the beginning of the play, "Did you ever wake up, well not quite wake up and you can't remember where you are?" All of Thompson's characters know this experience. It is, in fact, the inalterable rhythm of their precarious life in the social realm. They do not, as a rule, wilfully cast off the constraints of their defined social roles, in the manner of the most intriguing figures in farce. It is more a matter of their forgetting themselves, temporarily losing sight of where they are in relation to others and losing hold of whatever sense and order they normally depend on. The effect of this forgetting is beautifully rendered in John Ashbery's poem, "New

Ways of Knowing": "waking up/In the middle of a dream with one's mouth full/Of unknown words…." And then, in Thompson's vision, being compelled to speak those words and take on their emotions as an absolute pre-condition for having memory restored. One cannot reclaim one's place in the world of others until this alien voice has done what it can to bring its own dreadful imperatives to light.

Since there is no one in a Thompson play who is not subject to this kind of seizure, it is possible to be possessed in the presence of others without shocking them. Indeed, at least the *form* of most wild utterance is tolerantly absorbed by those who listen to it: its meaning is seldom fathomed even by the speaker, but this lack of comprehension is typically not a source of distress. In the scene segment with which I began, Mack precedes his entry into the dream space of obsessive speech with an apology to Dee for being honest about what he is thinking, or, as he tries to clarify, "I mean seeing in my brain." This brief, reflex concern with a code of correct behaviour seems very odd in a play where, from the outset, everyone seems equally driven to "go too far" in their speech and actions. In fact, Mack's friends are plainly more struck by his use of the word "sorry" than by the account of his father's (and dog's) heart attack that follows it. Moments after Mack has finished speaking, some brandy gets spilled, and everyone in the group, in a kind of imitative frenzy, cries out "SORRY! Sorry, I'm sorry." They seem to be experimenting, in the protective anonymity of a chorus, with the hypnotic *sound* of remorse, trying to bring the emotion closer as their voices rise, in a situation where there is no necessity to name (or even think about) the acts for which each of them most requires forgiveness. Mercy is openly disturbed by the repetition and asks why everyone is saying sorry. "You'd think we'd all committed a…" The unspoken word, sin, which refers both to real and equally tormenting imagined crimes is the core of the group's inner life, and the motive force of the constant invasion of their thoughts by "waking dreams."

The members of the group see violent agitation and loss of control as regular features of the social landscape. Such proclivities are understood to be *shared*, rather than a shameful and isolating mark of individual mental imbalance. Since circumspection plays so little part in Thompson's public realm, extremes of every sort are accommodated in the flow of the dialogue, and it is only the truly monstrous transgression that can close communication off. The startling spectacle of unfettered instinct running riot in scene after scene is movingly combined, as in the episode I just described, with a vestigial group memory of the traditional function of "limits" and the idea of moral accountability. The characters dream of a structure secure enough to hold them in check, and, at a deeper level, of a power comparable to grace which will deliver them from the "thing" that possesses them.

The comedy which is so prominent in Thompson's work dwells, in large part, on the borderline of madness. It generates an intoxicating aura of false freedom which, in turn, masks a process of enslavement. One would be wrong to conclude that the laughter Thompson's plays invite issues from a perspective rooted in caricature or from a heartless glibness about genuine suffering. Nor does Thompson take her license for inventing comic horrors from the always aesthetically defensible (but too often complacent) despair at being "alive in times like these." There is in her plays no poisonous embrace of vileness as the only condition left for us, with the implicit assumption that the artist is courageous for daring to say so. The nearest modern analogue for Thompson's form of comedy is the fiction of Flannery O'Connor, whose grotesque heroes are always moving, whether they realize it or not, towards "life and death" encounters with evil and grace. Hazel Motes, the preacher in O'Connor's *Wise Blood*, whose inability to rid himself of Christ's haunting image "in the back of his mind" leads him ultimately to blind himself, wrap his chest with barbed wire, and wear shoes filled with rocks and broken glass, could be seen as the prototype for Thompson's equally regressive and deranged seekers after truth. (Mrs. Flood, to Hazel: "There's no reason for it. People have quit doing it." "They ain't quit doing it as long as I'm doing it," he said.) "Freakishness," in Thompson's work as in O'Connor's, is treated as an emblem of our displacement from a condition in which sin, the redemptive value of suffering, and a love distinct from human love are realities—a "light" to see things by. Thompson's comic tone chiefly differs from O'Connor's in its closer alliance with emotion, which O'Connor generally distrusts because of its tendency to palliate the harsh truths that comedy exposes. Given this difference, it is perhaps not surprising that O'Connor's subject matter is always concerned with the mystery of faith, while Thompson is much more interested in the mystery of love.

O'Connor has declared, in her essay "The Grotesque in Southern Fiction," that "when the grotesque is used in a legitimate way, the intellectual and moral judgments implicit in it will have the ascendency over feeling" (O'Connor 43). Violence, to the extent that it is in harmony with O'Connor's comic instincts, is a blunt-edged, summary joke on human vanity. It is a calm "pronouncing of judgment" at the moment when the "very ground" of a character's soul has revealed itself, when the "spiritual lines of motion" are as clearly and sharply drawn as in a "child's drawing." There is a certain degree of "suffering with" in O'Connor's comic observation, but her involvement with her characters is never so strong that she cannot effect a clean break from them as they are lost, beaten, or murdered in their final ordeals. What makes her comic perspective somewhat forbidding is its sudden refusal of flexible response. A door seems to shut, and her initial amused patience with human frailty is on the instant replaced by a severity that accepts no excuses, that appears almost to delight in the righteous scourging of weakness.

Thompson, like O'Connor, manages to keep her concern with spiritual reality available to comedy by focussing primarily on characters who do not know how to *think* ethically. The surrealist behaviour of her characters is meant to erupt on stage with an unreasoning urgency severed from any effort of the moral will: 'life," which Hegel has termed "the kind that does not yet know itself." Even such "pure of heart" figures as Theresa in *The Crackwalker* (1980) and Pony in *White Biting Dog* (1984) maintain what I would call their passive rectitude in a region below conscious reflection. Their goodness dwells apart from their actions, and cannot be defined by reference to them. The rational mind has almost no access to this sort of spontaneous benevolence. It is clearly not the result of a steadily renewed choice to do good rather than evil. Their innocence, strangely combined with promiscuity and simple-mindedness in Theresa's case and an intensifying neurosis in Pony's, can best be understood as a gift for goodness, a grace that preserves the soul from infection, in spite of the frequent deep confusion of their conduct. No pattern of life that ethical conduct might enforce clearly emerges for Thompson's characters. Her comedy, however allied to a spiritual vision, is far less didactic than O'Connor's.

O'Connor's characters typically imagine themselves to be "good country people," and take comfort from the fact that their superiority to the "white trash," "niggers," criminals, and "ugly" folk around them "justifies" them in the eyes of God. O'Connor's dialogue draws much of its astringent humour from the incongruity of the vain and selfish person's assumptions that he is pious; his ostentatious self-approval condemns him every time he speaks, and tightens the noose around his neck. There will always come a moment of "abysmal life-giving knowledge" for this self deceiver: the sky will open, as it does for Mrs. Turpin in "Revelation," so he can be pierced with the realization of what it means to be human, which comes down to the question, "How am I a hog and me both?" Catholic dogma provides a lens for correcting the distortions in O'Connor's characters' hilariously awful pronouncements. But perhaps there is a hidden tendency to pride in the author's always possessing the correcting lens. It would appear that O'Connor herself is never in doubt, however mired in perplexity her characters may be, about what God is looking for. O'Connor claims that the fiction writer "cannot be an adequate observer [of the world] unless he is free from uncertainty about what he sees." But in an adjoining sentence she asserts that "Christian dogma is about the only thing left in the world that surely guards and respects mystery" (O'Connor 178). Any Christian writer would do well, I think, to ponder the implications of this second statement, but I don't feel that she is under any obligation to reconcile it with the arguably opposing requirements of the one preceding it. While it is reasonable to affirm that "open and free observation is founded [for the Christian artist] on our ultimate faith that the universe is meaningful," does the artist not limit the presence of mystery in nature and severely qualify her own acceptance of it if she always has a secure perspective on what she sees, one that *needs* to be free of uncertainty?

***

In the course of a 1987 interview in Toronto (July 23), Thompson was attempting to locate a passage in *White Biting Dog* to illustrate a point she was making when her attention was caught by the stage direction in Act One that instructs Cape to "gag" at the sound of his mother's love-making. Thompson had apparently forgotten the image, and laughed with a quality of delighted discovery, as though she had come up with the idea at that very moment. Then she exclaimed, "Isn't that amazing? ... That's just what he'd do." I have the impression that Thompson's comic sense operates in much the same way when she is writing. Her characters come to life in the act of making a full confession to her ("These were my *real* thoughts about that.... This is what I actually felt then, though it's a little hard to believe it.... How could I have done that? Well, there's no denying it. That's what I did"). For Thompson, "open and full observation" requires characters who hold no part of themselves in reserve, and who lack the good sense to defend themselves against almost certain misunderstanding. Thompson attends to their chronicles of misfortune with a kind of sympathetic wonder. This attitude does not exclude exuberant amusement at the impossible lengths to which they'll go in their dangerous, daft pursuit of a love "sufficient to their need." Ruth, the wisest character in Janet Kauffman's novel *Collaborators*, offers the young girl who narrates the novel two experiential truths that comprise the "soul of the action" in each of Thompson's plays: "As far as love goes, Andrea Doria, we are primitives, always primitives"; and, "I don't want to be in the middle. In the middle, everybody's lost" (Kauffman 51). In all likelihood, one will be lost at the extremes as well, but a more fluid, unscripted expression of identity may be attainable there.

Thompson does not ever sentimentalize or idealize her characters' displays of "authenticity." In the first place, they achieve their emotional honesty without much effort. It is not an existential decision, earned by a difficult repudiation of inherited social and moral values. In the second place, the full acknowledgement of their status as desperate human creatures is not their spiritual endpoint. It is rather the point where they begin a long, pre-ethical phase in the vale of soul-making. Before we can think ethically, Paul Ricoeur writes:

> We must discover that place where the autonomy of our will is rooted in a dependence and an obedience that is no longer infected with accusation, prohibition, and condemnation. This pre-ethical situation is that of "hearkening" [*l'écoute*]. In hearkening there is revealed a mode of being which is not yet a mode of doing and which thus avoids the alternative of subjection and revolt. Heraclitus said: "Do not attach importance to my words, but heed the logos." When word says something, when it reveals not only something about the meaning of beings but something about Being itself, as is the case with the poet, we are then confronted with what could be called the occurrence of word: something is said of which I am neither the source or the master. Word is not at my disposition as are the instruments of work... or the goods of consumption. In the occurrence of word I do not have anything at my command; I do not impose myself; I am no longer the master; I am led beyond the feelings of anxiety and concern. This situation or nonmastery is the origin of both obedience and freedom. (449-50)

Thompson's characters talk themselves out and enact their compulsions to the point of self-emptying exhaustion, in order that a space for hearing may finally be cleared within them. *White Biting Dog*, for example, builds in its last scene to a moment of unearthly silence when Cape and his mother, Lomia, sit apprehensive and motionless, as if prepared to listen for a voice other than their own for the first time. They have reached a juncture where it is possible for them to relinquish their posture of mastery. The obsessive, increasingly baroque enactments of the inner child's unfulfilled needs define the "substance" of the self's imagined autonomy, Thompson implies. The obedience to one's own desires (that is to say, the fixed, narrowly repetitive scenarios drafted by the unconscious) is demonstrably marked by the "overpowering ghost" of a child that the self can never leave behind. Each act that this self considers in its own "freedom" may well be inspired or prohibited by that implacable child, whose power vastly exceeds the shaping power of culture. What one's appetite chooses with the greatest insistence is that which the pre-ethical, "child-formed" self has least strength to refuse. Such choice does not lead to the actualization of a new being; it is a subjection to the will of our own past. Thompson treats this condemnation to repeat as a parody of the higher obedience to the life of grace. (Ricoeur describes the latter condition as an "obedience beyond fear," and a "consent beyond desire.") The name of God is hardly ever spoken by Thompson's characters, reminding me of Wittgenstein's injunction not to refer to those things that exceed the limits of one's discourse: "Whereof we cannot speak, we must remain silent." The action of Thompson's plays is the prelude to hearkening, in which the mortal counterfeits of love must be granted absolute primitive sovereignty before they can be recognized and (perhaps) overcome. The formation of a soul, in Thompson's world, depends on a moment of pristine clarity when one's whole being assents, for the first time knowing what ethical choice involves, either to good or to evil.

***

Of Thompson's three plays, *White Biting Dog* dramatizes the progression to the moment of choice most explicitly. In *The Crackwalker*, which from the time of its first production has been wrongly identified as a naturalistic play, the pressure of environment is such a palpable influence on the characters that the mental damage they exhibit and the brutal acts they engage in might appear to be wholly the consequence of poverty, ignorance, and heredity. The climax of *The Crackwalker* involves a father's killing an ailing infant son, born retarded, whom he has come to regard as the sole remaining proof of his own identity ("that boy in there he's my son, he's my son and without my son I'm nothing get it? NOTH-THIN... And I wouldn't *WANT* to be nothin, understand?" [52]). His wife, the slow-witted innocent Theresa, places the dead baby in a shopping bag and walks off with the intention of burying it. She alternately remembers and forgets what she has been told about being dead, as she speaks to the baby in the bag. ("It's okay, Danny, don't you be cryin now, you with baby Jesus sittin in the cloud and the Virgin lookin like me she with ya... Danny? You still live? You breathin if I breathin into ya? S'okay, I your Mum! [*tries to breathe into baby*] Danny? You dead, eh? You not live. You never comin back, eh" [56].) Alan, Danny's father, has killed him after a long, terrible struggle with the "ugly" images and thoughts that he can't "beat out of [his] head" (37). Danny is his last, dim image of himself surviving in the world beyond his psychosis. His strangling of Danny is a symbolic suicide, a helpless surrender to the dread of his own vanishing. Danny has been a "good" picture ("like lambs in a field") that he has tried to superimpose over the sickening obsessions that "burn holes" in his mind, as a form of protection. But all the pictures that Alan has constructed since childhood to hold evil at bay have eventually transformed themselves into what he is most afraid of. Danny has been his most solid picture, actually anchored in the real world, and he lavishes on this graspable image all the remnants of tenderness walled up behind his myriad fears. When he ultimately chokes Danny, he speaks words of love to him; there is no will to murder, only a hopelessly confused attempt to save what has already been lost.

Where is the point of spiritual departure in the frighteningly bleak circumstances of *The Crackwalker*? Where is there a recognition of (or a "hearkening" to) a voice that is not "in thrall," which it may be possible to obey? I would argue that there are two such points. Sandy, a character I have not yet referred to who has been distractedly involved with Theresa and Alan throughout the play, has a final monologue in which she moves impressively beyond the crude categories of her former "knowing." She demonstrates a willingness not to pass judgment on either of Danny's parents (in fact, claims continuing friendship with both of them) and decides that the child's death is a mystery that she would do well to leave alone. The spiteful gossip, Bonnie Cain, whose version of events Sandy has always been quick to accept in the past, is dismissed as a "fuckin hound dog" whose voice Sandy succeeds in silencing at the baby's funeral. ("*She* didn't say nothin more.") At the end of her monologue, Sandy refers for the second time to the "Christmas wreath" of flowers placed around the baby's neck in the coffin to hide the "strangle marks." Sandy declares she has seen the marks under the wreath. "The flowers never hid it they just made ya look harder, ya know? They just made ya look harder" (60). The repetition of this final phrase suggests, with a beautifully delicate obliqueness, that Sandy's perception has arrived at the threshold of a deeper dimension: a seeing/listening that is prepared to "dive and reappear in new places."

The other moment in *The Crackwalker* when the visible and invisible seem to converge is in Theresa's brief final scene, which concludes the play. Sandy, immediately prior to Theresa's appearance, has expressed concern that her fate will be to "go back down the Lido, start blowin off old queers again for five bucks" (60). But she has also acknowledged the compelling enigma of this fool-saint's nature. ("Jeez y'know I don't know what goes on inside that girl but it ain't what's goin on inside the rest of us.") Theresa's last gesture on stage is to fend off the advances of a lecherous "old buzzard," a decision she justifies by noting that he doesn't know who she looks like. Much earlier in the play, when Alan proposed marriage to her, he told her with utter conviction that she looks like the "madonna lady you know them pictures they got up in classrooms when you're a kid?" Theresa replied that she knew about her, that she loved the Virgin Mary and often asked her for "stuff." When Theresa later expresses doubt that she really looks like "that Madonna," Alan assures her that there's a perfect resemblance, and she believes him. As I noted previously, Alan has no success in planting "good pictures" in his own mind; all of them give way to the awful thoughts that possess him. However, the "picture" that he offers Theresa in the clear "first light" of his love for her is an image that survives his own descent into madness. Theresa's final line in the play (delivered after her refusal of the man who has propositioned her) is "You don't even know who I lookin like." The words are spoken, with slight variation, twice, in order to echo the repetition of the word "look" at the end of Sandy's monologue. Theresa lacks Sandy's power or desire to press beyond the surface of things. But her memory of Alan's fleeting response to her as Madonna furnishes her with a strong, literal image of value in which she can forever see herself. Her brief lines following the stranger's disappearance may, in effect, be saying: "I have no right to ask you to respect me. After all, I've done a lot of bad things. But if you knew *anything*, you'd be able to recognize the person I look like, and respect *that*. And if you can't see who I look like, then I don't want to be with you." The "picture" formed from what was least confused in Alan's love for her may not prove sufficient to prevent Theresa's destruction. But it has made her, through the mediation of a "felt" image of the good, visible to herself as one who "belongs to" another, and thus, paradoxically, Theresa becomes free to say no to those who claim authority over her.

I Am Yours, Thompson's third play, explores the phenomenon of demonic possession in a psychological force-field that seems modelled on the collective unconscious. The play begins with a dream in which a small boy (Toilane) approaches a house that he is certain is his own, only to be confronted at the door by a strange woman who calmly insists, against his increasingly loud protest, that his house is *hers*, that he does not live there, that he must live somewhere else. As he turns from the door, lost, a second dream involving two young sisters breaks in upon his. One of the sisters, Dee, is certain that she hears the scratching sound of an invisible animal inside her school. The sound fills her with dread and she refuses to enter, despite the reassurance and irritated urging of her older sister, Mercy. At this point, the boy becomes a participant in the sisters' dream, confirming Dee's fear that there is a scratching sound, since he can hear it as well. It suddenly grows dark, though the children are sure that it is still morning. Mercy, as the eldest in the group, does everything in her power to explain the terrifying situation rationally, then as a final measure urges her companions to concentrate on the "friendly" violets clustered in the grass, while they all take the "giant steps" associated with adults to a place of safety. As all defences fail and they surrender completely to their fears, the three children awaken "with a terrible start" in what Thompson calls their "separate adult spaces."

This remarkable opening scene prepares us for the collective dream quality of the play's entire action. The dream experience so dominates the "waking sense" of the "separate adult space" that it soon establishes itself as the primary reality. There is no separate, individualized space in which one can take refuge either from the "spell" of a private dream or the abrupt in-flowing of the dreams of others (equivalent to the child Toilane's discovery that *his* house has been mysteriously taken over by a stranger). The reason for the interlocking nature of the dream visions in the play has to do with the central mystery of Dee's demonic possession. The figures surrounding Dee are all projections of some aspect of Dee's "memory drowned" core experience, which brought into being and steadily nurtured the "great, hidden beast" that now borders her life at every point, waiting (she feels certain) to devour her. *Ich Bin Dein* (German for "I Am Yours") is the repeating phrase that serves as the primary clue to the beast's identity, as well as to the source of its power. The phrase operates as the formula of an evil spell or curse that somehow binds all of the figures in the play together. Dee's sister

Mercy's recurrent dream includes a medallion with these words inscribed on it. She seems always on the verge of deciphering their meaning when she is distracted by a stabbing recollection of betrayal and hurt. The translation that she and, by extension, each of the other characters is looking for can only occur beneath the ever-intruding personal sphere, at the level of what Friedrich Schelling has termed the "non-personal soul"; without that translation no spiritual integration can be achieved, and love will have no clear channel through which to flow.

When Dee, quite early in the play, opens herself to possession by "the beast," her long-standing dread of it is immediately transformed into the ecstatic freedom of merging with a stronger entity, and taking on its power. She feels a greater degree of self-possession than she has ever known before. Her first act of "freedom" is to betray her husband, Mack, in a sexual liaison with Toilane, who is now the superintendent of the apartment building in which she lives. Having driven Mack away with a vicious repudiation that seems largely unwilled, she persuades him to come back after learning that she is pregnant with Toilane's child. She tells Mack that the child is his, while secretly making plans to give the child up for adoption as soon as it is born, so that neither Mack nor the child's father (who desires to raise it) will ever be permitted to see it. With each advance in perfidy, she becomes less agitated; possession transfigures her into a radiantly single-minded presence, secure to a degree she has never been about the rightness of her own conduct. She is like the serenely frenzied Agave in Euripedes' *The Bacchae*, who displays the head of a "lion" she has killed on a pointed stake, blind to the fact that it is actually the severed head of her son Pentheus that she holds. Dee has a final recognition scene comparable to that of Agave, in which she is obliged once again to see herself in her actions. The awakening takes place in a hospital room after she has delivered her child. It is as though the "diabolic influx" that has subjugated her is expelled in the act of giving birth. She has lost the strong sense of shelter, of internal support that the inhabiting evil has given her. She remembers what it is to suffer, and to feel remorse. Having asked Mack's forgiveness, she has a vision of his face, and that of her sister, catching on fire; she cries out in panic as the fire spreads to their hands and hair. It is in the midst of this hallucination of her loved ones burning that Dee stands up and asks to talk to her mother. The "spiritual lines" of the play converge on this point in the action. As the faces of those she identifies with the reality of love are eradicated, feature by feature, Dee becomes conscious of a face *behind* theirs slowly taking form, the face she has refused to know as the face of the animal divinity she has "invited" inside her—her mother's face.

***

Throughout the play Dee's sister Mercy has regularly proclaimed the goodness of their mother, who made Mercy the centre of her life. She talks about her mother's "sandal" under a lawn chair that has become almost a sacred relic for her father after her death: something never to be moved. Only one of Dee's memories of her mother is reported in the play, and we learn that the experience caused her to shake for an entire night in Mack's arms. On the occasion of Mack's first meeting with her mother, Dee had mentioned in her mother's presence how scared she had been on the highway as they were coming to see her (unaware that it was the anticipated introduction that intensified her normally high level of anxiety). "In front of all of us," Mack recalls to her, "your mother turned to you and said, "Why? Why do YOU want to live so much?" In the initial phase of her possession, before losing herself altogether, Dee tells Mercy of a recurring nightmare of violent sexual release. Mercy, whose intuitions about her sister (if never about herself) have a clairvoyant accuracy, asks, without taking in the import of her words, without perhaps even hearing herself saying them: "How horrible could it be, were you devouring Mummy's brains and spitting out her teeth…."

Dee's profound fear of her mother's "inhuman" strength and her complete repression of a hatred for her that "cannot be justified" become entangled with the still arduous internal struggle to find some way of giving her mother a form of love—or submission—that will appease her. Dee needs some unspoken word or resolving gesture from her mother in order to make the love her mother could not accept into something fit to be offered to someone else. The mother's death has by no means put an end to their relationship, only moved it to a deeper level now that the possibility of acceptance by the living mother has been taken away. The pressure of Dee's conscious need for "atonement" combined with the complex of negative feelings that she cannot acknowledge, combine to spawn the "beast" that invades her. The logic of her possession (what the beast wants) is first to give Dee control of her relationships with others, then to enable her to "free" herself of the relationships, so that she can finally join her mother in a condition resembling death.

Mercy has a speech midway through the second act describing the two sisters in their mother's hospital room on the day she died, "holding her head and trying to help her breathe, and then the breath getting lighter and lighter until we'd all stop breathing." Mercy describes her own emergence from the hospital after "Mummy died"; she is released into a landscape of snow where "huge icy trees" were "just… showing themselves… showing. And I was so startled… to hear my own breath… keep… on…." By implication, Dee has elected to remain in "that dark hospital room," desperately prolonging the attempt to help her dead mother breathe, even if it means supplying her with all of her own "air," or building, in the powerful phrase of Henry James, Sr., "a literal nest of hell [for her] within [the child's] own entrails." When Dee suspects that she is pregnant, she executes a painting in a semi-trance, with a "yellow circle" (of energy, light, the life-force) enclosing a black circle (the dead mother slowly expanding inside the embryo, seeking to supplant it in the womb). Hence the idea of the child, from the very first, is hopelessly confused with the traumatically buried image of the mother struggling to breathe. Dee's original plan is to abort the foetus, but when she 'hears' the life inside her ("a breathing, a kind of breathing, a tone of voice, a step… [but also] a shudder of cold, your hand being squeezed, your eyes looking at me. Oh! you… are… you are") she is certain that the unborn child has communicated with her, and that she has no choice but to save it. No sooner, however, has Dee's maternal instinct been awakened, than she feels equally compelled to make arrangements to give her child away. "It could have his face!" she explains to Mercy, referring to Toilane, the child's father. "I couldn't even smile at it if it had his face! I could never touch it, never... nurse... it." Dee's actual dread, of course, is not of the confrontation with Toilane's face. By a massive act of dream-displacement that extends throughout her period of possession, Dee responds to every face she knows as though it were a mask worn by her mother. Her monstrous behaviour to others is a furious acting out of her inaccessible feelings for the presence behind them, whom she cannot succeed in identifying.

The hidden face finally becomes clear in the hospital room when Dee wakes up after childbirth. Dee stands up and announces her need to speak to her mother. Mercy, assuming that she is still hallucinating, gently reminds her that "Mummy's dead, she's dead." Dee is at last able to *know* this emotionally and accept it. What she wants to tell her, in death, is that she's sorry. Her voice builds in intensity as she repeats the words "I'm sorry" until she is wailing from the centre of her being. The words are no longer unfocused, as they were in the party scene I discussed earlier. They are discharged towards an image that has finally attained clear definition, as someone necessarily Other: "I am sorry that my love for you could never go anywhere" is perhaps the first recognition her deep cry brings forth. "I am sorry that I hated you, for I'm beginning to know and accept this hatred as a large part of what you were to me. I am sorry you could not forgive me for not being the child you thought you wanted or needed. I am sorry that I cannot be yours in death, if I am ever to learn to live as myself." This purging action, which embraces both the forgiveness of the mother and self-forgiveness (made possible only when the former, in its immense difficulty, has been achieved) is the play's single point of entry for the "non-personal" reality of grace. A point discovered, as so often in Thompson, on the far side of madness. But grace, whatever protection and healing it may bring to the sufferer who receives it, does not deliver her from confusion or the rending pain of loss. Our final image of Dee reveals her gazing at a row of cribs in the hospital nursery, certain that she has identified her child, who is actually in a hotel room in another city, being held by her "bewildered and lost" father. Dee softly assures the "wrong" infant that she is loved, and tells it what mother love will mean: "I want you forever because I love you." Love that is avowed in these terms is love already beginning to betray its worthiest impulses, "I am yours," the play's haunting title proclaims, but it has been the burden of the action to show us how these familiar words of self-surrender generally mean just the opposite, concealing a hard unyielding claim that "you are mine." In the constant revision of "yours" to "mine," of sacrificial giving to compulsive clutching, the would-be "lover" involuntarily pursues her own "perfected image" in the guise of another, "in whose existence [her] own experience is confirmed and amplified" (Updike 299).

Mercy's approach to love, like Dee's, is founded on the belief that it is reasonable to want to be "the centre of someone's life." When a person makes you his "centre," Mercy suggests, he is doing you a "kindness." In Mercy's reading of her past her mother has performed that kindness, but for all her "generosity" she could not compensate Mercy for her father's decision to ignore her. She feels that he chose Dee at an early age for "partnership" in an exclusive "company of love" where there could never be an opening for her. ("My DAD... thought I was kinda a dud you know? I even heard him introduce her [Dee] as his 'favourite daughter' once, and they had this special club and stuff.... He gave her a medallion with '*Ich Bin Dein*' German for... but RAYMOND thought I WAS AMAZING.") Mercy has made her one truth the lacerating (but after long nurturing, indispensable) idea that because of Dee, she will always be invisible to men ("all the boys always looked straight at you, straight through me"). She was originally Dee's childhood protector, then somehow fell behind her younger sister, and feels she was permanently eclipsed by her. Mercy's natural tenderness and powers of imaginative sympathy have gradually given way to a wholly negative self-absorption. Her experiences with men, with one exception, have involved "false offers" of herself, a parody of the freedom she remembers having experienced with her first lover, the father-surrogate Raymond. She submits to the role she believes defined her irrevocably in adolescence, that of "whoredog" victim. She is attracted chiefly to men she can't have, and makes herself available to them with a show of such pathetic, groping need that she insures either their contemptuous exploitation or humiliating refusal of her. In one of the most striking paradoxes of *I Am Yours*, she discloses that she is so afraid of her sister because she loves her. When Mercy abandons Dee in a crisis, as she does repeatedly throughout the play, she draws on her mother's "strength" to abandon her. Mercy must belong to her mother, as she sees it, because Dee was chosen first by her father to belong to him. Both sisters feel stifled wearing the rigid emotional apparel of the chosen/choosing parent (I am yours, but I wish I weren't). Their imprisonment only deepens, however, as they come to conceive growth as a switching of one parent's wardrobe for the other's. ("I will become mother, and then be free" is, in its barest formulation, the logic of Dee's possession, or, in Mercy's case: "I will take father away from Dee, in the form of Mack or whomever she is in love with now. Once I have father, then I will be his and he will be mine, and I will be free.") Toilane is yet another child yearning to break away from a parent (his mother, Pegs) whose "love" is a monstrous enclosure. Ironically, he intends to make his escape through Dee, whom he decides he loves at first sight. He finds himself drawn to her just at the point that she relinquishes all sense of personal identity, and disappears inside the demon embodiment of her mother's spirit. After Toilane and Dee make love, he tells her of the vision that came to him as he entered her: "I pictured in my mind this face lookin up at me... this face." The face swiftly merges with that of the omnipotent Pegs, who takes over his love affair as soon as he loses control of it, in an effort to secure her son's "rights." Pegs even goes so far as to preside over Dee's labour, sitting beside her as she struggles to give birth and assuming the office of her parent. While Dee suffers the agony of her contractions, Pegs's voice drones on interminably at her side, objectifying the mother image that Dee must recognize before she can expel the 'evil' that has taken hold of her. Pegs's recital concludes, fittingly, with a grotesque recognition scene from her own high school reunion. "'But Marjorie, here I am, I'm Peggy! Didn't you see me?' Well then SHE turned three shades of red and she SAID, 'Well yes, I did, but I wouldn't have known you... your FACE!' My face, had got so... it's true I guess, I don't look nothing like my wedding pictures."

***

Let us return once more to the excerpt from the play with which the essay began. Mack's story of his father's heart attack can serve as a concluding illustration of how identities metamorphose in the child's memory as he attempts to summon the parent who is "gone" yet still inside him. The father having his fatal attack at the top of the stairs is immediately displaced from the centre of Mack's tale by the stronger memory image of the dog who guarded him and refused to let anyone come near. The dog also becomes confused with Mack's mother. Both are female, and there is a marked ambiguity of pronoun reference as Mack tries to account for his mother's "failure" to know what the dog knew instantly, that his father was in danger ("she went berserk, you know, she was... the mother was in the kitchen, talking on the phone to the aunt, and she... the dog wouldn't let her near him"). The dog not only takes on the emotional response that Mack might see as "rightfully" belonging to the oblivious wife on the phone, but also reacts to her as if she were an enemy of the man who needs help, as much a stranger to his suffering as the "ambulance attendants" who arrive later. The father's fatal seizure is "relived" by the dog, who within two days of her master's death has a stroke of her own. In some sense, the father's death, because of this *imitation* of his heart failure, remains stalled just short of completion. He is not quite dead as long as his 'condition' is carried forward by his "paralyzed" but still surviving dog. The mother, for her part, is likewise imitated by the dog as she collapses in a daily alcoholic stupor on the couch, with the ailing animal stretched out alongside her. Thus, the Labrador with the "slurred bark" seems to contain whatever is left of Mack's parents. She is the mysterious emblem of what Mack must continue to take from them for his own life; Mack barks at the end of his story as if to acknowledge the fact.

Cape Race, the central character of Thompson's second (and finest) play, *White Biting Dog*, begins his on-stage existence in a situation that closely parallels that of Mack's story. Standing on a bridge contemplating suicide, Cape is confronted by a white dog with the power to speak to him. The dog tells him that he is "jumping to hell" and that he can only save himself by saving his father, who appears to be in the last stage of an incurable illness. Cape eventually learns (or, rather, thinks he learns) what he must do to save his father after meeting a young psychic named Pony, whom he regards as an unconscious emissary of the prophetic apparition. He believes he must persuade his mother to return to his father's house "for good" and agree to be his wife again. (She left her husband many years ago, and now lives with a "boy" named Pascal, who is even younger than her son.) The plot of *White Biting Dog*, however much it defies literal sense, has a beautiful simplicity of design, in notable contrast to the Byzantine intricacy of *I Am Yours*. As with all great plots, the mere process of recounting it seems to put one in touch with a mystery of experience that is at some deep level known to us, but whose truth lies just out of reach. The stories that get retold endlessly are those that appear to "live completely" within the action of their plots, yet manage to withhold (each time we hear them) something that is required to bring them fully to rest in our minds. The pattern seems to correspond to a pattern inside us; the plot invites us to see through it to a perhaps hidden "law" of our being that we may obey without comprehending. This law might be a prohibition or a fixed accusation or, as in the case of *White Biting Dog*, an impossible but inescapable task to perform.

The meaning of a drama, Thompson believes, should never be formulated for an audience in terms of a theme or idea that is already clear to them. When this happens, the intellect too easily safeguards the emotions against contact with that area in oneself that is still fluid and volatile. Thompson always aims her plays at the fault lines in our internal defence system, the places where the self has no "prepared responses." Unreality is the cost of the imagination settling for what can be seen and, with minor adjustments, stabilized. "Arrangements or structures reveal themselves, as Marx would have it, principally at the moment and in the act of breakdown" (Poirier 186). The plot of *White Biting Dog* is a structure that our feelings, however disposed to resist, know something about. Before we have had an opportunity to analyse this structure enough to gain some distance from it, it begins to "heave and buckle," threatening collapse. Thompson repeatedly dislocates the audience, as she propels the spectator, with no transitional scenes and few abatements of intensity, from troubling comedy, to nightmare panic, to breakdown, and back again. Every thought or impulse that arises in a scene immediately splits into its opposite, Pirandello-fashion, so that emotion and comedy both end up having the same source and the same value. An amusing declaration always modulates into raw feeling just at the point we enter comfortably into laughter. ("LOMIA. It's because I love being inside of my six layers of skin; it's de-licious in here—everytime I breathe I sort of—breathe out *seeds, seeds*. I feel—I inside I feel like... like... sewage" [68]). Conversely, feeling continually betrays itself, and drops unceremoniously into the comic. ("CAPE. Pony, Pony do you feel it? PONY. (*breathlessly*) I don't really like to say these things out loud. CAPE. (*kisses her*) Oh. Oh oh. That was—almost—good" [43].) Cape's emotion is no sooner acknowledged than it begins to disbelieve in itself. He instinctively turns against the person who has "tricked" him into a direct, uncalculated response.

One rationale for Thompson's characteristic rhythm of dislocation and her startling, surrealistic collisions of conscious and unconscious data is the necessity of keeping the thematic "machinery" of her plays invisible. She attempts to induce in us a prolonged sensation of psychic unsupportedness. We never quite know where we are in her plays, but it feels important that we should continue our efforts to find out. Thompson recently revised the final lines of *White Biting Dog* because she found them too sharply pointed. The original dialogue suddenly made explicit reference to the place where the moral consciousness of her characters had arrived by the play's end (in other words, bringing to light what they should learn from their experience). Thompson became convinced that the space of mystery, which all authentic experience inhabits, was falsified by the decision to impose clarity.

The "impossible task" paradigm that provides the basic plot situation for *White Biting Dog* derives, I think, from the common belief of young children that they must be the protector of their parents when they come into conflict, that it is up to them to "save" the marriage, to somehow bridge the gulf of enmity that has opened between the mother and father. (The child often assumes that he is the cause of the conflict.) Cape is essentially reliving this archetypal scenario as an adult, without under-standing his assigned role any better than he did as a child. (He is, of course, by implication, *still* that child.) The external challenge that was "botched" by the guilty, fearful young boy rephrases itself, in the adult psyche, as an *internal* challenge which must be met if Cape is to find his soul and restore himself to life. The central mystery of the play seems to emanate from the words "to save." What does the command to save one's father mean, when that father is on the verge of death and is clearly prepared to die? And what does it mean to save oneself? Cape finds a narcissistic solace in the romantic idea of his imminent suicide. Death of self, however (like death *to* self, its spiritual double) requires a form of courage, or at least decisiveness, that Cape does not possess. Cape seizes on the literal sense of the dog's message to him, and believes he is pursuing a noble objective as he lures his father back into a tenuous half-life with false assurances of his mother's renewed love for him. These assurances have far more to do with Cape's relationship with his mother and his own unacknowledged desires, than with his father's present need. The *real* task that the white dog has given him, whose directive he cannot hear through the ceaseless, drumming din of his fraudulent personality, is to bring his father and mother together inside himself, and to save some portion of his father's goodness, which he has not begun to understand, from dying *there.* Cape's conception of self, like Dee's, grows out of an unrecognized identification with his mother as destroyer. He allies himself, confusedly, with her "strength" in her long ago decision to "abandon" his father. Before the dog commanded that he save his father, Cape had abandoned him as well. He attempts to clear the way for a parental reconciliation by setting out to eliminate his mother's current lover, Pascal, a young man close to his own age. With an increasingly crazed confidence in his own rectitude, he seduces Pascal with the hope of "breaking him down." Through the act of sodomy, he imagines he is asserting his superior strength (superior to mother and Pascal, at once); what is actually being asserted is his greater fitness to take on the role of his mother's lover, a role to which the primitive child in him still lays claim. He moves backwards in the order of attachments to the original maternal bond, which he has neither actualized nor found any substitute for. Cape expresses most trenchantly what this bond means to him in the extraordinary encounter with her that concludes the first act. He kisses Lomia on the mouth, a stage direction informs us, as if he were "inhaling" her, after which she notes, with a mixture of bafflement and surprise, "We—we—touched tongues" (56). Cape then holds her tightly as he tries to articulate how he always feels in her presence. "I want to take you by the hair (*does so*) and then and then bash and bash and bash and bash and bash your head against the wall until you—" (56). Before he can complete either his threat or his half-fathomed thought, Glidden, his father, knocks on the door, re-establishing the interdict that prohibits Cape from usurping Dad's place in the torture chamber of this marriage. Glidden, who may well be suffering one of his mild hallucinations, has decided, child-fashion, to play a prank on his wife and son. Thus, he appears in the doorway on all fours, with a large bone in his mouth. Not losing sight of his obligation to be an authority figure as well, he offers (for their approval) a passable impersonation of Winston Churchill rallying the troops in Australia.

The only character in *White Biting Dog* standing somewhat apart from the closed circle of Cape's familial obsessions is Pony, the psychic, who initially resembles the eccentric "helping figures" in fairy tales. She is potentially the agent of self-integration and spiritual awakening for Cape, if he can be led to accept the uncorrupted love that she freely offers him. For the first half of the play, Pony possesses the remarkable ability to "listen past" the malign intent of his cunning, manipulative role-playing; she is in touch, as no one has ever been, with the helpless confusion and not quite strangled softness beneath his self-hatred. Moreover, she is comically as "starvin' to talk" as Pegs is in *I Am Yours*, so that Cape, with all his mental agility and shiftiness, is hard pressed to keep up with her. When Pony is not giving to others (and if she has any self-concept at all, it is that of "giver"), she lives enclosed in a kind of innocent reverie, which by some fortunate spiritual dispensation, is fragilely preserved from neurosis. Cape sees her as an agent of the white dog, having the power to help him accomplish the "impossible task" of saving his father from death. Pony's power, whose purpose he misconstrues, is all in the yielding. She is the white dog transformed from an immovable judge to a figure of mercy and atonement. Pony opens herself unreservedly to Cape, in an authentic gift of love. Because she holds "nothing back," she leaves herself deeply vulnerable to rejection. She has no capacity to defend herself emotionally against Cape's betrayal, when it comes. Nor does she know how to separate herself from him, and, in effect, return to the "old Pony" once it becomes clear that he has no further use for her. Pony's "mission," which she fulfills without comprehending, is to lead Cape to an acceptance of love that is *not* founded on control.

Cape's first moment of ethical choice in the play comes when he takes Pony to the bedroom and decides to make love to her. He is fully cognizant of the *reality* of her innocence. He also knows that there is a fundamental difference between what she is offering him and what he has previously been able to recognize in his relationships with others (especially other women). Finally, Cape may dimly apprehend that this is his last chance to surrender the mask that hides him not only from the world but from himself, rendering his entire being one great falsehood. Pony cannot be made into an extension or "reflector" of his mother (however much he would like to *find* his mother in her). She reveals to him no aspect of Lomia's nature, against which he might retaliate and which he could justify punishing. Rather, in her unselfconscious embodiment of the strength that dwells in vulnerability and sacrifice, she affords a basis of reconciliation with his father-image, which he renounced as pure "weakness" in early childhood. (Before the white dog's command to "save" him, Glidden was merely the impotent non-entity whom Cape occasionally visited for supper. Only in the process of dying has he become visible to his son as a man with an inner life, though Cape knows nothing about its contents.)

Cape's ethical choice, with respect to Pony, is not to "let her in" when he makes love to her. In the guise of tenderness (and in a darkness that is his private darkness writ large), he uses her body as a receptacle for the hatred that he has been unable to finish pouring out upon his mother. During her last monologue, at the end of the play, Pony describes, in spiritual terms, what transpired with Cape:

> I was invaded, Dad, Dad, filled, by the worst evil... you ever imagined—I guess it happened when I fell in love, on account of I had to open my mouth so wide to let the love in that the evil came in, too... and living with it was just like being skinned alive. (107)

By entrusting her whole being to Cape, she has quite literally *lost* herself in love. Initially confused by what has been done to her, she mistakenly identifies Cape's demon as the proof of his feeling for her, and embraces it as her own. A "marriage" of some sort *has* taken place, as she repeatedly reminds herself. As a result of her attempt to enter into Cape's will to destroy Pascal, she suffers a psychic collapse. In her panic at not recognizing herself, she realizes that she no longer recognizes Cape either, though she is now imprisoned in his "world." When she is made to see that Cape wants to be rid of her once his family rescue mission is accomplished, she appeals one last time to the *voice* of her psychic power. It was this voice, she believes, which brought her into Cape's life, in addition to being the force that shielded the "old Pony," somehow protecting her innocence. The voice grants her permission to take on herself the full weight of the sins that Cape has committed against her and Pascal, in the latter case with murder in his heart. (The truth of what Cape has done to Pony, while bearing the "likeness of love," is first imaged for her in his seduction of Pascal, which she witnesses.)

The cost of Pony's decision to translate the evil that Cape has wilfully imparted to her into a force of regeneration (so that he will not yet have damned himself to a place "beyond the interchanges of love") is an immense final yielding. She must lay down her life for him, an extreme instance of the Christian idea of "voluntary suffering in another's place." Charles Williams terms such a decision an act of "substituted love."[2] It can be persuasively argued that Pony's suicide is much more the consequence of mental disintegration than of a rational decision to "expiate" Cape's transgressions. Unable to cope with the agony of feeling that she is either two separate people, or no one at all, and believing that there is no way back to a self that she understands, and could claim as her own, she flees to suicide. It is the only available means of restoring psychic unity. Thompson fully acknowledges the operation of these forces in Pony's final scenes. At the same time, however, she insists that the ethical choice Pony makes as she is compelled towards death is meaningful and spiritually efficacious. It opens into the dimension of grace, and produces an atmosphere in the space occupied by Cape and Lomia that the mother and son can feel, and that is conducive to "hearkening."

***

I cannot conclude this critical investigation without strongly re-emphasizing my earlier observation that Judith Thompson is not, in any usual sense of the word, a didactic writer. She would be properly horrified at the thought of being found dogmatic about the appropriate distribution of suffering. None of her characters has earned by their worthy or dishonourable conduct the "loads" that they carry around with them. And Thompson does not wish us to have the confidence to make a final judgment of any of them. When I saw the Tarragon Theatre production of *White Biting Dog* in 1984, which remains one of the most vivid and powerful theatrical experiences I have had in Canada, I was forcibly struck by the persistent quality of "objective sympathy" in her presentation of all of her characters; it is the form of sympathy I associate with Chekhov. Thompson strives for (and frequently achieves) what Alan Williamson has described as the highest transaction of personal poetry.

> We feel a kind of tragic awe at entering into the inner language of a life, which is also its net of destiny; in that conjunction we come close to the essential causes of human things. But we also learn a method or discipline of possible escape from the limitations of selfhood, and from the necessity of judging and being judged by others. Or, at the very least we learn, in William Blake's terms, to judge 'states' and not 'individuals,' by seeing how different states are built up out of the same basic human materials. (It is at this level that a deeper, earned universality rewards the reader [viewer] who has refrained from demanding a shallow one.) (Williamson 13)

One not sympathetic to Thompson's work might wish to argue that her relentless concentration on extreme behaviour (her characters seem always to be hovering near psychosis) makes her range far too narrow for the creation of a large spirited, humanly various drama. Such a critic might also dismiss what I have tried to characterize as her religious vision as a sado-masochistic simulacrum of spirituality. If the readings I have offered have not been adequate to modify these objections, I rather doubt that a fuller attention to specifically theatrical gifts (her unparalleled grasp of rhythms and sound patterns, for example) would make my high regard for Thompson's work more intelligible. In my judgment, her three plays give ample evidence of a powerful, utterly distinctive, fiercely independent theatrical voice. She may well be Canada's best playwright.

(1988)

Notes

[1] This passage does not appear in this way in the published final text of *I Am Yours*, but see 152 for the final variation. Toles is apparently quoting from the script for the first production. Many quotations from *I Am Yours* throughout are either not identical to or are not traceable to passages in the available texts, and are therefore not provided with citations here. The original publication of this essay did not provide full publication information for all if its quotations, and I have not been able to trace all of them, but have done my best to convert the essay into standard MLA format (ed.).

[2] The phrase, Toles says, is Charles Williams's, but he does not provide a precise citation (ed.).

Works Cited

Kaufmann, Janet. *Collaborators*. New York: Knopf, 1986.

O'Connor, Flannery. *Mystery and Manners: Occasional Prose*. Ed. Sally and Robert Fitzgerald. New York: Farrar, Strauss & Giroux, 1981.

Poirier, Richard. *The Renewal of Literature: Emersonian Reflections*. New York: Random House, 1987.

Ricoeur, Paul. *The Conflict of Interpretations: Essays in Hermeneutics*. Ed. Don Ihde. Evanston: Northwestern UP, 1974.

Thompson, Judith. *The Crackwalker*. Toronto: Playwrights Canada, 1981.

———. *I Am Yours. The Other Side of the Dark: Four Plays by Judith Thompson*. Toronto: Coach House, 1989. 115-76.

———. *White Biting Dog*. Toronto: Playwrights Canada, 1986.

Updike, John. *Assorted Prose*. New York: Knopf, 1965.

Williamson, Alan. *Introspection and Contemporary Poetry*. Cambridge, Mass: Harvard UP, 1984.

Spatial Metaphor in the Plays of Judith Thompson

by Robert C. Nunn

Ici, dans le champ du rêve, tu es chez toi.
—Jacques Lacan (qtd. in Bowie 140)

Judith Thompson is in my opinion one of the best playwrights this country has seen, now or ever. This judgement by no means reflects a critical consensus; indeed her plays arouse strong passions for and against.[1] It does reflect my own experience. Her plays are impressive enough in the theatre, but in a sense have most of their impact days, months, years later, like certain dreams that bring to consciousness metaphors that only slowly reveal their meanings and continue to colour our lives. This is the mirror opposite of the process by which the plays came into being: for Judith Thompson it takes years for images and characters to rise from the unconscious or suddenly present themselves in a chance encounter. Chance and dream: the two royal roads to the unconscious for the Surrealists. I am reminded of André Breton's famous saying: "Desire discovers those objects which permit it to take shape." In a recent interview, Judith Thompson "describes herself and the way she thinks with the metaphor of a 'screen door swinging between the unconscious and conscious mind'" (Hunt 10-12).

As my title indicates, metaphor is the thread that I wish to follow into the labyrinth of Judith Thompson's plays. Metaphor in her plays is specifically theatrical in that the dominant metaphors are always spatial, like the image of the screen door; that is, conceived in spatial terms and inviting realization on the stage. The sets for the three productions I have seen (*The Crackwalker* at Toronto Workshop Productions in 1982, *White Biting Dog* and *I Am Yours* at Tarragon in 1984 and 1987 respectively) have been multileveled and have called attention to vertical and horizontal dimensions and to walls and partitions between one part of the set and another. In the texts there are many metaphors of surfaces and what is beneath or behind the surface always threatening to become visible, for example, the last lines of *The Crackwalker* (Sandy is describing the funeral of the baby strangled by its father):

> They had them flowers round Danny's neck so's to hide the strangle but I seen it. The flowers never hid it they just made ya look harder, ya know? They just made ya look harder. (92)

To anticipate the direction I am going to take, I would like to point out how very close that is to the dreamwork as Freud describes it in *The Interpretation of Dreams*: as in the mechanism of displacement, the accent is shifted from the latent content of the "strangle" to the manifest content of the flowers, which serves to censor the unacceptable content yet at the same time serves as its vehicle of expression, to allow what Pony in *White Biting Dog* calls "the underneathness" to become visible.[2]

These spatial metaphors are the vehicles with which the plays penetrate two specific areas: social structure and the structure of the psyche. Anne Ubersfeld's chapter on theatrical space in *Lire le théâtre* is full of insights which apply to Judith Thompson's plays:

> *Toutes les métaphores qui soulignent le caractère spatial des activités humaines peuvent trouver une application féconde dans le domaine du théâtre. Grossièrement, on peut dire que spatialiser le monde, c'est non seulement le rendre compréhensible, mais le rendre théâtralisable.* (158)
>
> [All metaphors which stress the spatial character of human activities can find fruitful application in the realm of the theatre. Broadly speaking, we can say that to render reality in spatial terms is not only to make it comprehensible but to make it open to theatricalization.] (my translation)

One system of spatial metaphors in particular is the series of spatial representations of the structure of the psyche which Freud developed. Ubersfeld observes:

> *Une célèbre note de Freud dit: "la psyché est étendue. Ne le sait pas." Freud et après lui Lacan ont donné de l'appareil psychique toute une série de formalisations spatiales.* (160)
>
> [A famous note of Freud's says, "The psyche has a dimension in space. Does not know it." Freud and after him Lacan have attributed a whole series of spatial formalizations to the psychic apparatus.] (my translation)

Taking my cue from Ubersfeld, I build the following analyses on a foundation of Freud's spatial representation of the psyche as divided between the "conscious" and the "unconscious" and Jacques Lacan's post-structuralist rethinking of this seminal concept.[3]

I

The Crackwalker, Judith Thompson's first play, was first produced at Theatre Passe Muraille in 1980 as a seed show. It was revived in 1982 as a co-production by Passe Muraille and Montreal's Centaur Theatre. Clarke Rogers directed both times; the first production was designed by Patsy Lang, the second, by Jim Paxton. It is about two couples who are friends. Sandy and Joe fight, part, and reconcile. Alan, whose sanity is very fragile, marries Theresa, who is retarded. They have a baby, whom Alan strangles. The play ends with Sandy's recollection of the baby's funeral. The plot is a minimalist rendering of the "tragic rhythm of action." Theresa and Alan's *hamartia* lies in conceiving a child in defiance of Theresa's social worker who wants her to have her tubes tied. Alan tries to transform the two of them into a normal married couple who make a good mum and dad, an effort doomed by Theresa's fecklessness and his own descent into psychosis. The height of Theresa's tragic recognition is: "Danny? You dead, eh? You not live. You never comin back, eh" (85). Alan's *anagnorisis* is: "I done what I done and I done it..." (89). Joe and Sandy, the witnesses of this tragic action, experience "horror and pity, the old Aristotelian twosome" (Thompson, "Happy" 133) and grow in stature before our eyes.

The Crackwalker: the title itself tells us something about the metaphors that figure in Judith Thompson's imagination. She has said that the play is not about poor people in Kingston, it is about "the abyss" (Thompson, conversation), the depths that are hidden from us, the opaque surface, the cracks in the surface that give us dizzying glimpses of the abyss.

According to Joe, *The Crackwalker* is the bogeyman that keeps Sandy awake and shaking at nights (70). It is the play's dominant metaphor, related specifically to an actual person, well known to Kingstonians, who obsessively avoids stepping on cracks in the sidewalk, and related more generally to the childhood game played on sidewalks: "step on a crack and you break your mother's back": playing with a breach in the taboo against the unthinkable and the unsayable. Cracks are the gaps and fissures in a surface that allow it to be breached. The central expression of this, pivotally positioned at the beginning of Act 2, is Alan's monologue about the terrible image of a cauliflower-like growth in a woman's vagina which he can't stop thinking about:

> Did youse ever start thinkin somethin, and it's like ugly...? And ya can't beat it out of your head? I wouldn't be scared of it if it was sittin in front of me, I'd beat it to shit—nothin wouldn't stop me—but I can't beat it cause it's in my head fuck. It's not like bein crazy, it's just like thinkin one thing over and over and it kinda makes ya sick.
>
> Fuck I'll be doin the dishes where I'm workin down the Tropicana there and it's like pictures burning holes in my brain I try all the time to like put other pictures overtop of that, nice things that I really get off on, eh, that I really like—lambs in a field... I try puttin pictures of these baby sheep over top of the cauliflower and I'll do it and it's okay for a second then the lamb its eyes'll go all funny like slits lookin sideways just like them snakes and then it'll open its mouth and there'll be them long sharp teeth and a bunch of worms inside and the nice little sheep goes all ugly on me and the cauliflower comes back worse than ever like it ate the sheep or somethin... (55-56)

This metaphor of the eruption of repressed content through the defenses of the "conscious" is another version of the play's controlling metaphor. This is what comes through the cracks. Two languages are spoken in the play, the language of the "conscious" with its clear demarcation between what is sayable and what is not, and another language registering the presence of the "unconscious" and erupting and in a sense rewriting the text, a violently poetic language, at the same time horrifying and beautiful.

This other discourse is like a subterranean stream running through the play, frequently breaking through the surface, particularly in the monologues. There are four, one for each of the principal characters. Theresa's, which begins the play, is very lightly censored. Theresa's command of the rules of language and behaviour is weak to say the least. Her language is full of contradictions to which she is indifferent, as indeed she is to the reality principle. She takes equal pleasure in eating donuts ("I love em") and in defecating: she proudly announces "You shoulda seen the pooh I done today it was hardly long!," to which Al says: "Theresa married ladies with babies ain't supposed to say things like that!" (59). Joe's monologue reflects the fact that he is sane and of normal intelligence. He speaks working-class flawlessly. But his whole monologue flows towards his recollection of the aftermath of the automobile accident that killed his buddy "the Mayor." He comes to in the ambulance to hear an inarticulate stream of words from the Mayor's sister which after great struggle he deciphers: "She was saying she did like his boots" (33). An eruption of irrational language. He doesn't speak it but he can just make it out. Alan's monologue as we have seen is precisely about that eruption. The final monologue is Sandy's. She like Joe speaks the language of the sane and normally intelligent: she is neither indifferent to the eruption of unconscious discourse like Theresa nor helpless to stop it coming through like Al. To her it is like a foreign language which she cannot understand. But she refuses to pretend it does not exist. She remains loyal to both Theresa and Al, refusing to turn away from the mystery of their thought processes and behaviour:

> Jeez y'know I don't know what goes on inside that girl but it ain't what's goin on inside the rest of us... I don't blame Trese though, I still feel for her even... I'll tell ya who else I stood up for at that service... Al, and he done it. Oh yeah, I still consider him a friend. No matter what he done, nobody can say what happened in that room... (91)

Beneath these levels of discourse, beneath even Theresa's, is the Man's. He is so drunk and drugged that the only language he speaks is an entirely uncensored dreamlike babble of unconnected images: "Hee lice Church'n Mondee all dee Mondee hee hee hee! ... Breakin my fa fa pheno phenobarbidoll—barbidoll—NIGGER, YOU NIGGER!" (87): a language which Alan begins to speak in his final moment on stage:

> ALAN. Bye Joe. (*Crouches in previous position, zipping and unzipping his jacket*) Nobody here—but us chickens—nobody here but us guys—don't bother me we got work to do and eggs to lay—and guys to see— (90)

The different levels of speech, from the rational language of Sandy and Joe to the psychotic speech of Alan and the uncensored speech of Theresa, to, finally, the Man's chaotic outpourings, are precisely matched by different social levels. Joe and Sandy are working-class. Alan is a distinct step downward. He has great difficulty holding down a job; his mental instability not only relegates him to the most poorly-paid unskilled jobs, such as washing dishes, but he cannot keep them. Theresa's retardation limits her likewise to the most menial work, eked out by prostitution. The two are on the margins of the welfare class. The Man is at the very bottom of the social ladder, lumpenproletarian, Indian, and drunk and drugged. The psychological and social levels function as metaphors of each other.

What happens in the play is that from each psychological/social level one is invited to look downwards, towards the next level down, with revulsion and disgust but at the same time with compassion and most importantly a feeling of kinship... the old Aristotelian twosome. Sandy overcomes her disgust at Theresa for screwing her husband, in spite of her lies about the incident, because she understands that Theresa cannot be judged by the same standards she uses to judge Joe's behavior. Her responses to Alan are much the same:

> ALAN. I said take that back you ugly bitch.
> (*He grabs her. She throws him to the floor*)
> SANDY. You're sad, you know that? You don't scare nobody.
> ALAN. I'm no fag.
> SANDY. (*goes back to lie on couch*) I seen ten-year-olds fight better than you.
> ALAN. Why?
> SANDY. Why what?
> ALAN. Why don't I scare nobody?
> SANDY. Cause you're a wimp that's why. Like one of them dogs that starts shakin when ya go to pat it.
> ALAN. How come.
> SANDY. How am I supposed to know?
> ALAN. Don't say nothin to Joe, eh?
> SANDY. What, about takin a fit?
> ALAN. About you thinkin I'm like one of them dogs.
> SANDY. I won't.
> ALAN. Or Trese.
> SANDY. Don't worry about it. (44-45)

Similarly we see Joe place compassion over revulsion in his response to Alan after the murder of the baby:

> ALAN. I done what I done and I done it and I fucked it up so I'm payin for it, get it? I'm payin for it.
>
> JOE. I don't know what ya done. (89)

Alan has the same mixture of revulsion and compassion for the Man to begin with, but cannot keep the balance once the Man tries to dry-hump him, and in a later scene vomits on his sock. Can the tragic emotions penetrate that far down into the abyss?

In production, the audience takes its place in this system of layers. A predominantly middle-class audience, as most theatre audiences are, is likely to find itself looking at Sandy and Joe with mixed feelings. On the one hand they visit such bitterness and emotional violence on each other that the audience is likely to see them as examples of working-class self-hatred. But they regularly throw us off guard by showing compassion towards Alan and Theresa and, as the play progresses, towards each other. Our kinship with them is established by the clear signals that their response towards Alan and Theresa is offered as a model for the audience's response. Their refusal to judge or reject them in their extremity poses a challenge to the audience (a challenge which the figure of the Man pushes to the limit and beyond).

The audience's feeling of kinship with Alan is ensured by the direct appeals he makes in his monologue, that is, at the moment he begins his descent into psychosis and toward murder:

> No offense or nothin I don't mean no offense I wish youse all good luck in your lives I was just—like I just wanted to know if any of youse like knew of a medicine or somethin ya might take for this... (55)

An audience who cannot of course prescribe for a fictional character must perforce follow him along his terrifying downward path. Alan's initial response to the Man, "Hey buddy—hey can I do something for ya?" (51) places the audience in the position of seeing the Man through Alan's eyes. There is a sense then of receding depths, Alan mediating between the utter degradation of the Man and the relative health and well-being (and wealth) of the audience.

The many-leveled set which Jim Plaxton designed for the Passe Muraille-Centaur coproduction reinforced this multileveled psychic and social reality in a general way, that is, the whole set in its many leveledness was a broad metaphor of the psyche and of society.[4] The dominant visual image, however, was the sewer outlet, the opening of a large concrete sewer pipe, entrance to which was barred by a heavy steel grate. Thompson's note on staging, which appears for the first time in the fourth printing of the play (1988), indicates that the scenes involving the Man take place around the sewer, "which is prominent throughout the play" (ix). The sewer has been incorporated into the script. It is a metaphor of the permeable barrier separating the world of the "conscious" from the world of the "unconscious," waking from dreaming, sanity from psychosis. In social terms it is a metaphor for the permeable barrier between those who survive economically and those who do not. The image of a sewer as the access and passage to the "unconscious" is in keeping with the play's dual stress on the fearfulness of what is just on the other side and on its familiarity—that is our stuff down there, always hidden under our feet. In the Centaur/Passe Muraille co-production there was a thin trickle of foul-looking water issuing from the pipe, but there was room for a torrent.

II

White Biting Dog is the most difficult of Judith Thompson's plays to grapple with, so far. Critical opinion of it is divided. For example, George Toles considers it her best play (Toles 129). (Ric Knowles, who directed a production at Mount Allison, would probably concur); Richard Plant, although applauding "her vigorous imagination, her theatrical sensibility, and her poetic gift," considers that the play "is so overburdened with imagery that [to an audience in the theatre] it is finally inaccessible" (Plant 23). I have seen it, read it countless times, am deeply impressed by it, and it slips through my fingers like quicksilver.

Maybe the best way to get hold of it is to consider it a kind of truncated *Hamlet*, Ernest Jones-style, in which the only relationship which finally matters is that between Cape and his mother, Lomia. Cape has come back to the house where his father, all alone, is dying, in order to save his life. He tells the audience at the beginning of the play that as he was about to jump off the Bloor Street viaduct a white dog spoke to him and told him that he was going straight to hell unless he saved his father. He goes about this by recruiting the help of Pony, who is psychic, and who determines in a trance that the only way to save Glidden is to bring Lomia back to him. Lomia turns up with her lover Pascal shortly after having been forced out of their apartment by fire. Finally, Cape's efforts to save his father destroy Pony (who witnesses Cape seduce Pascal in order to destroy his mother's relationship with him); they destroy Pascal, shattering the persona he has created; and they destroy his father, who brings on a final, fatal attack in disillusion on learning that Lomia has only come back to him because she has nowhere else to go. An impression in the last few seconds of the play that the deaths of Glidden and Pony are sacrificial and redemptive seems to me so unconvincing that it is tempting to think of it as a dream-displacement. Supposedly these deaths have cracked the shell of egotism that has always prevented Cape and Lomia from feeling. But the displacement of accent does not disguise the fact that between the two of them they have cleared the stage of all but mother and son; that the only genuine feelings Cape expresses throughout the play are monstrous extremes of love and hatred for his mother; that the only connection with another which Lomia does not fake is with her son:

> CAPE. You don't feel anything.... You've never felt anything! ... Not for others, and neither do I. We can't help it. Nothing-gets-in.
>
> LOMIA. Yes it does, it does get in, it, certainly does it—no it doesn't you're right. (*whispers the next line*) I hate saying it though because saying it—sort of makes it true, no? I want to, I try to feel things—I hate it in here, in this-thick-pitch—everything I do, I do to get OUT. Are you the same?
>
> (*CAPE pulls LOMIA to him and kisses her on the mouth, not sensually but as if he's inhaling her*)
>
> We-we-touched tongues.
>
> CAPE. (*holding her closely, starts in a whisper*) I'll tell you one thing I feel. I feel—I always feel—I want to take you by the hair (*does so*) and then and then bash and bash and bash and bash and bash your head against the wall till you— (56)

White Biting Dog was first produced in January 1984 at Tarragon Theatre. Bill Glassco directed; Sue LePage designed a set rather like Jim Plaxton's design for *The Crackwalker*. It too was multileveled and functioned as a constant visual metaphor of the multiple layers of reality in the play. It is obvious that Judith Thompson's plays have an affinity for multi-leveled sets. It is difficult to imagine them working behind a proscenium arch.

The multi-layered reality is psychological primarily, although subtextually there is a multilayered social reality: Lomia is from a wealthy and privileged background in Rosedale; Glidden does not belong in her world (he is from Gravenhurst); Cape is an ex-lawyer; Pascal is actually Gord from Oakville, a suburban kid under a layer of hip; and Pony is the daughter of a projectionist from Kirkland Lake, very working class. A part of the destructive mix of these characters comes from this clash of social strata.

In contrast to *The Crackwalker*, the most important spatial dimension in this play is the distinction between inside and outside. Both spaces are represented on the stage. The interior of Glidden's house, as in a cutaway drawing, shows a living room, stairs leading to two bedrooms, the first of which, Glidden's, has transparent walls, and two exits to the kitchen and the street. The world outside the house is signified by a narrow ramp that projects out into the auditorium so far that characters can enter from and exit to the lobby. It is the sidewalk that runs in front of the house. At times throughout the play the mysterious sound of a skateboard seems to come from the sidewalk, always heard and commented on by Glidden ("What—What the heck is that sound do you know I've heard it every day now for..." [Thompson, *White Biting Dog* 5]); it sounds for the last time at the moment of Glidden's death. Judith Thompson indeed associates the sound with death, an escape from pain (Letter). The sidewalk thus is associated metaphorically with death.

Inside the house, Glidden has been making peace with his impending death, that is, before the arrival of his son with his mission: "Look at the kettle and think of me, I'm water now, I will be steam" (7). The penetration of the house by Cape and the others reduces him to absurd hope, utter humiliation, and abject suicide. Outside the house, the sidewalk comes to function as a metonymy of the external forces which penetrate and destroy. It is on the sidewalk that the most vicious scenes take place.[5] It is there that Cape seduces Pascal, exploiting what he senses is Pascal's fascination with him. It is there that Pascal rejects Lomia with the utmost cruelty. Finally it is there that Cape informs Pony that he cannot love her after all, leaving her in a terrible state compounded of her possession by the evil she feels she has opened herself up to in loving Cape, the crushing of her hope that she can save him, and grief at his final rejection of her. The sidewalk is the place of the most dreadful pain, of loss and of the shattering of the self:

> PASCAL. STOP. It's not... YOU, Lomia, it's me. Gord, *Gordon. From OAKVILLE*; something's—snapped— ...I'm different I'm Gord, Gord I got... different blood now I'm not I'm not who I—who—who—you— (85-86)

> PONY. How could I go home, eh? How could I go home to the very people I would have Judas-licked for you? They wouldn't know me anyways 'cause the old Pony's almost squished... (101)

It is no accident that the sidewalk is located in the midst of the audience and literally connects the fictional world of the play with the real world outside the auditorium.

The contrast between inside and outside is evident in the set design and in the blocking. These function as metaphors of a pervasive mapping of the characters' psyches in terms of inside and outside. Cape to Lomia: "You've never felt anything! Not on the inside you know that.... Not for others, and neither do I. We can't help it. Nothing-gets-in." Lomia to Cape: "I try to feel things—I hate it here, in this-thick-pitch—everything I do, I do to get OUT." Cape kisses her on the mouth as if inhaling her (56). Lomia to Pony: "...I—love being inside my skin; it's de-licious in here—everytime I breathe I sort of breathe out *seeds, seeds*. I feel—I inside I feel like... (*honest*) sewage" (68). Pascal on language: "like box cars-shuts *out*, and kinda locks *in*. It's corrupt to the—colon—" (23). Cape on Glidden's illness: "His insides are rotting. It's Latin for that. In-something" (53).

Lomia has the most appalling metaphors of the insides of the psyche: recalling the deaths of their three dachshunds, run over by a car: "the poor things were bacchic, gobbling up each others' viscera..." (72); she can hear her food digesting, "floating along in my bloodstream like cows in a flood in India" (84). As Pascal is leaving her she begs him:

> ...You can... feed me. You can stuff me! You can stuff me and stuff me and stuff me till my skin won't hold any more fat and it bursts. And then you can burn me! (88)

Metaphors of eating and vomiting, defecating and farting, occur throughout the play. Cape gags at the thought and later the sound of his mother's lovemaking. Pascal to Lomia: "You wanted to be treated like shit. YOU WANTED TO BE TREATED LIKE SHIT!" To which Lomia replies: "...only because when you treated me like... fecal matter, the pins and needles would start, see?" (87). Pony stuffs herself with batter and, she claims, meat hacked from the frozen bodies of the dachshunds, and claims to have vomited a prodigious amount of this revolting mixture in the toilet and in the cups in which she serves Cape and Glidden tea.

All these metaphors of inhaling, ingesting and expelling carry emotional and psychological connotations of penetration and destruction. Likewise Cape's sexual penetration of Pony and of Pascal is an invasion of their very sense of themselves, an invasion and a destruction, like the "monster of black smoke that hurl[s] itself" at Lomia when she opens the door of her apartment (25). Pony, explaining to her dad why she has just killed herself, says:

> I didn't... kill myself 'cause I couldn't hack it or because the man I loved couldn't love me back, it was 'cause... I was invaded, Dad, Dad, *filled* by the worst evil... you ever imagined—I guess it hap-

> pened when I fell in love, on account of I had to open my mouth so wide to let the love in that the evil came in, too... (107)

These metaphors of invasion and internal corruption are contradicted at the end of the play by metaphors of invasion as salvation. Pony says to Cape just before she exits to hang herself:

> I'm gonna swoop down inside myself and pull out the old Pony, and I'm gonna give her over to you. And when she's inside you, you're gonna be saved. (102)

Glidden says to Lomia just before he goes to his room to bring on his fatal attack: "...you'll be okay if you let me in. Will you let me in?" Lomia replies, "I'll *try*," but once he has left she cries:

> "Let me in, let me in, let me IN" WHAT DOES HE MEAN? I know what he means, but I CAN'T, I'm SHUT, I'm JAMMED I—ohh GOD let me let him— (104)

The stage directions at the end of the play indicate that Lomia "feels a totally unfamiliar feeling; something inside her is cracking"; as she takes two very deep breaths, her face close to the face of her dead husband, "her body must look as if a strange chemical has entered it" (105). She is joined by Cape carrying Pony's body: "deep within them [both] something has cracked" (108).

The pattern that emerges from all these ins and outs is a disturbingly ambiguous one. Evil in this play is the inability to let other people in, a psychopathic indifference to their reality other than as instruments. It is at the same time the power to penetrate and destroy the other. Redemption is possible once that shell cracks, letting love in. Yet Pony's utter lack of shell, her uncompromising openness, lets all of Cape in, to her destruction. The same can be said of Glidden, whose openness to Lomia dooms him. This contradiction is certainly not resolved by the apparently redemptive ending, with two dead bodies sharing the stage with their destroyers, two ravening egos locked in a repetition of the Oedipal fantasy.

III

Spatial dimensions are once again a rich source of metaphor in *I Am Yours*, Judith Thompson's most recent play, which was produced at Tarragon Theatre in the late fall of 1987. Derek Goldby directed, and the set—again, multi-leveled—was designed by Jim Plaxton.

A brief outline of the play: Dee, on the verge of a breakdown, and alone and shaky, having driven her husband Mack away, has a wild one-night stand with Toilane, the new superintendent of her apartment building. She conceives. Toilane learns that she plans to give his baby up for adoption and takes her to court, urged to declare war by his formidable mother, Pegs. He is forced to drop his suit when Dee with the backing of her sister Mercy counters with a false charge of rape. Dee goes into labour while Pegs and Toi are visiting to "forgive and forget." Toi and his mother, a retired RNA, deliver the baby and abduct it.

The play begins and ends with an image of profound loss: the loss of the dyadic relation between mother and child. The play begins with Toilane's dream of a closed door which will not open—"Where's my mummy?" he cries. In the last line of the play, Pegs has just had a stroke and is unconscious or dead, seated in an armchair, her eyes staring straight ahead. Toilane is holding his baby in his arms and says, bewildered, "MUM?" (66).[6]

The first scene is worth looking at in detail. It not only presents a dream, but its meaning is overdetermined like a dream, and since it is played in darkness with only a tight spot on Toi's face, it includes the audience in the dream:

> (*The stage is dark. TOILANE walks slowly towards the audience, on a ramp that juts out into the audience, in shoes with a heel that clicks. There is a tight spot on his face—he is his six-year-old self, in a dream he is having as an adult. He is walking up to what he sees as a giant door, the door of his own home.*)
> TOI. Mum! Muum, I'm home!
> TOI. Hey, Mum, I'm home!
> TOI. Where's my mummy? (*PAUSE*)
> TOI. But this is my house! I live here.
> (*PAUSE*)
> TOI. I do so! My parents are in there! I do so live here, they're in there! I do live here, I do live here! I do live here! I do live here!
> (*The "door" slams. The audience should serve as the door. Do not bring in a real one.*) (1)

The loss that this scene signifies reaches far beyond the emotionally-charged memory-trace of a six-year-old child in front of a closed door. That is a screen memory: displaced onto it is the "lack" that is the key term in Lacan's reading of Freud: the lack that first comes into being in the mirror stage, in which the infant seeks an imaginary recovery of fullness of being in identifying with an object (above all the mother's gaze); the lack that finally and irrevocably defines the subject with its entry into the symbolic order. The Oedipal prohibition and the simultaneous acquisition of language finally shut the subject's being behind the slammed door of repression; at that moment the "unconscious" comes into being on the other side of the door. In Toi's dream, he recapitulates these stages: The "mummy" in whom he locates his very life transforms into the two parents on the other side of a shut door, which henceforth cuts him off from his life: "I do live here"—On the other side of a locked door is where I live. I am shut out from where I live. The I who speaks is shut out from the I who lives: "here" is where the "I" who speaks of himself is not.

An explication of Lacan by Toril Moi could supply the subtext of this scene:

> ...When the child learns to say "I am" and to distinguish this from "you are" or "he is," this is equivalent to admitting that it has taken

> up its allotted place in the Symbolic Order and given up its claim to imaginary identity with all other possible positions. The speaking subject that says "I am" is in fact saying "I am he (she) who has lost something"—and the loss suffered is the loss of the imaginary identity with the mother and with the world. The sentence "I am" could therefore best be translated as "I am that which I am not".... To speak as a subject is therefore the same as to represent the existence of repressed desire: the speaking subject is lack... (Moi 99-100)

The desire that animates Toi throughout the play is born in that moment recapitulated by the dream, born of that lack. His through-line is to pass from one object of desire to another—from wanting to be "intergutted" with Dee to wanting the child he has fathered—a through-line which leads him full circle to the cry of loss with which the play began.

The play is filled with lament for the loss of an intimacy whose only possible model is the relation of mother to infant, signified by the look that passes between them. "Eyes" and "looking" matter a great deal in the play. Dee walks out of the hospital where she was about to have an abortion because she has a vision of the fetus speaking to her, its eyes looking at her (28). In the second-to-last scene, Dee perhaps dreams of searching for her baby in the hospital nursery where she has been assured it is (actually it is in a hotel room in Sudbury):

> (*DEE opens a door. A light blinds the audience. She walks forward on the ramp towards the audience. The audience, to her, is the nursery. She is looking for her baby. She feels purified—through birth—and also through understanding her self hatred, her guilt about her mother—she is now able to love after having grappled with her "shadow" or "animal." She is infused with this love. She sees the baby somewhere in the audience. [Not picking out an individual, of course.]*)
> DEE: Ohhhhh! Which... one are you, baby? Which.... Oh!! I see you!! I see you now! Oh! You are so... beautiful. so!!! I want you baby I want you forever because I... love you. I LOVE you Oh! Oh! Your eyes are opening...... Hello! hello! Hello!!! Hello! (66)

In this scene a door opens, in contrast to the slammed door of scene 1. An intense light pours out of the open door, almost too strong to look at directly. The baby's eyes open. The mother and infant greet each other. There is an illusion that this love will be forever. Yet the baby is not there. Its absence is what is crucial about this scene. It is an absence metaphorically linked to the absent, dead gaze of Toi's mother as we crossfade to the hotel room for the final scene of the play, linked as well by the white light Pegs sees as she loses consciousness. We see a montage of the severed bond between Toilane and Pegs and the imaginary bond between Dee and the baby (who is not there). The fact that Dee's greeting is directed to every single person sitting in the theatre includes the whole audience in a dialectic of desire and absence.

Pegs laments the loss of that unity of mother and infant (speaking to a taxi driver who is not listening):

> ...What happened? What happened to the baby who looked up at me with eyes when the doctor first showed me [sic] to me, blackberry eyes, the baby I musta walked ten miles a day in our little apartment, back and forth, back and forth, eyes closin, lookin at me, lookin at me. Why is it that look goes away? (38)

The mothers—Pegs and Dee—find in that gaze an echo of that lost identity: so does the Dad. When Toi, eavesdropping, hears that Dee is pregnant, he says:

> It's funny, I sorta knew I madja pregnant. I pictured you know? While we were doin it. I pictured in my mind this face lookin at me, this... face. (30)

Toi on the bus gazes at his baby and says:

> It's like there's a well, you know and when I seen her, Tracy, somethin pumped that water up and it filled my whole head, you know it filled my whole head! (62)

The play is full of lament for lost intimacies which momentarily revived that feeling of identity: Mercy's Raymond (the older man with whom she "did everything but" in his car when she was fifteen) and the honey that seemed to pour everywhere when he kissed her, a feeling she "certainly never... ever... had... again" (18); the wild sex Toilane has with Dee, leaving him desiring her and mourning his loss from then on. In stark contrast are couplings so empty of feeling that they are parodies of desire. Mercy recalls having sex with her husband: "we'd just do it in the dark facing separate directions" (35). She quotes him: "If you can get it up, you can have it, but I'm watching the Brady Bunch" (25).

The locket inscribed *Ich bin dein*—the title of the play—ironically holds out the offer of eternal love, of the desiring subject finding its lost complement in the other, but in fact, for the two sisters who possess identical lockets, Dee's from her Daddy, Mercy's (maybe only in dreams) from Raymond, the locket signifies loss. The promise is always already broken, the desired object is always already a signifier of that which is absent. Indeed the German poem from which the line comes even while speaking literally of eternal love speaks metaphorically of loss:

> ...You are locked in my heart
> The key is lost
> You will always have to stay inside it .
> For always. (45)

Raymond, meeting Mercy again (perhaps Mercy only dreams this), says:

> I dreamed about you too, you know, several times a year every time the season changed. Swimming, swimming in cold blue water, clear; striped fish and dark, inky seals jumping around us, and I turn, and

> look at you and your eyes, your eyes are toooo... blue.... And then I'd wake up, look out the window and see the first snowfall, or the leaves had turned... overnight... (64)

Dee's appalling behavior toward Mack and towards Toi has its source in something the very opposite of desire yet intimately related to it, which she describes as an animal on the other side of a wall, always about to burst through.

That animal on the other side of the wall, the recurrent images of shut doors, of locked hearts, of walls.... Perhaps it is significant that Dee feels liberated from the terror of all the life that swarms on the other side of the wall just after she has given birth, and momentarily imagines that she is looking into the eyes of her baby. For a moment the split subject is whole. That split subject—the I who speaks/the I of which one speaks, and is estranged from—the "conscious" in the "prisonhouse of language"/the "radical otherness of the unconscious" (Eagleton 157)—is the subject of Mack's story of the six-foot tall beehive swarming with 50,000 bees, on the other side of the wall in his bookstore, while on this side, people are "doing cash, taking inventory." The first inkling that it is there is the "slow return of the repressed": "First just one, buzzing around, then two, three we barely notice, then wham! someone gets stung, something's going on.... Someone could have an allergy, DIE" (27). Yet when the hidden is revealed, honey pours into the store.

Mack offers this to the audience as a parable of Dee's "Animal." Dee is terrified of the animal on the other side of the wall, and has been since she was little. Now that her dreams are getting worse, and her behaviour towards Mack is more and more out of control, she is afraid: "It's like it got out of the wall" (25). "I'm afraid that the dreams will seep into the day. That I'll do things..." (26). Is the other side of the wall the location of the most extreme contradiction: desire born of lack—that impossible sweetness—and its opposite, a murderous rage at the primal loss—directed at the mother? Of corresponding guilt at having these feelings? Mercy guesses at the content of Dee's nightmares: "How horrible could it be, were you devouring Mummy's brains and spitting out her teeth...?" (26). Possibly the greatest loss referred to in the play is Dee's and Mercy's loss of their mother, whose death Mercy recalls in Scene 21. But whereas Mercy's memories of her mother are filled with yearning to once again be the centre of someone's life, as she was of her mother's, Dee's are filled with a rage at being emotionally abandoned—a rage so powerful it must be repressed and only appears as dream-displacements: the animal behind the wall, the shark "banging at the shark cage and sliding out" (25):

> MACK. ...Your mother, your mother. Remember the first time I went up to meet your mother; you were going on about how scared you'd been on the highway, how you would never drive on the highway again and your mother in front of all of us, your mother turned to you and said, "Why? Why do YOU want to live so much?" Remember what you did? Remember what you did?
>
> DEE. Don't.

MACK. Remember how you shook, you shook in the sleeping bag with me all night you shook with your head in my arms.
DEE. No. (7)

If one pole of the emotional structure of this play is the pairing of loss and desire, the other pole is the pairing of loss and rage. While Mercy turns to one substitute after another for the lost complement of herself, Dee's rage erupts at the signifiers of her lost complement. In the astonishing scene 6, Dee swings violently back and forth between the two extremes of desire and hatred toward the same object, her husband Mackie. As she does soon after with Toi. As she does in her nightmares: "I have these dreams, I have orgasms, I have orgasms in my sleep, I wake up with my nipples hard but the dream, the dream that carried it was so horrible, so horrible that..." (25). As Mercy warns her she might do with a child. What Mercy says of her relation with her younger sister suggests that she was the first victim of this pairing of desire and rage. When they were young, Mercy protected Dee from the nightmare she was already terrified of, sang to her, cared for her in a very maternal way. Later as Dee reached adolescence, she turned on Mercy and took advantage of her own sexual attractiveness to torment and humiliate her sister, leaving deep emotional scars: "How can anybody like me, eh? How can you like me?" (37). The series of pictures of the growing fetus Dee paints during her pregnancy are by turns beautiful and grotesque. Mercy too swings violently between the two poles of desire and hate in the memory or dream of the day Raymond gave her the locket with its inscription "I Am Yours." In contrast to Dee, the object of these contradictory feelings is finally her father, whom she addresses in a dream as "you FUCKER DADDY" (17), whose preference of Dee over her, signified by the locket, is as evident as their mother's preference of Mercy over Dee. Mercy, like Dee, is driven in the present by these buried feelings. At one extreme she found in Raymond an object who would seem to satisfy the longing for the withheld love of her father; at the other extreme is her ten-year marriage, just collapsed when the play begins, to a cold and distant man who repeatedly replayed the original rejection. In the course of the play she halfheartedly tries to seduce Mack away from Dee; as George Toles argues, she is attempting to take father away from Dee in the form of Mack (128). But the difference between Mercy and Dee is this: while Dee is "taken over" by the inconsolable and unappeasable animal within, which seeks to destroy the displaced objects of her desire and hatred, Mercy seems to recognize a dream-displacement when she sees one, so that the subtext of her unsubtle pursuit of Mack is clearly "I can dream, can't I?" Perhaps the most touching moment in the play occurs when Dee, intending to bribe her sister into perjuring herself, passes over the symbolic locket with its inscription from Daddy, *Ich bin dein*, a conflation of metonymy and displacement.

Toi's relation with his mother, which we witness on the stage, bears clear traces of the same opposition of desire and hatred. (In the Tarragon production Toi had large very visible tattoos on his forearms, LOVE on one, HATE on the other.) The dream of the giant door is the key to both feelings: the hatred is hinted in his initial violent and hurtful rejection of his mother's suggestion that he come back home and be taken care of: it is displaced onto his murderous hatred of male homosexuals:

> ...he just kept, like we'd kick his head and he'd move again so we'd kick it again and he wouldn't stop moving and I started see like a monster from the cartoons with all these snake heads and everytime ya kick one off, it grows another one, right? And he kept growing snake heads so I kept kickin them kickin them off and he goes "I think I'm swallowing blood" in this voice... like Gramma or something but he's a *guy*, he's a guy, right, he's not GRAMMA, he's makin like he's Gramma and he's a GUY. (11)

The reference to the figure of Medusa points to what is going on here. At the other extreme is his loyalty to his mother, his appeal to her to help him get his daughter, and finally his apology for a cruel rejection of her when he was in grade four (65). He succeeds in recapturing a trace of the original identity just moments before he stands staring in bewilderment at the empty gaze of his dead or dying mother.

This system of opposites—loss/desire at one pole, loss/hatred at the other—constitutes not only the emotional structure of the play but also its Action. It consists of two parallel through-lines, Toi's and Dee's. They complement each other. Toi's, as we have seen, moves from loss through desire to a repetition of the loss. Dee's moves through more and more violent eruptions of the repressed pairing of desire and hatred, towards a recovery of the lost object that is its source: the imaginary gaze between herself and her child releases her from her repressed hatred of her mother and the attendant "self hatred and guilt" she has felt (66). Dee's swelling tummy is the index of both of these Actions, and of the "animal" that in nine months breaks through the wall: Dee's labour begins with "a leak, a trickle of water," through a little tear from a little fingernail, which triggers a nightmare vision of "a lion, breaking through the wall a lion roaring all the stones breaking..." (53).

For Judith Thompson, the personal cannot be detached from the social. The wall that divides Dee in two is also the wall that separates her class from the proletariat. She is equally terrified of the "seepage" from the other side in both respects. Several times in the course of the play, the "animal" metaphor is applied to the working class. Pegs recalls with hatred how the middle-class women she cleaned house for would talk to her "like ya talk to a dog or a baby" (47). Confronting Mercy after her son has dropped the suit, she cries, "We're human beings. We're not animals you know" (51). That animal must be kept shut out. Toi cries out to Dee after their night together, "You showin me your... your animal," and she screams "NO!" (21). Later, when she is pregnant, she refuses to consider giving the child to Toi: "I couldn't... give... one of us... to a person... like that, how could I?" (30). Something very like the return of the repressed happens several times in the play when the working-class characters burst through the door of Dee's apartment to confront her with what she denies so strenuously: significantly, they appear to claim Toi's right to the baby shortly after Dee regales Mack and Mercy with a condescending account of her ride with a taxi driver who hates his job and hates what he calls "the riding public": from her illusory safe distance she can find proletarian resentment amusing. Two scenes later that wall has given way.

The metaphors I have discussed cry out for realization in spatial terms, which the designer, Jim Plaxton, accomplished brilliantly. Clearly taking his cue from the text, he designed a multi-level playing Space.[7] At stage right was the superintendent's apartment, later the motel room in Sudbury; it was at the lowest possible level; one seemed to be looking down into a pit. At stage left on the same level was a space that served as a seat on a bus and the interior of a cab, always occupied by at least one proletarian—the Italian labourer into whose uncomprehending ear Mercy pours out her story about Raymond as they bus to Toronto; the bored resentful cabbie to whom Pegs laments the loss of the infant's gaze; and finally Toi and Pegs on the bus to Sudbury. Floating above this space, like a different world, is Dee's apartment. The door of her apartment, then, is the breach in the wall through which what is denied and ignored makes its way: from the other side; from below. An easel bearing the series of paintings of the growing fetus stands near the door, its surface thus associated metaphorically with the breach through which the unconscious contents seep.

One element of the set, the ramp projecting into the audience, is specified emphatically in the script; and I would like to conclude with some thoughts about its function. In some sense the experience of seeing a play is always that there is an invisible fourth wall between the audience and the drama. All the things we see—the set, the actors-are "derealized" and exist only as signs (Elam 7-10). They are what they are not. That is, theatre, in its relentless conversion of everything it touches into a sign of something else that is not there, incorporates in its very being that "absence" or "lack" of which Lacan speaks. That perpetual dialectic between alienation and empathy, whose political connotations interested Brecht, is also a model of the psyche. Our awareness of the difference between our reality and the de-realized signs—absences—in front of us can in a moment transform into an imaginary identification that can shake us to the core. As Anne Ubersfeld says in *L'école du spectateur*, our pleasure in the theatre is by its very nature double:

> *il est va-et-vient entre le sentiment d'une absence et le jeu avec une presence.* (330)
>
> [it consists of a continual movement between the feeling of an absence and playing with a presence.] (my translation)

Such an approach to the relation between the work and the spectator's desire and imaginary identification is by now familiar territory in film and television studies:[8] coincidentally, a moment in the play that bears on this is couched in terms of television—Mercy's passionate defense of television: "IT IS A VOICE A WARM VOICE. THERE ARE FUNNY TALK SHOWS WITH HOSTS WHO THINK EXACTLY LIKE I DO" (31).

Judith Thompson is gifted at momentarily lowering the level of repression, letting the contents of the "unconscious" seep through, catching us by surprise with something that seems for a moment more than a signifier whose signified is an absence, leaving us shaken with momentary presence.

We have seen how *White Biting Dog* also uses a ramp projecting out into the audience to foreground this play of presence and absence. Its use in *I Am Yours* is even more telling. In *I Am Yours*, nine scenes out of thirty-six are played in whole or in part on the ramp: notably, Toi's dream of the open door, Mack's parable of the beehive behind the wall, Dee's vision of the fetus calling to her, Toi's declaration of war, Toi's abject apology to the judge, Mercy's dream-reunion with Raymond, Dee's vision of her baby in the nursery. The ramp is the focal point of the extraordinarily powerful affects that the play releases to seep through the wall of repression of which the "psychic distance" of the audience is a displacement. Significantly, the play takes its time with this: only three scenes are played on the ramp in the first act (fully two-thirds of the running time); all the rest are in the second act. Significantly too, the audience is directly addressed in ways which further accomplish the breaching of the wall. We are the door which slams in Toi's face, and twice we are the infant whose voice and gaze seem to erase all absence and restore all that has been lost:

> SCENE FOURTEEN
> (*Location-hospital*)
> (*DEE walks up ramp towards audience She has felt the life of the fetus inside her and cannot go through with the abortion. She now walks toward the audience where she feels the 'flashes' coming from, her hands outstretched to feel them.*)
> DEE. (*looks at audience*) Is that you?? Are you... speaking... to me? I can hear you. I can hear you—I hear... your voice, are you... I can hear your voice speaking. It's you!!! IT issss you, you are talking to me You're talking to me, yes I can hear, I can feel these, yes, I can hear you breathing, breathing, your voice, your step—the way you will step on the stairs, a small intake after you laugh, you laugh, the way your mouth... when you sleep; curves down; the swell... inside you when you see a tree, a beautiful tree one day, a shudder of cold, your hand being squeezed, your eyes looking at me! Oh! you are... you are... you... ARE!!!!!!!! (28)

Lack and desire; presence and absence; a wall that is and is not breached; an identity of mother and child that is at once uncannily familiar and a signifier referring to something which is not there... *I Am Yours* by Judith Thompson.

IV

In all three plays I sense a dramatic imagination that seizes on spatial metaphors in order to explore the human condition on stage. I also sense a progression, towards a stronger and stronger perception of social and psychological contradictions and oppositions: desire and rage, love and hate, good and evil, Eros and Thanatos. Always there is a permeable barrier, a "screen door"—the cracked surface in *The Crackwalker*, the door between the house and the sidewalk in *White Biting Dog*, the walls and doors in *I Am Yours*. On the one side is the waking world, where everything is clearly one thing or the other, the world of rationality, common sense, the "conscious," where language functions as a way of organizing and codifying experience.[9] On the other side is the utterly strange, yet uncannily familiar, world of dream, nightmare, the "unconscious," where opposites and contradictions coexist, where another language is spoken, where the dreamlike play of metaphor and metonymy disrupts all efforts to make simple, unequivocal matches between signifier and signified. Judith Thompson's plays are increasingly bold journeys into the abyss of the unconscious.

(1989)

Notes

1 E.g. at one extreme, the woman who stormed out of Centaur Theatre during a performance of *The Crackwalker*, "bellowing over her shoulder, "'Call the chauffeur, George, we're leaving!'" (Carley 46). At the other, Clare Coulter, who said that "the power of Thompson's writing... and her experience of playing Pony in *White Biting Dog* 'made me feel I should examine the way I approach my life'"(Hunt 12).

2 Judith Thompson has studied Freud intensively. See Steed.

3 Writings by and about Lacan on which I have drawn are Lacan, *Écrits* and *The Language of the Self*; Bowie; Eagleton; Wright; Moi, and Silverman.

4 Mark Czarnecki, in his review in *Maclean's* commented on the "ingenious multilevel set, which provides the precise spatial co-ordinates required to chart the pilgrimage of Thompson's characters from oblivion to oblivion."

5 Information on blocking comes from the prompt script of *White Biting Dog* which I consulted at Tarragon Theatre.

6 All quotations from *I Am Yours* are from a pre-publication manuscript, and don't necessarily correspond to the published version.

7 Information on set and blocking comes from the prompt script of *I Am Yours*, consulted at Tarragon Theatre.

8 See for example Mulvey, and Metz.

9 Thompson: "People don't believe contradictions exist. You're a nice person, or you're a bad person. It's difficult, because the people that go to the theatre are the very people most difficult to convince" (qtd. in Colapinto).

Works Cited

Bowie, Malcolm. "Jacques Lacan." *Structuralism and Since.* Ed John Sturrock. London: Oxford UP, 1979.

Carley, Dave. "A Canada Nobody Knows." *American Theatre* (Feb 1988): 46-47.

Colapinto, John. "Playing With Fire." *Radio Guide* (Sept 1985): 7.

Czarnecki, Mark. Review of *The Crackwalker*, directed by Clarke Rogers at Centaur Theatre. *Maclean's* 15 Feb 1982: 63.

Eagleton, Terry. *Literary Theory.* Minneapolis: U of Minnesota P, 1983.

Elam, Keir. *The Semiotics of Theatre and Drama.* London: Methuen 1980.

Freud, Sigmund. *The Interpretation of Dreams.* Trans A.A. Brill. New York: Modern Library, 1950.

Hunt, Nigel. "In Contact with the Dark." *Books in Canada* (Mar 1988): 10-13.

Lacan, Jacques. *Ecrits: A Selection.* Trans Alan Sheridan. New York: Norton 1977.

———. *The Language of the Self.* Trans Anthony Wilden. Baltimore: Johns Hopkins UP, 1968.

Metz, Christian. *Psychoanalysis and Cinema: The Imaginary Signifier.* London: Macmillan 1982.

Moi, Toril. *Sexual/Textual Politics: Feminist Literary Theory.* London: Methuen 1985.

Mulvey, Laura. "Visual Pleasure and Narrative Cinema." *Screen* 16.3 (1975): 6-18.

Plant, Richard. "Opening Lines." *Books in Canada* (Apr 1985): 23.

Silverman, Kaja. *The Subject of Semiotics.* New York: Oxford UP, 1983.

Steed, Judy. "Thompson Different From Her Characters." *The Globe and Mail* (Toronto) (11 Feb 1982): E5.

Thompson, Judith. Conversation with Robert Nunn. July 1988.

———. *The Crackwalker.* Toronto: Playwrights Canada, 1981.

———. "The Happy Vessel." *Still Running... Personal Stories by Queen's Women Celebrating the Fiftieth Anniversary of the Marty Scholarship.* Ed. Joy Parr. Kingston: Queen's Alumnae Association 1987. 133.

———. *I Am Yours.* Unpublished manuscript. Jan. 1988.

———. Letter to Ric Knowles. 24 Oct 1984.

———. *White Biting Dog.* Toronto: Playwrights Canada, 1984.

Toles, George. "'Cause You're the Only One I Want': The Anatomy of Love in the Plays of Judith Thompson." *Canadian Literature* 118 (Autumn 1988): 116-35.

Ubersfeld, Anne. *L'école du spectateur.* Paris: Editions Sociales, 1982.

———. *Lire le théâtre.* Paris: Editions Sociales, 1977.

Wright, Elizabeth. "Psychoanalytic Criticism." *Modern Literary Theory.* Ed. Ann Jefferson and David Robey. Totowa N.J.: Barnes and Noble 1982. 113-33.

The Implicated Audience: Judith Thompson's Anti-Naturalism in *The Crackwalker*, *White Biting Dog*, *I Am Yours* and *Lion in the Streets*

by Julie Adam

In the 1990 Tarragon Theatre [revival] of *The Crackwalker* the Indian Man (Clayton Odjig)—the absolute outsider—remained on stage for some time after one of his encounters with Alan (Randy Hughson)—a relative outsider. In fact, he was uncomfortably close to those who sat in the first row of a very intimate auditorium (Tarragon's Extra Space). He sprawled diagonally across the invisible barrier between illusion and reality. One constantly had to remind oneself that this was an actor portraying a character. Would it have been easier or more difficult to think of him as a theatrical sign had he looked less "real" and had one not been aware that in another part of Toronto a similar figure would be lying on the street, perhaps spilling from sidewalk onto road, possibly ignored by passers-by, many of whom might be touched by the same sight in the theatre? How different would this stage image have been had someone from the street lain down on stage in the same manner? Would this intrusion of life into art have been tolerated by the people who applauded the intrusion of art into life, a perfectly convincing artificiality?

Audiences experience different forms and varying degrees of discomfort when the action enters the auditorium and they become involved, perhaps even implicated, in the plot. This discomfort results from emotional, intellectual and moral uncertainty in experiencing changes in distance between life and art. As long as the fourth wall, however thin and unstable, separates illusion and reality, one can delude oneself into believing that one is in control of one's reaction to the performance. When the action remains in the designated area—the area demarcated for performance—then any breach of the naturalistic contract is understood as a foregrounding of the process and the mechanics of performance, as in the case of Brechtian practice. When through any number of demystifying techniques illusion openly declares itself illusion—that is, it points to the reality of illusion rather than the illusion of reality—passive consumption is precluded. If, however, the playwright or the director tampers with spatial conventions and has the action enter the auditorium, then one begins to wonder whether this is an illusion or the thing itself. Of course, in the extreme version of this, in participatory theatre, naturalistic illusion gives way to another form of illusion. After all, audience participation is itself an illusion.

Brechtian anti-illusionist theatre, or its offshoots, insists that audiences become intellectually and politically engaged viewer-participants, in ideal cases able to take the ideological battle from the theatre to the street. Other theatres use anti-illusionistic devices and fluctuations in aesthetic distance for reasons that are not strictly, or not at all, political. For instance, in *The Glass Menagerie* Tennessee Williams uses these techniques to adjust and readjust the spectator's vision. Because the play is authored by memory and coloured by desire, the "dollying" is aesthetic and emotional, rather than political.

Judith Thompson engages in this second type of manipulation of aesthetic and emotional distance and in a constant readjustment of the fourth wall. Although the ostensible subject matter of her plays—human suffering, both physical and psychological, especially of the so-called underprivileged—is such that audiences frequently respond as if her plays were slice-of-life studies, *The Crackwalker* (1980; published 1989), *White Biting Dog* (1984), *I Am Yours* (1987) and *Lion in the Streets* (1990) belong to that tradition where a surreal day-dream or nightmare spills into a naturalistic picture. Many of her individual scenes—that is, basic units of dramatic presentation—may be naturalistic, but their juxtaposition takes the plays outside the restrictive domain of naturalism.

Thompson is interested in the dramatization of "Truth," that transcendent something that speaks to a collective unconscious. In fact, she has said that she wishes to explore those context-free moments of supposedly universal validity (Interview 98). She attempts to probe fundamental human problems and desires, but because she provides a very specific, indeed often narrowly defined, context as well as characters recognizable as particular types, and yet insists on universalization, her work is open to various ideologically based attacks.

White Biting Dog is a case in point. Its wealth of mythical material superimposed on a traditional tale of family discord has made Paul Walsh in his review of the published text state that "behind the straw dogs of excess… stand the familiar values of patriarchal authority" and that "the play seems unaware of its own ideological commitments." Furthermore, Walsh sees in the play an "unexplored conflict between a desire for formal innovation and an acquiescence to a perniciously powerful ideology of conservative authority" and maintains that "we are left with a grim morality of good and evil" (Walsh 146). I agree with Walsh's description of the play, but would argue that the "grim morality of good and evil" is not the embarrassing reality of the play to be unearthed by an astute critic, but its proud centre.

What resembles explorations of class issues, for instance in *The Crackwalker* and in *I Am Yours*, is only a superficial rendering of class warfare; the battle lines are usually drawn differently and the images and metaphors in *I Am Yours* take the play in another direction. It is not only Toilane, the working-class character, who literally declares war after his long-suffering mother gives him a consciousness raising speech, but also the other characters. The wars Mercy, Mack and Dee wage are not class or gender wars, but wars against the abyss, their personal darkness that threatens to engulf them. The class war is just one concrete manifestation, like Dee's emotional breakdown, of this more abstract and universal war. Similarly, while Thompson makes explicit the specific socio-economic context of

The Crackwalker, she insists that her "characters just don't have a particular social group" (Interview 97).

Since Thompson's plays deal with the walls people erect to keep out "the monster that's hovering around the periphery of civilization" (Interview 95) and with the doors they try to open to enter each other's lives, it is only fitting that her plays should rely on the constant shifting and repositioning of the fourth wall. To varying degrees, Thompson implicates spectators in the action of her plays and seldom allows them to remain uninvolved observers. In a 1989 interview she comments on the "penetrative effect" of plays in a comparison of "the ideal theatrical experience" with the way in which one dreams: "...when you go to sleep you dream. They're your dreams, but it seems as if they're just happening to you... I hope I have stumbled upon a kind of collective unconscious so that it's like a dream happening" ("Revisions" 19). This, I believe, implies that in a dream one is narrator, actor/character and observer, both insider and outsider, both active and passive, and it is this configuration that Thompson tries to replicate. Furthermore, she seems to wish to draw the audience into this dream-theatre and believes that they can relate on a subconscious level to the images that she places in characters' waking and sleeping dreams.

In *The Crackwalker*, in *I Am Yours*, and to a limited degree in *White Biting Dog* and *Lion in the Streets*, she uses a type of soliloquy or direct address to interrupt the action and to communicate with the audience on a different level than the linear plot. Without completely violating the fourth wall convention or engaging in participatory theatre, Thompson implicates an unsuspecting audience in the action of each play. Of particular interest are her openings where the audience contracts are drawn up and which, together with the closings, establish a frame that contains the audience.

Designers and directors, among them Thompson herself, have tended to translate the anti-naturalistic elements in her plays into the stage design, breaking up surfaces and creating multi-level sets with several acting areas to accommodate an episodic structure that emphasizes conceptually and visually, rather than sequentially, related episodes as well as fragmented psyches. In an illuminating article Robert Nunn discusses *The Crackwalker*'s reliance on spatial metaphors, especially its use of levels—social, psychological and linguistic—and comments on the images of rupture and seepage that dominate the play. There is another manner in which the play seeps corruption and pain, desire and love, and this has to do with seepage from stage into auditorium and with an energy that passes from performer to spectator and back.

The play opens with Theresa rushing out onto the stage and addressing the audience. In the 1990 Tarragon production Debra Kirshenbaum did not establish eye contact with the audience but her gaze included them in her field of vision as she stared at the wall behind them, and beyond. (*In White Biting Dog* there is a similar approach to audience address when Pony speaks to her father in the imaginary projection booth.) Kirshenbaum's touching portrayal of this lumbering, towering figure left a lasting impression. Theresa's long speech is a complaint and a confession of sorts and the audience functions as a confidante. They are asked to accept this "fool-saint," as George Toles terms her, and her vision of reality. By having Theresa speak to them directly, Thompson ensures that they hear her plea and see her deliver it. Theresa's first words to the audience, presumably following an argument with someone off-stage, are, "You know what she done to me?" (19). The play is an answer to this question. Appropriately, the play closes with a very brief scene, a final flicker of an image, where after a "Small struggle offstage. Theresa runs onstage" and says: "Stupid old bassard don't go foolin with me you don't even know who I look like even. You don't even know who I lookin like" (71). The lines are spoken to an off-stage male figure who wants sexual favours. The audience, unlike the "stupid old bassard," knows who Theresa "lookin like": in act 1, scene 4 Alan tells Theresa that she looks just like "that madonna lady; you know them pictures they got up in classrooms when you're a kid? ... Cept the madonna picture got a baby in it" (35-36). This is a testament of love and the audience can either laugh at Alan for his naivete or marvel at his innocence.

In *I Am Yours* the audience is drawn into the emotional fabric of the play and implicated in its action; in fact, it is made to become one of the characters the way the film camera can render the spectator the receiver of a speech, a look, or an action. In each case the character is positioned on a ramp that extends into audience space. The audience plays several roles: that of Toilane's mother and of the door that slams in his face in his nightmare of a childhood experience (119); of the judge as Toilane admits his guilt (164); of a confessor as Mack tells the story of his own nightmare and his attempts to tame the beast within (142, 162); of the fetus and then of the baby as Dee tries to make contact with her physical and spiritual self that leads her to grace (143, 176). Thus the audience finds itself both facing the main characters and inhabiting them. The action "happens" to the audience as it does to the characters in their dreams. Throughout the play, and especially at the end, the audience is made to accept the role of mediator. In the penultimate scene, Dee reaches a moment of communion with the audience—the "baby"—and in the last scene with Toilane, through the actual baby, whom he holds in his arms. Toilane's final question "Mum??" must be answered by the audience who has participated in the drama and has through the course of the play opened the door, so to speak. The play is framed by the opening scream "Mum!" and the closing question "Mum??," spoken by Toilane, in the first instance to his oblivious mother and to the audience, and in the second to his absent mother ("passed out or maybe dead" [176]), to the audience and to Dee, the new mother. Although Toilane and Dee are not speaking to each other in these last scenes—scene 35 cross-fades to scene 36 (176)—they communicate to and through the audience via their collective dreams.

White Biting Dog and *Lion in the Streets*, two melodramatic fantasies, are less dependent on direct audience address. In these plays the nightmarish images, now an integral part of the plot, are enacted rather than described. If the setting of *White Biting Dog* is hell, as Cape seems to suggest, that of *Lion in the Streets* is purgatory. *White Biting Dog* opens with Cape, a "very handsome silky young man who could seduce almost anybody" and who "flirts with the audience while telling them the most terrible things about himself" ([ix]), drumming on his bongo drums and then uttering the first line, to the audience: "Did it even happen?" (1). Together with Pony, a "deeply ethical" ([ix]) saviour/sacrificial victim, the audience is drawn into the vile games Cape and the vampiric matriarch Lomia play with the dying patriarch Glidden, a Norman Rockwell enthusiast, and Pascal, Lomia's young lover. Pony delivers her long posthumous speech towards the end of the play from the "edge of [the] stage, and directs... [it] to where the projectionist would be if the theatre were a cinema" (106); that is, to the wall behind the audience. She tells her father, invisible but somewhere at the back of the auditorium, how she was invaded by the worst evil, what Thompson calls "radical evil" (Interview 103). If through the course of the play the audience was not sure whether what they had just seen did "really happen," this scene places them in direct contact with Pony, the source of grace and redemption.

In *Lion in the Streets* the first lines are once again spoken to the audience, this time by Isobel, a child martyr, guardian angel and lost soul trying to gain peace. Isobel, murdered seventeen years ago, invites the audience to journey with her through a series of overlapping vignettes of contemporary life and to witness scenes of psychological and physical violence. When at the end of the play she finally confronts her murderer and instead of avenging herself she utters the purifying words "I love you," she is allowed to enter heaven. As she ascends, the audience is left behind, on earth, in purgatory.

The position of the audience and of the fourth wall varies from play to play. The audience is most intimately inside the characters in *I Am Yours*, sharing their dreams and visions. Character and spectator are as closely linked as the pronouns in "I am yours."[1] Naturalistic illusionism is precluded but scenes of communion between characters and audience rely on another form of illusion, that of art and life inhabiting the same realm. This provocative illusionism is achieved also in *Lion in the Streets*, by a different technique. Isobel, the central character who establishes brief but important contact with the audience, is an outsider: she is dead and invisible. She functions chorally as prologue/narrator, and although physically she moves through the action, conceptually she exists in a zone between stage and auditorium. Unable to enter heaven till the end of the play, lost and trapped, she turns in desperation to the audience:

> Hey! Who gonna take me home? You? You gotta car? What kinda car you got? Trans Am? What about bus tickets? You gotta bus tickets? C'mon. Come on. COME ON. SOMEBODY. What I'm sposed to do, ha? Who, who gonna take me home? Who gonna take me home? (10)

Although the fourth wall has been brought down for long enough to unsettle a complacent audience, given the nature of conventional non-participatory theatre, no answer will be forthcoming.

Many of Thompson's characters inhabit the space that both separates and fuses illusion and reality. It is the exploration of this magical zone that is at the centre of Judith Thompson's theatricalism.

(1992)

Note

[1] A translation of "*Ich bin dein,*" a line from a twelfth-century lyrical poem from the *Tegernseebriefe*, written by a young nun to a cleric who was her teacher.

Works Cited

Nunn, Robert. "Spatial metaphor in the plays of Judith Thompson." *Theatre History in Canada/Histoire du théâtre au Canada* 10:1 (Spring 1989): 3-29.

Thompson, Judith. *The Crackwalker*. Thompson, *The Other Side of the Dark: Four Plays by Judith Thompson*. Toronto: Coach House, 1989. 15-71.

———. *I Am Yours*. Thompson, *The Other Side of the Dark: Four Plays by Judith Thompson*. Toronto: Coach House, 1989. 115-76.

———. Interview with Judith Rudakoff. *Fair Play: 12 Women Speak (Conversations with Canadian Playwrights)*. Ed. Judith Rudakoff and Rita Much. Toronto: Simon & Pierre, 1990. 88-194.

———. *Lion in the Streets*. Toronto: Playwrights Canada, 1990.

———. *The Other Side of the Dark: Four Plays by Judith Thompson*. Toronto: Coach House, 1989.

———. "Revisions of probability: An interview with Judith Thompson." By Sandra Tomc. *Canadian Theatre Review* 59 (Summer 1989): 18-23.

———. *White Biting Dog*. Toronto: Playwrights Canada, 1984.

Toles, George. " 'Cause You're the Only One I Want': The Anatomy of Love in the Plays of Judith Thompson." *Canadian Literature* 118 (Autumn 1988): 116-35.

Walsh, Paul. Review of *White Biting Dog* by Judith Thompson. *Canadian Theatre Review* 45 (Winter 1985): 143-46.

Constructing Fictions of an Essential Reality, *or*, "This Pickshur is Niiiice": Judith Thompson's *Lion in the Streets*[1]

by Jen Harvie

In the opening scene of Judith Thompson's most recent stage play, *Lion in the Streets*,[2] "[t]he ghost of ISOBEL, a deranged and very ragged looking nine-year-old Portuguese girl, runs around and around a large circle, to music, terrified of a remembered pursuer, in fact, the man who killed her in this playground seventeen years before the action of the play.... She is terrified" (*Lion in the Streets* 15). She says:

> Doan be scare. Doan be scare. [*turns to audience*] Doan be scare of this pickshur! This pickshur is niiiice, nice! I looove this pickshur, this pickshur is mine! [*gesturing behind her*] Is my house, is my street, is my park, is my people! You know me, you know me very hard! I live next house to you, with my brother and sisters, Maria, Luig, Carla and Romeo we play, we play with your girl, your boy, you know me, you know me very hard. But... when did tha be? Tha not be now! Tha not be today! I think tha be very long years ago I think I be old. I think I be very old. Is my house but is not my house is my street but is not my street my people is gone I am lost. I am lost. I AM LOOOOOOOOOST! (15)

One of the things I find interesting about this passage—and, for that matter, the rest of *Lion in the Streets* and much of Thompson's other work—is the way that it may be seen to combine a powerful level of realism with equally powerful deconstructions of reality. Isobel may seem "real" because she exhibits characteristics which, in traditional psychological realism, might indicate she was a unified subject—a real person with a real problem. She tells us she has a home, a family, and is afraid she is lost. And the idiosyncrasies of her naturalistic speech seem to corroborate her reality, suggesting further that she is young, perhaps speaks English as a second language, and is frightened. Read as a unified realist text, and the play may be seen to invite this kind of reading, Isobel appears to be a little girl in a classic state of psychic fragmentation which she and the audience will presumably move from through the course of the play to a state of unity and resolution.

But as much as Isobel may seem real and may seem to confirm our preconceptions of reality, her reality may likewise be seen as problematic. For instance, she describes her home, what frames her reality, as a "pickshur"—specifically a representation, not a reality. Moreover, she undermines the truth of her own description of herself and her "life" when she claims she is very old although she seems young, and she contradicts her own story—her own construction of reality—with comments like, "Is my house but is not my house...." Later in the play, Isobel realizes that long ago she was kidnapped and murdered. "I am gone," she observes, "I am no more!" (36). Realistically, these lines suggest that Isobel "went missing" and is now dead. In a poststructuralist sense however, these lines suggest Isobel is missing—she is absence, not realistic presence.

As a critic concerned with issues of cultural heterogeneity, the reason this combination of the apparently real and the real problematized interests me is because it seems to allow for the mimetic depiction of contemporary social realities—realities, say, of age, gender, class, and race—at the same time as it deconstructs our ideas of reality, problematizing the objectivity with which we may think we perceive what seems "obvious," and positing reality not as essential, homogeneous, and therefore static, but as provisional, heterogeneous, and changeable. Informing a reading of gender issues, this combination might allow us to recognize gender as, in one respect, "true," and, in another respect, socially constructed. Acknowledging gender as true, we may recognize it as a common condition for oppression and confront and challenge that oppression. We may also allow for gender identification as a form of empowerment. Reading gender as socially constructed, on the other hand, we may perceive it as an ideologically loaded fiction, in Julia Kristeva's terms a "slogan," a myth of a static idea in a world which might more constructively be considered ever changing.

These two positions—one seemingly affirming an essential reality and the other apparently deconstructing that reality—might both benefit a project of recognizing and communicating cultural difference, but they might also appear inherently to negate one another. However, I think they may be seen as compatible if we consider a concept of an essential reality as perhaps necessary but only ever provisional, in other words, as a fiction of an essential reality.[3] I would like to suggest that Thompson's *Lion in the Streets* constructs necessary but provisional fictions of reality. This allows that some concept of a static or essential reality may be helpful to a project of cultural emancipation, but also that such a concept should be considered provisional, and in that sense fictional, so that reality may furthermore be seen as not intractable but open to change.

To begin, I would like to look at how Thompson's *Lion in the Streets* may be read as a linear, unified realistic text, and how such a reading may, first, serve a project of recognizing cultural heterogeneity and, second, impede that project. In serving that project, *Lion in the Streets* mimetically depicts a recognizable current Canadian society, specifically that of a semi-gentrified neighbourhood in urban Toronto. The play "shows," and evokes audience empathy for, a vast gamut of oppressed subjectivities differentiated by, among other things, age, race, class, sexuality, gender, religion, occupation, and ability. With twenty-nine characters, including a young girl of ethnic minority, a woman with cystic fibrosis, and a gay male Maritimer, the play presents a cultural spectrum broad enough to be the envy of any Canadian federal government advertising office. And importantly, the play evokes empathy for these diverse subjectivities. Thematically, *Lion in the Streets* acts as an exhortation to recognize the sources of one's oppression and to rise up and challenge them, a worthy theme for any oppressed subjectivity. But a realist reading may also impede a project of effecting cultural change because it may be inherently conservative, seeming to confirm a world we think we already know, reifying the truth of the oppressions we identify, and comfortably closing off any will to change stimulated in the audience in the course of the play by providing the catharsis of resolution.

To demonstrate how *Lion in the Streets* may be read as a unified realist text and how this may serve the recognition of cultural heterogeneity, I would like to turn first to characterization, attempting to identify character as unified by realistic psychological motivations and objectives.[4] The play has been described by Thompson herself as a relay play and by *The Globe and Mail* critic Robert Cushman as a daisy chain play (Cushman). Structurally, this means one character from the play's first scene appears in the otherwise apparently unrelated second scene, from which another character appears in a similarly unrelated third scene, and so on, until we accumulate twenty-nine characters and roughly thirteen main scenes. Thus, the play may be seen to resist unity, particularly unified characterization. But through the length of the play, Isobel is present, appearing in her ghostliness on the fringes of every scene, sometimes commenting, sometimes remaining silent, but providing throughout recognizable character objectives which are reflected or even reverberated by numerous other characters in their individual scenes. In act I, Isobel's objective is to find her home, and in act II, this alters slightly, becoming the need to find her killer, whom she refers to as the "lion." In both acts Isobel seeks resolution or, in Thompson's etymology, escape from the "abyss" (Interview 95). And it is in identifying each character's "abyss" or "lack" that we may further identify some of the ways and reasons people or groups are oppressed in the current social formation.

For instance, we may say Isobel's age and gender are part of what renders her vulnerable to the suffering she experiences—abduction, probable rape, and murder. Another scene presents a character named Scarlett who has cerebral palsy and is confined to a wheelchair. Her "abyss" is boredom, partly the result of patronizing social attitudes and assumptions which construct the disabled as predominantly unable to participate in "normal" activities like, for instance, sex. Scarlett's objective might thus be read as the need to escape from her boredom by challenging social attitudes which diminish the interests and abilities of the disabled and reconstructing herself as someone who can, as she puts it, "git it ONNN" (46). Other scenes show a woman whose abyss is the fear of her impending death from bone cancer and whose proverbial "home" or resolution is the possibility of "d[ying] good" (35), and a daycare worker whose abyss is the snobbish insults she suffers from the parents and whose objective is to confront and challenge their classist assumptions with a comment like Scarlett's spoken to her interviewer, "You think you're bettern me, dontcha?" (46). Repeatedly throughout *Lion in the Streets* apparently real characters are presented in situations which mimetically portray some of the diverse possibilities of oppression in a heterogeneous urban Canada.

The play's structure may likewise be read as unified, providing a through line from disorder to resolution and catharsis. As in a quest narrative, Isobel searches for her home and her killer and other characters search for their respective homes or resolutions. And as in a revenge tragedy—or perhaps more specifically a revenge comedy, because Isobel ultimately forgives her killer—Isobel and the other characters seek to triumph over their oppressors and oppressions. Again these through lines suggest "real" conditions of oppression and "real" responses to that oppression, responses which include self-recognition (especially as this relates to recognizing the sources of one's oppression) and confessing or giving forgiveness, methods of achieving catharsis or, again in Thompson's words, "grace," which she describes as happening "through penitence.... Through seeing who you are and changing things" (Interview in Rudakoff and Much 103).

Imagery may also act as a unified signifier of meaning in *Lion in the Streets*, serving to help make sense of or comprehend the play's unified meaning. Typically for a play by Thompson, the strongest image pattern is Christian, predominantly Roman Catholic. Images of angels and saints and private heavens and hells abound. [5] Through the course of the play Isobel acts as a Dantesque guide through inferno and purgatory to heaven—a pattern reflected in actors' vertical movement up and down the set of the premiere production directed by Thompson at Toronto's Harbourfront in June, 1990. And Isobel's final monologue, which invokes her own apotheosis or at least her ascension, makes repeated reference to her breath, another strongly loaded Christian signifier. The play's title itself comes from Proverbs 26:13, the whole of which, in conjunction with verse 14 reads,

> The sluggard says, "There is a lion in the road! There is a lion in the streets!" As a door turns on its hinges, so does a sluggard on his bed. (May and Metzger 798)

The passage implies that for fear of oppression, evil, or Thompson's abyss, some people retreat, refusing to challenge their oppressions. Thus the title, along with the play's other Christian imagery, may act implicitly as an exhortation to the play's characters and audience to search out and confront the sources of oppression in their "lives." In interview, Thompson has said that all of her plays "show how we hang onto what brings magic to our lives," adding that "*Lion [in the Streets]*, which ends with an ascension, is about the power of Isobel's spirit—the power to confront evil and walk away with something even though life may be forfeit" (Kaplan 55). The play's Christian imagery may be seen to bolster this theme of self-recognition and self-challenge, what Thompson has referred to elsewhere as "finding that Force in yourself and using it" ("An Interview" 37).

A second strong image pattern in *Lion in the Streets* is that of pictures which characters repeatedly refer to or imaginatively construct in order to contain and stabilize what might otherwise be threatening situations and experiences. Isobel, for example, refers to her home as a "pickshur," thereby rendering her desire attainable because it is now somehow "concrete." Joanne, dying of bone cancer, imaginatively interpolates herself into a pre-Raphaelite painting of Ophelia drowning beautifully in a stream, thereby capturing and controlling a death which she otherwise fears (34-35). Again, if we read this picture imagery as signifying unified meaning—and its repeated occurrence in similar patterns may suggest this approach—we may see it also as supporting the emancipatory theme I have identified since it suggests an active recognition and construction of what one wants.

Finally, language in *Lion in the Streets* may often act as a realistic indication of unified meaning. Presenting so many characters so quickly, Thompson often uses "textural" detail provided in language as much as or even more than the information provided literally through language to establish the psychological realism of her characters and to identify their various "lions." In a meeting with her charges' yuppie parents, a daycare worker named Rhonda attempts to assimilate by speaking the type of language sported by the parents. But when her practice of occasionally giving the children sugar comes under the direct attack of one parent as the first step in what will then become the children's inexorable plummet to cocaine addiction, Rhonda speaks in her own defense in language which gradually alters from her best yuppie-friendly to include numerous ellipses, the occasional grammatically "incorrect" space holder, the expression "I seen" for "I have seen," and the word "youse" for the second person plural (29-31). Thus, Rhonda's language acts realistically to assert what she perceives as her class difference, which she further perceives as a reason for her persecution (cf Thompson, "An Interview" 37).

Altogether I think it is possible and indeed worthwhile to construct a unified realist reading of Thompson's *Lion in the Streets.* Such a reading allows for the construction of unified subjects or representatives of certain subjectivities, mimetically depicting a vast range of personal characteristics for which individuals may suffer social persecution or oppression in a heterogeneous urban Canadian community. Read as a unified realist text, *Lion in the Streets* is a profound modern parable on the value of recognizing and overcoming some of the conditions which act as grounds for oppression in our current society.

What this type of reading may also do, however, is naturalize our constructions of reality or truth, making them seem essential, transcendental, or at least somehow static and in that sense intractable. Recognizing the "real"—real people marked by their "human nature," real problems, and real situations—we reify that reality, potentially enforcing its hegemony. Thus, although a realistic reading of *Lion in the Streets* may generate an interpretation of the text as promoting change, such a reading may also inhibit change by enforcing a linear—in other words deterministic—world view. A unified realistic reading may thus counteract or undermine its own theme of progress and change because such a reading requires and therefore reifies a recognition of the status quo.

Which is why I think it is worthwhile to frame this realistic reading, and an idea of an essential reality in general, as a necessary but provisional fiction, a myth of stasis, an indication not a prescription of some of the potential conditions of contemporary society. Such a reading would show that what appears real might be considered more constructively as a fiction or a discursive construction of an essential reality. This perception of reality would allow for the possibility of change—as alternative "realities" may be seen to be constructed equally easily—and would also stimulate a recognition of reality not as essential and homogeneous, but plural and heterogeneous. The social problems identified in a realistic reading of the play could thus be seen as not intractable, but open to change. Furthermore, a reading that does not carry the objective of unifying and universalizing meaning and closing off conflict and change with a neatly arrived at resolution may instead allow to flourish a plurality of meanings and a will to change. Thus, a thematics promoting change need not be restrained by a reading practice of containment.

To problematize a unified realistic reading of *Lion in the Streets*, this second type of reading which I am identifying might attempt to show how the play presents itself and the reality to which it seems to refer as discursively produced texts. Characterization might thus be read not as unified and based in a single objective, but rather as fragmented and based in often conflicting and changing objectives. Feminist theatre critic Elin Diamond calls this "refusing the romanticism of identity," where a concept of unified identity is seen as hegemonic, acting to conserve the status quo. According to this type of reading, characters in *Lion in the Streets* may be seen as split subjects who construct and adopt, often self-consciously, fictions of subjective unity that will help them to 'comprehend' and confront their constantly changing and often threatening situations.

I have already looked at how Rhonda, the daycare worker, switches languages in order to find and adopt a subject position which is, as Richard Paul Knowles has written, "useful and meaningful in a particular context" (36).[6] Other characters self-fashion in other ways, attempting to contain themselves and those around them by constructing and adopting a dominant narrative, picture, or fiction selected from an implied range of potential realities. When a character named Bill is attempting to leave his wife Susan for another woman, he refers to Susan as a "cartoon mum" (22), finely constructing what is for him a pejorative image and rejecting it in favour of an image of a woman he does want, his lover Lily, whom he likewise constructs as his "sweet whore."[7] Susan, in her turn, attempts to prove she too can be libidinous and constructs herself as a temptress, painting a verbal portrait of a scene where she once danced for Bill. When this image is similarly rejected by Bill, Susan reverts to a characterization of herself as a caregiver, nursing Bill through an illness she also imaginatively constructs. The exaggerated unity or obvious construction of conflicting interpretations of reality in this scene and others suggests that these "pictures" are not "complete" representations of characters' realities but are adopted as "slogans" which help characters to make sense of or contain only provisionally the "lion" of a chaotic or threatening experience.

In another scene Scarlett, who is by all appearances severely disabled and confined to her wheelchair, claims she has a lover with whom she can dance. "I can MOVE when my boy comes," she explains, having risen from her wheelchair. "I am movin, I know I am, I am turnin and swishin and holdin," and she and a character referred to in the stage directions as "*MAN*" "dance romantically around the set" (47). Apparently mutually exclusive narratives of Scarlett's disability and ability make equal claim to truthfulness or reality. Thus, the desirability and indeed functionalism of a static concept of reality is allowed and even encouraged while the exclusivity of any dominant reality is severely problematized. And this goes for the audience as much as the characters. The audience partakes in these various realities without necessarily knowing which reality has a stronger truth claim. Thus the audience may recognize that in constructing a dominant narrative it does so actively and only ever provisionally. Realistic and unified character objectives and narrative through lines may be read but are perhaps best seen as provisional, allowing for the coexistence of diverse and sometimes mutually exclusive realities.

In terms of plot and structure, *Lion in the Streets*' rather unorthodox relay pattern may also be seen to disrupt a traditional realist reading of plot as linear and unified, usually following a single protagonist's "journey." In reference to writing *Lion in the Streets* Thompson has said, "I thought, I just can't bear some giant narrative, somebody taking this immense journey" ("A Conversation" 188). The resulting fragmented text, with its rapid cutting from scene to not necessarily related scene, may disrupt narrative linearity and thus narrative predictability, further interrupting audience expectations and identification. Through constant interruption the audience may come to perceive its sense of identification and resolution in any given scene as always merely provisional, a possibility which further suggests all perceptions of identity should be considered provisional.

Disrupted narrative flow in *Lion in the Streets* may also interrupt audience expectations, problematizing a traditional realist reading of reality as predictable and in that sense intractable. Thompson has also been quoted as saying that in writing *Lion in the Streets*, "I just couldn't cope with the idea of a huge body of narrative.... I started to find that kind of narrative tedious, because your expectations are usually fulfilled" (Knowles 34). Disrupting audience expectations allows for the expansion of potential realities. For instance, if we consider the play to have a through line offered by Isobel and her apparent objective of revenge, we may expect the play to end with that revenge enacted, with Isobel killing her killer. Instead, the play ends with Isobel forgiving her killer, the very unexpectedness of which may challenge the pre-dictability of "human nature" and reality. This unexpected conclusion implies an act of will on the part of Isobel to forgo a tragic conclusion and instead to construct a narrative ending which is more like a comedy. Isobel's achievement or construction of grace requires not only an act of will on her part, however, but also on the part of the audience. In her last lines, Isobel switches the focus from the play to the audience, making the direct address, "I take my life. I want you all to take your life. I want you all to have your life" (63). Isobel may provide a through line for the play, but she does not provide a closed discourse. The audience is invited to close the discourse with a happy ending, but the act of constructing this narrative ending is foregrounded, allowing for the benefit of a static reality—a "happy ending"—but also emphasizing that this reality is fictional or constructed.

Imagery in *Lion in the Streets* may also be seen as a potential destabilizer of meaning as much as a unifier, as it is more commonly read. In scenes like the one where Scarlett describes herself as a living hell and threatens, quite literally, to swallow her interviewer Christine (48-49), the play's imagery may be so overt or blunt as to call attention to itself and to its role as a unifier of meaning, effectively alienating the audience from a passive acceptance of the imagery as unified and unifying. Foregrounded like this, the play's imagery may be seen to invite the audience to acknowledge the tools it uses to construct meaning and to perceive such constructions as single possibilities chosen from a range of potential meanings. Reading imagery as a unified indicator of meaning may thus be seen as helpful and constructive, but also potentially reductive, as choosing one paradigm of meaning may implicitly disallow other options. The play's picture imagery, if we read it as metarepresentational, may act particularly strongly to interrogate the potential of any representational apparatus—like a play—to portray unified truth. Characters may adopt "pictures" or images as subject positions but the possibility of ever achieving such stasis is nevertheless problematized throughout the play with comments like Rhonda's to Joanne: "You can't become a picture, do you know what I mean? I mean you can't... BE... a picture, okay?" (32).

Finally, language in *Lion in the Streets* may be seen to foreground its own textuality, further problematizing the play's realism. Thompson's naturalistic language, with its acute details connoting class, age, and psychology, often segues into a sort of "magic realism" in which the details of the realist language are exploded and its writerliness is foregrounded. In one scene, Isobel's mother is telling her neighbour how she was folding laundry: "I fold. I fold clothes one pile for Antony, one pile for me, one for Maria, Romeo, ISOBEL and Luig, my hands fold the clothes...." And her narrative gradually carries her into the body of her husband, standing on a subway platform where he will fall to his death:

> ...I am his head, circles and circles like red birds flying around and around I am his throat, tight, cannot breathe enough air in my body the floor the floor move, and sink in, rise up rise like a wall like a killin wave turn turn me in circles with teeth in circles and under and over I fall!... I fall on the silver track nobody move I hearing the sound. The sound of the rats in the tunnel their breath like a basement these dark rats running running towards me I am stone I am earth cannot scream cannot move the rats tramp... trample my body flat-ten and every bone splinter like... (27)[8]

The switch to this sort of magic realism here and elsewhere in the play may draw attention to the textuality of language, emphasizing that even when, as in naturalistic speech, language appears "natural," it is always constructed.

Thus through analyses of character, plot and structure, imagery and language,[9] we may read *Lion in the Streets* as non-unified, foregrounding its own construction and, therefore, its own manipulation of "reality." Characters are shown to construct, adopt, and adapt their own realities, and the audience's complicity in constructing the fiction of the play's realistic through line and theme is foregrounded through the unorthodox exaggeration of the tools of imagery and structure which an audience may often use unconsciously to order a play's unified meaning or reality. What we often perceive as reality is revealed to be constructed, and what is potentially liberating about this is that "reality" need no longer be seen as essential or transcendental but subject to change. Recognizing the imposition of unity, we allow for the possibility of plurality, alterity, and heterogeneity. The different oppressed subjectivities we identified in our unified realist reading need not be totally deconstructed and disallowed by this second reading, but may be contextualized as historically and culturally contingent fictions, not transcendental realities. Similarly, the thematic movement from oppression through self-recognition to liberation identified in our first reading need not be read as universal and timeless but historically and culturally contingent. After all, a timeless thematics of liberation requires and therefore ensures a timelessness of oppression.

The "realities" which we read in our unified realist reading may thus be seen as necessary but only provisional. As Thompson has said in interview, "I really think that in many areas it is possible to turn our sense of being victims around" ("A Conversation" 192). We may recognize "our sense of being victims," our identities, as fictions but, nevertheless, we may also occasionally construct them as real to help us in certain oppressive situations.[10] We may take both the essentialist or realist reading and the poststructuralist reading because both are helpful to a project of cultural emancipation. And I mean to suggest this as a potential reading strategy not just for this play.

As Isobel says, "This pickshur is niiiice." We know it is a picture, a fiction, but we still like it, need it, and invoke it however it may help us. This is a politics of the provisional, allowing Isobel and her audience to save their respective "neighbourhoods," if not the world.

(1992)

Notes

1 This is a revised version of a paper presented to the Association for Canadian Theatre Research/Association de la recherche théâtrale au Canada at the University of Prince Edward Island on 29 May 1992. Both versions are based on research done at the University of Guelph in 1991 for my Master's thesis, "Problematizing 'Truth': The Stage Plays of Judith Thompson." My MA thesis supervisors were Ric Knowles and Ann Wilson and to them I would like once again to extend my thanks.

2 *Lion in the Streets* was first produced by Tarragon Theatre for the duMaurier World Stage Festival, Toronto, in June 1990, with Thompson directing. The stage script was developed from Thompson's earlier radio play, *A Big White Light.*

3 My ideas on this approach are informed primarily by my understanding of feminist standpoint theory. Briefly stated, according to some versions of this theory, a practice of deconstructing identity is considered valuable because it may, for instance, dismantle patriarchal inscriptions of femininity. But standpoint theory also encourages the adoption of the fictional position "woman" in order to safeguard against a rampant deconstruction which might reduce all differences to an absolute Difference, erecting a new universality and once again "silencing" the gender specific interests of feminism. Feminist standpoint theory rejects both the supposed "view from nowhere" of humanism and the idealistic "dream of being everywhere" of poststructuralism, and adopts instead a cautious "view from somewhere." For a more elaborate discussion of this idea, see Bordo.

4 Throughout this unified realist reading, the reader will recognize the indebtedness of my terminology—"motivation," "objective," "through line,"—to Stanislavskian acting technique. While my intention here is to delineate a reading strategy that seeks a "unified" character's "through line" to a "super objective," a corresponding ("Method") acting strategy would have many of the same emphases and effects.

5 Consider, for instance, halo imagery in Maria's description of her dying husband (27) and in Father Hayes' narration of the child David "dancing *on* the water" (40, italics added).

6 This article on Thompson's dramaturgy provides the basis for "The Fractured Subject of Judith Thompson," Knowles' shorter introduction to the published version of *Lion in the Streets.*

7 Bill does not call Lily his "sweet whore" in the play's published version, but did so in the Tarragon Theatre production directed by Thompson in November 1990.

8 It is important to note that it is not "really" Maria who speaks these lines but the neighbour's husband, George, impersonating Maria. This layered and self-conscious role-playing may serve again to de-naturalize the play's realism and to emphasize unified subjectivity as something which is constructed and adopted rather than unified and true.

9 Both my reading strategies have emphasized approaches to the play as a written text. For performance and production, similar strategies could be employed to examine the unity and potential disunity of direction, acting style(s), and set, costume, lighting, and music design.

10 It may be argued that the freedom to construct different realities is not itself an absolute, but is available rather in varying degrees to different groups or individuals. Access to emancipation through self-construction must thus be seen as a function of privilege. I think this is a valid and important criticism of the "standpoint theory" approach, but I would also like to suggest that while it indicates limits to the usefulness or applicability of this theory, it does not entirely deny this theory's value. I also think this criticism is worth considering in reference to *Lion in the Streets*. One might ask, to what extent does *Lion in the Streets* provide feasible or constructive encouragement to oppressed subjectivities, and to what extent does it romanticize, and therefore continue to oppress, objectify, or appropriate for uses of a privileged group's fantasy, various oppressed subjectivities? In an interview with Thompson, Zimmerman suggests that some characters' constructions of liberation in *Lion in the Streets* are unlikely. Part of Thompson's reply is, "...it is mysterious" ("A Conversation" 192). To what extent does this reply mystify Thompson's interest, as a relatively privileged member of society, in generating texts which portray but may not facilitate the emancipation of oppressed individuals, and to what extent does it, in its very ambiguity, capture her commitment to unlikely and, for that very reason, powerful challenges to oppression?

Works Cited

Bordo, Susan. "Feminism, Postmodernism, and Gender-Scepticism." *Feminism/ Postmodernism*. Ed. Linda J. Nicholson. New York and London: Routledge 1990. 133-56.

Cushman, Robert. "Exploring a Limitless Domain of Human Misery." *The Globe and Mail* 4 June 1990: C8.

Diamond, Elin. "Refusing the Romanticism of Identity: Narrative Interventions in Churchill, Benmussa, Duras." *Performing Feminisms: Feminist Critical Theory and Theatre*. Ed. Sue-Ellen Case. Baltimore and London: Johns Hopkins UP, 1990. 92-105.

Kaplan, Jon. "Mini-fest Probes Thompson's Unsettling Visions." *Now* 8 November 1990: 55.

Knowles, Richard Paul. "The Achievement of Grace." *Brick* 41 (Summer 1991): 33-36.

Kristeva, Julia. "Woman Can Never Be Defined." Trans. Marilyn A. August. *New French Feminisms*. Ed. Elaine Marks and Isabelle de Courtivron. Amherst: U of Massachusetts P, 1980. 137-41.

May, Herbert G. and Bruce M. Metzger, ed. *Oxford Annotated Bible*. New York: Oxford UP, 1962.

Thompson, Judith. "A Conversation with Judith Thompson." By Cynthia Zimmerman. *Canadian Drama/L'art dramatique canadien* 16.2 (1990): 184-94.

———. Interview. *Fair Play: 12 Women Speak (Conversations with Canadian Playwrights)*. Ed. Judith Rudakoff and Rita Much. Toronto: Simon & Pierre, 1990. 187-204.

———. "An Interview with Judith Thompson." By Eleanor Wachtel. *Brick* 41 (Summer 1991): 37-41.

———. *Lion in the Streets*. Toronto: Coach House, 1992.

Going North on Judith Thompson's *Sled*

by Sherrill Grace

> North.
> Where north?
> Far. (Richler 413)

> What happens to the North... when women enter the northern landscape? (Atwood 88)

It is no exaggeration to say that Canadians are fascinated by what Glenn Gould called "the idea of North."[1] This fascination can be traced from the mid-nineteenth century to the present, and what is understood by the term "North" has both changed with the changing geo-political realities of Canada and, paradoxically, even stubbornly, remained the same. Judith Thompson's new play belongs to a long line of texts that contribute to and participate in what I call (after Foucault) the discursive formation of "North," and it is her use of "North" as idea and symbol that I want to examine here.[2]

"North" is central to all aspects of Thompson's play, but the play is extremely complex, and my focus on one element means that many other interesting issues cannot be considered. Nevertheless, looking at *Sled* through a northern lens facilitates both a close reading of the internal dynamics of the play (its themes, symbols, setting/staging, characters, language, structure, and intertextuality) and an evaluation of its place within a series of wider, interconnected contexts of Canadian culture. To go "North" on Thompson's *Sled* is to enter an imagined space, on page or stage, that is already crowded with southern constructions of "North." But why should anyone want to go "North" in the first place, and what happens when you get there? What does going *North* mean?

Sled is a hybrid play that mixes dramatic modes in a bravura combination of styles and voices: without warning, the play shifts from a detailed realist presentation to a lyrical expression of emotional states; ghosts appear to characters who are otherwise firmly situated in a gritty material reality that is created through props, costume, and language; characters suddenly break from familiar modes of dialogue into song or expressionist monologue; linear time, although asserted at intervals, is disrupted by flashbacks and flashforwards, and space (notably the stage itself, as described in the stage instructions) is multiple and fluid so that it can be both realistic and symbolic and allow "North" to be superimposed on a Toronto urban scene. The characters contribute to this hybridity in that they represent a range of ethnic and linguistic groups, from the First Nations, the so-called founding races, French and English, to immigrant groups like the Irish and the Italians. Moreover, they are neither fully developed as people, whose psychology is explored and thickened through action and dialogue, nor merely symbols or stereotypes; they can be read and performed in multiple ways.

Thompson's attempted inclusivity has an epic scope and intention. In *Sled* she tries to create her image of Canada, from its assumed beginnings to its present precarious position as a nation at the end of the twentieth century, and she attempts to construct this vision of the country from a highly problematic combination of metonymy and metaphor. The metonymic setting is Toronto, more specifically a small neighbourhood called Seaton Village, which lies between Dupont and Bloor, west of Bathurst, and the metaphoric setting is the Pickerel and Jack Lake Lodge with its extensive snowmobile trails and "a wilderness farther north" (*Sled* 12). Seaton Village is constructed as the part that represents the whole, where the whole is understood as Toronto, which, in turn, is offered to the audience/reader as representative of civilized, urban, southern Canada. The Lodge, its trails, and the "wilderness farther north" function metaphorically as the Other, a vast, empty, undifferentiated space lying somewhere up there and bearing whatever fantasies and values southerners project upon it.

The setting of the play calls for a juxtaposition of this metaphoric "North" with this metonymic southern neighbourhood, although, at times, the two spaces merge, with "North" superimposed upon Clinton Street. When the play shifts from Annie's opening song, "Oh heavenly time of day," the stage instructions call for precisely this kind of superimposition: "*A residential street, with mostly red brick houses with high pointed roofs, some three storey, but most, two-storey workers' houses. The houses, however, look as though they are in the middle of a forest. The birches remain*" (15). The effect of this staging is to stress the presence of "North" in the mind's eye, or imagination of the characters, to indicate the degree to which "North" permeates everything we do and are in southern, urban Canada, and to remind us that it (whatever *it* is) is always up there to escape to when the violence and degradation of urban life threaten to overwhelm us.

The plot of the play is circular and mythic. The story line is simple: a middle-aged Toronto couple, Annie the singer and Jack the cop, go to the northern Ontario lodge for a weekend's respite from the city and a faltering marriage. When Annie goes for a midnight walk along the snowmobile trails she is shot by a drunken local who has stolen a snowmobile to poach moose and may (or may not) have mistaken her for game. Meanwhile, back in the city on Clinton Street, a young woman called Evangeline waits for the return of her lost brother and shares memories and monologues with an Italian-Canadian neighbour, Joe, who recalls the violence that shattered his family. After Annie's violent death, Kevin, the man who killed her, makes his way to Toronto to find his mother and sister, while Jack, the bereaved husband, returns to his house, which is almost next door to Evangeline's and Joe's. Kevin turns out to be Evangeline's lost brother, kidnapped by a babysitter when he was only four and whisked away to North Bay, but because he is only her half-brother he sees nothing wrong in insisting upon a possessive sexual relationship with her. Inevitably, Kevin and Jack confront each other over Evangeline, but when Jack realizes that Kevin killed Annie he tries to murder him. Less predictably, Evangeline picks up a gun and shoots Jack before he can strangle her brother, and the two siblings flee "North," following the North Star. The story ends with Evangeline and Kevin on "the hill where Annie was killed" (109). Evangeline is soon to give birth, Kevin is about to die, and the Northern Lights fill the night around them, while Annie (or her ghost) sings once more "Oh heavenly time of day" and a Snowy Owl hoots.

II

In addition to the setting, with its dominant spatial metaphor of northern lodge, wilderness, and snowy trails, and the cyclic action that returns us, as in a ritual of life and death, to the northern scene of Annie's death, Thompson inscribes "North" in the discourse of the play through the phrases, images, symbols, and allusions that are repeated and developed verbally in the text. A few examples will illustrate my point.

Two of the most important words, which gain emphasis through their repetition, are "sled" and "Northern Lights." The importance of "sled" is obvious from the title of the play, but readers and spectators bring their understanding of the word from personal experience to what they learn about it from its use in the play.[3] Sled is cognate with sleigh and sledge, all vehicles pulled on runners over snow by people, dogs, or horses. A sleigh is associated with convivial winter outings or the delivery of news and supplies, and sleighs are familiar from poetry, novels, and paintings. Sledges are more serious affairs that are used by trappers, loggers, or explorers pulling heavy loads great distances over remote and dangerous terrain. In my experience, sleds signify children's sports or the Winter Olympics. The term "sled" in Thompson's play carries all these associations, but it is also slang for the modern snowmobile which, however useful it may be, signifies noise, efficient predation, violence, and an intrusion of technology into the wilderness on a new destructive scale.

When Kevin speaks of sleds or sledding he is describing snowmobiling, either on the trails around the Pickerel and Jack Lake Lodge or in the Northwest Territories. In his hands, the machine is synonymous with speed, violence, macho adventure, and death. As he slits Mike's throat he reminisces about "the greatest sled of my life" and boasts about "pullin' off a ride in the interior of NWT" (52). By contrast, when Evangeline speaks of sleds, she is thinking about loss of control and death in what sounds like a child's wooden sled: "I just feel things are going in a certain way. And there's nothin' I can do to stop them. Like I'm in a sled, right? In a runaway sled goin down a mountain of ice" (84). Either way, a sled evokes "North" and, by association, winter, cold, snow, danger, and violent death.

The other major sign for "North" in the play is the Northern Lights, which on the level of language connect with the North Star that Evangeline and Kevin follow and with the name Evangeline imagines for her child: "Annie Northstar" (106). Well before their first appearance at the end of Act 1, the Northern Lights are present in the troping on "North" that gives us North/Norse/Northern/ Northern Lights/North Star/Northstar. Moreover, for *readers* of the play, the significance of the Northern Lights, as of the sled, is established by Thompson's prefacing quotation from Candace Savage's *Aurora*: "Suddenly, [the shaman] would notice a sled descending out of the sky. It would land nearby, and the shaman would climb on board. Once he reached the land of the moon, he might meet dead relatives or watch spirits playing ball in the northern lights" (10). Just as this passage connects and situates both terms and both objects (if the aurora can be called an object), it also contextualizes them in important ways. Sleds and the aurora are important in circumpolar and northern mythology, where they are signs of power and are always associated with death, be it a violent death through loss of blood or a joyful state of spiritual travel and transformation.

But Kevin is no Inuk shaman, and Thompson's close association of the sled (through the snowmobile) and the Northern Lights with him is puzzling. As he is killing his friend Mike, who has wanted to go to the police after Annie's death, Kevin delivers his "greatest sled of my life" speech. And while he speaks, the stage instructions tell us that "*the Northern Lights appear in the sky, lighting up Kevin and darkening him, flashing across his face and body*" (51). Then, as he is slitting Mike's throat, Kevin asks: "have you ever seen...? the lights? ...the Northern Lights?" (52).

The last time we see the Northern Lights is at the very end. Following the advice of Annie's ghost—to disappear into the northern forests of Canada (105)—Evangeline leads Kevin north to "the hill where Annie was killed" (109). Some months have passed since their flight from Toronto; it is winter again, there is a blizzard, and Kevin is freezing to death. He hears wolves howling, and the "Northern Lights light up the sky" to "surround" Evangeline and Kevin as he dies (109). Thompson links this appearance of the aurora with the earlier scene, in which Kevin murders Mike, by having Evangeline say: "They're every bit as lovely as you said, Kev" (109). However, by having Evangeline describe them, Thompson reaccentuates, rather than merely repeats, the words "Northern Lights." From Evangeline's perspective, they are "Something kind.... Dancing spirits," and "They've finally come for us" (109). They are still linked with death, but this time no one is being murdered. Most importantly, Evangeline indigenizes them by giving them their Cree name: *Cheepyuk Neemeetowuk* (109).

The implication is that Evangeline and Kevin have, in some sense, finally come home linguistically, geographically, spiritually, and psychologically. Given that they have returned to the spot where Annie died and that her ghost sings the song that opened the play, I would suggest that this multiple return (to the opening of the play, to the song, to the murder scene, to the Northern Lights, and to "The North") signifies reconciliation and transformation held out to us (albeit without conviction) by Annie when she quotes Corinthians 1. 15-20: "Behold I shall tell you a mystery. We shall not all sleep but we shall all be changed" (21).

Thompson further connects this notion of transformation with "North" through the use of the North Star, *Keeweetinok Atchak* (99), as a symbol. The stars are generally associated with "North" from the beginning, when Annie sings "Oh heavenly time of day." Annie's song includes the stars in a cluster of stereotypical northern references (snow, silence, birch and pine, darkness, Great Snowy Owl, and wolves), but it is not until the climax, in Act 3, that the North Star becomes significant. When Annie's ghost appears to the distraught Evangeline on Bloor Street (after Jack's murder), she tells Evangeline to flee the city by walking north, following the North Star (105). Kevin meekly follows his half-sister north to the "Fuckin' cold, fuckin' wolves" (107) and his own death, but Evangeline gathers strength and determination as she goes north to bear the daughter she will call "Annie Northstar." This name marks the child semiotically as a complex sign—of hope for the future, of reconciliation, perhaps of atonement for Annie's death, and of the verbal completion (and icon) of the play's troping on "North"; the name also serves as a symbol of reunion for Evangeline with Kevin and with her Northern Cree roots and heritage, and of culture with nature (a point I shall return to).[4]

This construction of what Thompson repeatedly calls "The North" and inscribes as *northern* through word, image, and symbol, establishes "North" as the binary opposite of "South" in the discourse, as well as the diegesis, of the play. The entire play rests on this fundamental binary of North/South, where "North" is situated no further north in Ontario than, at most, Algonquin Park, and "South" is a central Toronto neighbourhood. Thompson's description of her experience on a ski trail in Algonquin Park provides insight into her construction of "The North" in *Sled* and, thus, of the binary in which "North" is inscribed. "I was alone," she explains, "with this exquisite stand of birch and the light going down and I felt this rush of a kind of St Francis of Assisi ecstasy, in communion with nature, and I thought 'only in Canada'. At the same time I felt this note of a deeper kind of danger. I felt fear with a kind of ecstasy."[5]

This combination of alone-ness in the North, ecstasy, communion with nature, and fear is a commonplace in Canadian culture and the arts. It has been represented and re-articulated in poetry, music, painting, fiction and non-fiction (including criticism), film, and drama for at least 150 years. Moreover, it is a formulation central to the construction of a Canadian (as northern) identity. Think, for example, of the opening and closing sequences of *Thirty-Two Short Films About Glenn Gould* (1993), a painting like Blair Bruce's *The Phantom Hunter* (1888), classical compositions like Harry Somers's *North Country* (1948) or Malcolm Forsyth's *Atayoskiwin* (1984), the closing scenes of *Tay John* (1960) or *Gone Indian* (1973), and the plays of Herman Voaden. "Only in Canada," indeed.

Drawing on her own experience and on this wider formulation, which she can assume we share, Thompson mystifies "North" as Other, that space at once Canadian and yet *unheimlich*, the site of our uncanny "home and native land." For Thompson, "North" lies beyond precise articulation or realist representation; it signifies, instead, a psychological and verbal excess, an aesthetic object that can only be hinted at because to bring it down to earth would oblige her to write a different play and to deal with a host of social realities that undermine the symbolic power of "North" to invoke communion with nature, ecstasy, and fear. "South" (Toronto/Seaton Village/Clinton Street) is, by contrast, highly particularized, densely populated, familiar, and historied. However, this neighbourhood is a late twentieth-century urban centre that "cannot hold," and the rough beast slouching toward it (Yeats 211) is one of its own orphaned sons. That Kevin comes from the north and will return to it in death must be weighed against the fact that he was born in Toronto and returns to his family home there. Kevin is not of Thompson's "North"; North Bay, or so-called northern Ontario (like Diane, who kidnapped him [56]), is not his true mother country. If he belongs anywhere, it is in the "South"—in Toronto, in Millhaven. He is a product of contemporary, urban alienation and failed communion, or community.

Evangeline, like Annie, however, is identified with "North." Annie wants to go there to find answers to her troubled marriage and to a deeper alienation (92). According to Jack, Evangeline is *like* the "North"; he finds her beautiful and "mysterious. A forest. In winter" (98), which is, as dialogue, an odd *non-sequitur* (he has just been praising the Toronto Botanical Gardens), but, as metaphor, consistent with the North/South binary of the play. Both Annie and Evangeline are increasingly identified with Thompson's "North"—Annie because she experiences (as Thompson had) ecstasy, peace, and joy in the snowy forest and dies there, Evangeline because she discovers her Cree identity and follows Annie's lead. By the play's end, both women have *become* "North"—"mysterious. A forest. In winter." They are at home there, in communion with "North" and each other; they are not, finally, *like* the "North," not simile, but one with it: metaphor. Jack and Kevin are urban creatures who could never understand or accommodate themselves to a space that represents either wilderness danger (Jack) or a force to be dominated (Kevin), and Joe is separate from anything northern; he is, after all, the son of Italian immigrants, and his sphere is the city.

In other words, Thompson's binary is gendered along the most conventional lines (see Grace, "Gendering"): North = wilderness, mystery, otherness, and the feminine; South = civilization, familiar norms and social reality, and the masculine. Thompson pushes this binary further, although still working within conventional parameters, to construct "North" as the empty, idealized space of death and transfiguration and "South" as the crowded space of hard realities, disillusionment, and corruption. Nevertheless, this "South," for all its negative aspects, remains the centre of the action (literally and thematically) and, paradoxically, its hegemony is not weakened or dismantled so much as reinforced by the binary opposition that constructs "North" as a function of the southern imaginary and as an obscure object of southern, urban desire for the Other, without which it cannot survive. Whether we are men or women, of course, we cannot actually live in or with this "North." We, like Thompson's characters, are southern Canadians. As men we will attempt to crash through it on snowmobiles, hunting, testing our masculinity, and seeking adventure; as women, we will escape into this feminine "North" only to find that it is ourselves—as welcoming Mother or devouring Monster.[6] Either way, escape from the masculinized "South," as Thompson envisions it, is an escape into death that is figured as regression (a kind of return to the womb) or, possibly for the women, as homoerotic.

The emphatic heterosexuality in *Sled* is undercut by Thompson's feminist critique of masculinity and misogyny, while the close bond between Annie (more properly her ghost) and Evangeline hints at a lesbian alternative to the destructive heterosexuality of their lives, albeit one displaced in death and projected onto "North."[7]

Finally, and most significantly, Thompson's "North" exists in what Elaine Showalter has called the feminine "wild zone" beyond reason, logic, and denotative language (30-31). In the play, we experience "North" through Annie's songs, through sound effects (wolf howls, a hooting owl), lighting, and staging: indeed, as a play, *Sled* foregrounds the fact that "North" is always *staged*, is always a simulacrum. As a wild zone, "North" is the absence of "South," all that the south is not. As such it can be used to define us (southern Canadians), while it eludes our grasp—as it must, if it is to retain its power. "South," however, is represented through the density of talk—dialogue, monologue, argument—and physical sets.

III

There are two major strategies for constructing Canada, or Canadian identity, in *Sled*: one is the obvious inclusion of languages, races, ethnicities, classes, religious practices, and histories; the other is the deployment of (both as participating in and con-tributing to) the discursive formation of North. I have said little here about the inclusivity of the play, but it is important and contributes enormously to Thompson's epic impulse.[8] As I see it, this striving to include, through constructing a representative history of the nation, conditions the inner dynamic of the plot and operates most forcefully in the "South"; Joe's memories, for example, contextualize Seaton Village in time and place. The other strategy, invoking the already familiar discursive formation of "North," contributes to the representation of a Canadian identity by pointing beyond the limits of one text, or one evening in the theatre, to a broad cultural context and an ideology that exists outside the play in what Benedict Anderson calls the "imagined community" of nation.[9] *Sled*, with its representation of urban hybridity and apparent northern purity, successfully interpolates itself into that wider context by recalling a host of other texts.

Since the twenties, Canadian playwrights have attempted to stage the North; Herman Voaden's plays provide the best known example. But Voaden's understanding of the North was shaped by the imagery and ideology of the Group of Seven, notably Lawren Harris, and work by the Group quickly became a formative influence on Canadian art in general. Poets like A. J. M. Smith and composers like Harry Freedman were directly inspired by a particular canvas (see Grace and Haag). In the introduction to his centennial sound documentary, *The Idea of North*, Glenn Gould acknowledged the popular and omnipresent influence of the Group and the profound fascination the north had held for him since childhood. He found himself obsessed with "the idea of north [which] began to serve as a *foil* for other ideas and values that seemed... depressingly *urban-oriented* and *spiritually limited* thereby" (liner notes, n.p., emphasis added). While he recognized that his "metaphorical manipulation of the north" was highly romantic and ultimately a construction, Gould nevertheless put his finger upon that very North/South binary that D. C. Scott describes in "The Height of Land" and that Thompson reinscribes in her play:

> Upon one hand
> The lonely north enlaced with lakes and streams,
> ....;
> On the other hand
> The crowded southern land
> With all the welter of the lives of men. (Scott 108)

By the late sixties, as Thompson was growing up, "the idea of North," more particularly a Group of Seven-inspired construction of "North," was sufficiently familiar to be assumed as part of a shared Canadian identity and iconography. More than that, as Gould notes, this "North" had acquired a set of spiritual, mystical, and moral values that were embedded in its representations by southern Ontario artists. This mysterious, spiritually uplifting, if also overwhelming "North," that was (still is) purveyed as Canada, is largely based on the imagery of the country north of Lake Superior, of Algoma, and of Algonquin Park, where Tom Thomson canoed and died, and to a lesser degree on the *pays d'en haut* of Quebec (see Warwick).

I am not suggesting that Judith Thompson was directly influenced by this or that painting, poem, novel, or media account. Unlike Atwood's story "The Age of Lead," where the explicit intertext is a television program about opening nineteenth-century graves on Beechey Island (Grace, "Franklin"), *Sled* participates in a more general, diffuse cultural practice that renders the pursuit of such influences irrelevant and, ultimately, uninteresting. What is interesting, however, is the way in which *Sled* resonates with, takes up a position beside, and contributes to the discursive formation of "North" that I have been sketching. Consider, for example, Howard O'Hagan's *Tay John*, where the reader is left with the unforgettable image of Tay John heading north and pulling the dead Ardith Aeriola behind him "Always deeper and deeper into the snow [until] he had just walked down, the toboggan behind him, under the snow and into the ground" (264). Like the characters in *Sled*, O'Hagan's are mythic figures of hybrid racial and ethnic origins, and they are unable or unwilling to adapt to modern values and urban life. It is as outcasts escaping the violence of so-called civilization that Tay John and Ardith withdraw further and further north until, in death (she from childbirth, he more mysteriously from the story itself), they are united with each other in the northern landscape on the timeless stage of myth. Or consider Jeremy Sadness, the central character of Robert Kroetsch's postmodern parody *Gone Indian*. Despite its crucial ironies and parodic mode, *Gone Indian* constructs a "North" where "extreme cold, the long nights, the solitude of *unbounded* space... induce that northern ecstasy" (123) also central to *Sled* (see Grace, "Robert Kroetsch"). Moreover, Kroetsch also feminizes his "North," constructing her as a muskeg mother "redolent of all our beginnings" (147) or as a "cold, blank, oblivious... amoral virgin" (43). Whatever we decide she is, she claims Jeremy and his lover, Bea, at the end, when the two disappear on a snowmobile into the northern night. Tay John and Ardith, Jeremy and Bea, Kevin and Evangeline—all couples, all ethnically hybrid, all in search of origins and identity, and all finding their identity in escape from southern civilization that brings an ecstatic and fatal union with something called "North."

But "North" in *Sled* is a composite construction that develops from a set of tropes, as a well as from a narrative action culminating in a death figured as ecstatic union with a frozen landscape. One key trope is "sled," and the sled associated with Kevin is the snowmobile, that familiar sign for "North." Even classical music has recognized the snowmobile, and in *North/White* R. Murray Schafer brings the machine on stage and scores it to represent the "rape of the Canadian North" by southern governments "in conspiracy with business and industry" (62). Whether or not Thompson knows *North/White*, she clearly shares with Schafer the belief that, as Schafer puts it (quoting Gould), "the 'idea of the North'... is at the core of the Canadian identity [and] the North is a place of austerity, of spaciousness and loneliness; the North is pure" (62-63).

Finally, there are the Northern Lights, perhaps the most frequently re-presented (indeed clichéd) of northern images, and in this instance Thompson has been precise about at least one of her sources: Candace Savage's *Aurora*. However, Savage's book, like *Sled*, is itself only one example of the re-presentation of the Northern Lights in the discursive formation of "North." Two other recent examples of their re-presentation are Peter Mettler's film *Picture of Light* (1994), in which a film crew travels to Churchill, Manitoba to capture the mystery of the Lights on celluloid, and Paterson Ewen's painting *Northern Lights* (1973). During its screening at the 1994 Toronto Film Festival, dramatic posters for *Picture of Light* appeared on Toronto streets, so that, in addition to media attention, simulacra of the Lights were everywhere to be seen. Ewen's painting, from the collection of the Art Gallery of Ontario, is less accessible to the public imagination and, of course, it appeals to a different public than Mettler's film. Nevertheless, *Northern Lights* does circulate within the public domain and does participate in the construction of "North." Moreover, it played a dominant role in the 1996 Paterson Ewen retrospective at the AGO, where it was hung in a specially lit room equipped with benches and earphones so visitors could study the painting while listening to Ewen, Mettler, and others meditate upon the Northern Lights. The result of this attention by Ewen, Mettler, and now Thompson is an accentuation of the Lights as powerful *natural* images of an ethereal beauty, sublime mystery, and romantic mysticism, constitutive of the Canadian landscape and, thereby, of Canadian northern identity.

IV

Sled, however, is a play, and if it can be placed within the larger cultural and discursive context I have described, it must also be returned to the stage and to the sphere of dramatic literature. Amongst the Canadian plays about the "North" with which I am familiar, Thompson's *Sled* occupies a problematic position because it represents a return to the romantic themes, set-designs, and use of music of Herman Voaden, for whom "North" was the mystified space of idealized spiritual encounter ending in death and of the feminine Other. Her birches, pine trees, stars, Northern Lights, and snow recall his and, in that recall, reinforce the hegemony of the Group of Seven in the collective imaginary. She has done this, moreover, at precisely the same time that our national identity, as defined by the Group, has been re-constructed and re-staged in our largest art galleries through the massive retrospective exhibition called *The Group of Seven: Art for a Nation.* But there are other norths and other ways of imagining and staging "North" and Canada-as-North—for example, Geoff Kavanagh's *Ditch*, Philip Adams's *Free's Point*, and Mansel Robinson's *Colonial Tongues.*

Ditch deconstructs the mythology of the last Franklin expedition, which has been presented, since the 1850s, as the tragic destruction of heroic Englishmen. *Free's Point* is a dramatic reconstruction and interpretation of an actual RCMP case in northern British Columbia, and it shares much with mad-trapper narratives like those about Albert Johnson. *Colonial Tongues*, set in 1995 in a small northern Ontario town, with flashbacks to the early 1940s and mid-20s, is the closest to *Sled* in that it takes Ontario as its frame of reference, opposes "North" and "South," and makes the fate of a small northern Ontario town a metaphor for the fate of the nation. However, the resemblances end there because Robinson refuses to mystify northern experience or to romanticize the northern Ontario landscape. Instead, he presents and legitimates a northern reality—the destruction of company towns and a way of life by southern greed—without pretending that all northerners are idealists prepared to sacrifice themselves for something called Canadian identity or that those dreamers who remain in northern ghost towns have anywhere to escape to. Death in the transfiguring great white "North" is not an option.

By comparison with *Ditch*, *Free's Point*, and *Colonial Tongues*, *Sled* is both extremely ambitious and, in most respects, deeply conservative. To be sure, it is the only one from this quartet of recent plays about the North to create a central role for women within a critique of masculinist values, but this role is highly problematic. Escape from a masculinized, violent, urban "South" into the peace and purity of a silent, white, frozen "North" is an escape into death, which we are asked to believe will be spiritually transfiguring, at least for Annie and Evangeline. A nice thought, perhaps, but part of an idea of "North" circumscribed by the Cartesian binaries that identify woman with nature and both with a realm open to male domination and exploitation. In her rejection of the city for the wild zone of "North," Thompson refuses to challenge this binary, and she turns her back on the hybridity and social practice that Homi Bhabha calls for in his theory of "dissemi-*nation*" (299). As a consequence, her attempt to empower women, and a part-Cree woman at that, reinscribes both the feminine and the native as the silent/silenced Other in a binary dominated by the kind of white, heterosexual masculinity critiqued in the play. Jack and Kevin may be dead by the play's end, but nothing fundamental has been changed (as Annie feared [21]) because no new voice or alternative vision has been introduced into the narratives of gender, race, and nation. Insofar as *Sled* offers us an image of Canada at the end of the twentieth century by using the regional to represent the national construction of identity, there is little room for optimism because this vision merely repeats Donald Creighton's outdated Laurentian paradigm for imagining Canada.[10]

According to Thompson, the initial idea for the play came from a story told by one of her students, who remembered seeing a frozen man whose snowmobile had crashed through the ice; the man was alive, even though frozen stiff, like a statue. "There was something about the frozen man," Thompson explains, "that made me think about Canada and the North and our frozen emotional landscape in this country" (Thomas 47). Thompson's *Sled* is, finally, an image of that emotional landscape, and she uses her idea of "North" to construct a disturbing representation of an individual and collective identity that finds little hope of redemption except in death. To go "North" on *Sled* is to enter the bleak, lifeless scene of Lawren Harris's *North Shore: Lake Superior* (1926), and that is cold comfort indeed.

(1998)

Notes

1 This is the title of Gould's sound-documentary composition. In *Canada and the Idea of North* I examine the development and ideological fabric of this "idea" in Canadian historiography, geography, political thought, and the arts.

2 I use the term "North" to designate a discursive and semiotic construction of place and meaning that has little to do with the physical and material realities of northern Canada; "North," as represented to most Canadians and marketed to the world, is a southern Canadian construction.

3 The play was originally called "Last Things," but Thompson changed the title during the workshop process of 1995-96. Possibly she chose the new name when David Ferry brought her a copy of Candace Savage's *Aurora* (Duchesne and Fletcher 36). Thompson used two passages from *Aurora* (33, 35) as an explanatory note to her published text of Sled (10).

4 In addition to being part Cree, Evangeline is a figure of the patient woman searching for a lost lover and homeland. She is Longfellow's Acadian heroine who has given her name to the area of Nova Scotia called "the land of Evangeline" (see McLeod).

5 For this quotation, see Walker. It is important to remember that this sense of communion mixed with dread does not occur "only in Canada," or only in connection with northern wildernesses. It is Thompson's conviction that matters here.

6 In *Strange Things* (87-116), Atwood analyses several representations of "North" as female in Canadian literature (excluding drama) and speculates about what happens when a female character goes "North."

7 In conversation with Colin Thomas, Thompson remarks that "if you create a society that hates women, you're going to create Kevin" (48), and she goes on to link him with Marc Lepine and Paul Bernardo. She also explains that *Sled* is about the "compromise" a heterosexual woman makes when marrying in our patriarchal culture. In *Strange Things*, Atwood speculates that, when a woman goes into a female "North," she may find there "a kind mother or sister or lesbian lover" (89).

8 In the early drafts, Thompson had a wider spectrum of characters, languages, stories, and ethnicities, but in reducing the playing time by half she cut much of this material; see Knowles 12-16.

9 In this connection, see Bourdieu's concept of the "habitus" (54-59) and Bhabha's description of the "nation-space" (299-301).

10 Despite the title of his major history of Canada, *Dominion of the North*, Creighton argued that the country was developed by eastern (Ontario/Quebec)

powers operating along the St Lawrence river in accordance with what has come to be known as his "Laurentian thesis"; "North," for Creighton, signified the eighteenth-century "northern colony," which was "the old empire of the St Lawrence" (165), and the Canadian North scarcely existed for Creighton. This view of Canadian history was first challenged by W. L. Morton in *The Canadian Identity*, in which he argued that the West and the North were equally, if not more, important to Canadian historiography.

Works Cited

Adams, Philip. "Free's Point." Unpublished manuscript. 1996.

Anderson, Benedict. *Imagined Communities: Reflections On the Origin and Spread of Nationalism.* Rev. ed. London: Verso, 1991.

Atwood, Margaret. "The Age of Lead." *Wilderness Tips.* Toronto: McClelland and Stewart, 1991. 157-75.

———. *Strange Things: The Malevolent North in Canadian Literature.* Oxford: Clarendon, 1995.

Bhabha, Homi K. "DissemiNation: Time, Narrative, and the Margins of the Modern Nation." *Nation and Narration.* Ed. Homi K. Bhabha. London: Routledge, 1990. 291-322.

Bourdieu, Pierre. *The Logic of Practice.* Trans. Richard Nice. Stanford: Stanford UP, 1990.

Creighton, Donald. *Dominion of the North: A History of Canada.* 1944. Toronto: Macmillan: 1957.

Duchesne, Scott, and Jennifer Fletcher. "*Sled*: A Workshop Diary." *Canadian Theatre Review* 89 (Winter 1996): 33-41.

Forsyth. Malcolm. *Atayoskiwin: Suite for Orchestra.* 1984. Canadian Centre for Music: Tape #1907.

Foucault, Michel. *The Archeology of Knowledge.* Trans. A.M. Sheridan Smith. London: Routledge, 1972.

Freedman, Harry. *Images* [1957-58]. Toronto: EMI Canada, 1960.

Gould, Glenn. *The Idea of North.* 1967. *Glenn Gould's Solitude Trilogy: Three Sound Documentaries.* CBC Records: PSCD2003-3, 1992.

Grace, Sherrill. *Canada and the Idea of North.* Montreal and Kingston: McGill-Queen's UP, 2001.

———. "'Franklin Lives': More Atwood Ghosts." *Various Atwoods: Essays on the Later Poems, Short Fiction, and Novels.* Ed. Lorraine York. Toronto: Anansi, 1995. 146-66.

———. "Gendering Northern Narrative." *Echoing Silence: Essays on Arctic Narrative.* Ed. John Moss. Ottawa: U of Ottawa P, 1997. 163-81.

———. "Robert Kroetsch and the Semiotics of North." *Open Letter* 5/6 (1996): 13-24.

Grace, Sherrill, and Stefan Haag. "From Landscape to Soundscape: The Northern Arts of Canada." *Mosaic* 31.2 (1998): 101-22.

Kavanagh, Geoff. "Ditch." Unpublished manuscript, 1993.

Knowles, Richard Paul. "'Great Lines Are a Dime a Dozen': Judith Thompson's Greatest Cuts." *Canadian Theatre Review* 89 (Winter 1996): 8-18.

Kroetsch, Robert. *Gone Indian.* Toronto: New Press, 1973.

Longfellow, Henry Wadsworth. *Evangeline.* 1847. Halifax: T. C. Allen, 1901.

McLeod, Grace Dean. *Stories of the Land of Evangeline.* Boston: D. Lothrop, 1891.

Mettler, Peter. *Picture of Light.* Montreal: Domino Film, 1994.

Morton, W. L. *The Canadian Identity.* 1961. Madison: U of Wisconsin P, 1972.

O'Hagan, Howard. *Tay John.* 1960. Toronto: McClelland, 1974.

Richler, Mordecai. *Solomon Gursky Was Here.* New York: Knopf, 1990.

Robinson, Mansel. *Colonial Tongues.* Toronto: Playwrights Canada, 1995.

Savage, Candace. *Aurora: The Mysterious Northern Lights.* San Francisco: Sierra Club, 1995.

Schafer, R. Murray. *North/White: On Canadian Music.* Bancroft, Ont.: Arcana, 1984. 62-63.

Scott, D. C. "The Height of Land." *Poets of the Confederation.* Ed. Malcolm Ross. Toronto: McClelland, 1960. 107-10.

Showalter, Elaine. "Feminist Criticism in the Wilderness." *Writing and Sexual Difference.* Ed. Elizabeth Abel. Chicago: U of Chicago P, 1982. 9-35.

Somers, Harry. *North Country.* 1948. *The Spring of Somers.* CBC Records: SMCD5162, 1996.

Thomas, Colin. "Sex, Dreams, and a Bucket of Snake." *Georgia Straight.* 3-10 Apr. 1997: 47-48.

Thompson, Judith. *Sled.* Toronto: Playwrights Canada, 1997.

Walker, Susan. "A Woman of Letters." *Toronto Star* 9 January 1997: G3.

Warwick, Jack. *The Long Journey. Literary Themes of French Canada.* Toronto: U of Toronto P, 1968.

Yeats, W.B. "The Second Coming." *Collected Poems of W.B. Yeats.* London: Macmillan, 1967. 210-11.

From "Judith Thompson: Social Psychomachia" (in *The Buried Astrolabe: Canadian Dramatic Imagination and Western Tradition*)

by Craig Stewart Walker

from IN PURSUIT OF THE CHTHONIAN

A non-dogmatic use of Christian sensibility (similar to that in *Lion in the Streets*) appears in the stage version of *Tornado* (1992). [...] [T]here are substantial differences between the two versions of *Tornado*; in the stage version Thompson has not merely changed names and details but added a new subplot, additional characters, and made a significant shift in tone. For example, though both versions begin, as so many of the Grimms' *Tales* do, with a couple who as yet have no children, the relation to fairy tales only really becomes evident in the more pronounced "magic realism" of the stage version.

In the radio script of *Tornado* the central female character is Mandy, a social worker. Mandy's husband, Bill, is having an affair with one of their middle-class friends, Jane, and is trying to work up the courage to tell Mandy he wants to end their marriage. Among the reasons Bill is attracted to Jane is her readiness to conceive a child, a prospect Mandy openly disdains. Once Mandy discovers the affair, however, she is determined to have a child herself in order to keep Bill. On Mandy's caseload is Rose, an impoverished young mother of four who is expecting a fifth and who suffers occasional epileptic seizures. When Mandy proves to be sterile, she devises a plan to confiscate Rose's baby at birth, convincing her that fourth and fifth children of epileptic mothers often die in their mothers' homes because of a mysterious virus. Mandy tells Bill she has paid a surrogate mother, but her ruse is exposed, and the play ends on the Scarborough bluffs, with Mandy deliriously insisting that she is the real mother of the baby and finally suffering an epileptic fit herself.

In the stage version of *Tornado* Mandy has become Viola, who is not a social worker; Bill has become Dexter, who is even more pathetically ineffectual than Bill was. More extreme is the transformation of Jane into Velveteen, a nineteen-year-old lower-class stripper who is pregnant by Dexter. Shirley, Jane's confidante, re-emerges in a much larger role as Red, a lesbian colleague of Velveteen's who is in love with her. The chief changes in the plot have to do with Viola's attempts to take legal custody of Velveteen's baby, a fate Velveteen avoids by leaping into Niagara Falls; only subsequently does Viola plan to take Rose's baby. Rather than playing on Rose's simple gullibility, as in the radio play, Viola makes a bargain with Rose. Rose has custody of only one of her children, Jake, the eldest (here a boy of fourteen, whereas he seems about ten in the radio play). Viola offers to pay for home care for Rose and thus allow her to recover custody of her other children, provided she hands over her newborn baby. In agony, Rose agrees, though when Jake discovers the plot, he is enraged and vows revenge. In the climactic scene on the cliff's edge he first attempts to cut off Viola's hands ("red" on stage, "big" on the radio) before being persuaded to show mercy. Then, as in the earlier version, he helps Viola through an epileptic seizure; but, rather than ending here, the stage *Tornado* ends with Viola surrounded by the comforting attentions of Rose and the ghost of Velveteen.

Significant as the changes to the characters and the plot are, most striking is the overall shift in tone. Whereas the radio play *Tornado* was, albeit unusual and slightly stylized, a fundamentally realistic portrait of a woman driven to madness in her desperation to keep her husband by becoming a mother, the stage version assumes a more poetic overtone, employing more surrealistic imagery and a more explicit symbolic framework. The stage *Tornado* begins just outside a church, and the entire subsequent action of the play is haunted by religious perceptions of one kind or another. It is specifically revealed that each of the main characters is a Catholic, though their diverse interpretations of their religion ensure this does not imply any one stable ethical context for their behaviours. To take the most obvious example, Viola insists that her marriage cannot be allowed to end because, she tells Dexter, "We're Catholics, remember?" (50)—although that has not prevented her from having three abortions (54). Clearly, in so far as the characters themselves invoke their Catholicism, it represents for them religious authority of a kind that has more to do with their personal desires than with any official teachings.

By no means, however, should we assume that Thompson's invocation of Catholicism is intended to be simply ironic. She has a manifestly serious interest in the more profound aspects of Catholicism lying beyond moral dogma. One may identify in Thompson's work variations on all the main theological apparatus by which Catholicism aspires to bring meaning to human life: the notions of evil and goodness, of sin and purity, of confession, atonement, and forgiveness, of redemption, transcendence, and grace, of epiphany, and, not least, of teleological mystery: the final unknowability, despite moments of apparent revelation, of the mind of God. These concepts do not emerge in anything like an orthodox shape under Thompson's hand. But their presence in other forms is persistent enough that a recognition of them is fundamental to understanding Thompson's poetics.

One of the most compelling and uncanny, religious themes in *Tornado* is the occasional bald identification of characters as God or the Devil. Thompson takes a metaphor that is often used casually and facetiously, but then pushes it, so that real meaning is wrung from what might otherwise be discarded as stale hyperbole. For example, Dexter and Velveteen are "making out" at one point, when the conversation turns from the familiar and foolish and escalates into something disturbingly portentous:

> DEXTER. Oh God I sometimes think you must be a witch... you... have you put a spell on me? I think of you and it rips through my

> body, this desire, it is stronger than than, my marriage, than my beliefs, than... than...
> VELVETEEN. Than God.
> DEXTER. Oh no.
> VELVETEEN. Yes it is.
> DEXTER. Vel, there is nothing stronger than God.
> VELVETEEN. Then it must be Her will.
> DEXTER. God is a Father, Vel, you don't call God HER.
> VELVETEEN. God is my mother.
> DEXTER. You're taunting me with this God thing, aren't you? Playing with me?
> VELVETEEN. Is that what you think?
> DEXTER. Like a cat, and and you know what a cat makes me think of?
> VELVETEEN. What, Dex?
> DEXTER. The devil. You tempt me, and play with me, and try to keep my child from me and call God a mother, I sometimes I really think you're from the other side. [...] I'm beginning to think you're not human.

Then, a few lines later, the tables are turned:

> DEXTER. The judge has ruled in my wife's favour, Velveteen. Yesterday. [...] Shall I tell you what he said?
> VELVETEEN. Why? Are you the devil? (56)

The conversation externalizes what Thompson has described as the "constant struggle inside—a sort of St. George and the Dragon [...] Was this an evil thought? Was this a good thought?" She adds that "certainly in the Catholic religion the struggle between Satan and God is a constant thing" ("Conversation" 185, 186). In having the characters project the elements of this internal struggle upon one another, Thompson has created something like religious expressionism: the inward psychic battle between spiritual forces is imposed in broad symbolic figures upon the social world.

All the same, were the externalization of the spiritual struggle to go no further than the name-calling seen above, there would be nothing very remarkable about it. We might consider it an unusually intense rendering of common hyperbole, but little more. However, that there is something far more important at stake in these religious references becomes evident when they are considered within the thematic pattern of the play as a whole. In an earlier scene Velveteen and Dexter discuss her pregnancy:

> VELVETEEN. The quickening has started. The kicking. THE BABY IS KICKING.
> DEXTER. Oh! Oh my God in heaven is it? Is it?
> VELVETEEN. It's not an it, it's a she. SHE.
> DEXTER. Oh a she? A she? How do you know, Vel?
> VELVETEEN. I'm going to call her Jesus.

> DEXTER. Vel. Please. This isn't funny.
> VELVETEEN. Actually, I'm going to call her god.
> DEXTER. Vel, isn't that kind of sacrilegious?
> VELVETEEN. No. No it's not, Dex. My baby is going to be god [...] I'm not joking.
> DEXTER. Our baby is going to be god. Yeah. I can see it. Cause she's from you and me, she's from love. (54)

Dexter has found a comfortable platitude with which to apprehend Velveteen's extravagant claim. But it is evident that Velveteen—and Thompson—mean something more.

One of the chief departures the stage *Tornado* makes from its predecessor is in a stronger parallel between Rose and Velveteen than had been possible between Rose and Jane. The new parallel amplifies the symbolic significance of the two expectant mothers. Asked once about the numerous mother and son relationships in her work, Thompson answered (perhaps a little jocularly) that "the obvious answer as to why I write about mothers and sons is that I was brought up a Catholic and there's one big mother-son relationship!" (Interview 99). As I suggested earlier, another explanation that applies in certain cases (e.g., Lomia and Cape in *White Biting Dog* or, less surely, Pegs and Toilane in *I Am Yours*) would be the importance of the Oedipal complex to Freudian thought. Yet in *The Crackwalker*, and certainly here in *Tornado*, the Madonna-Christ archetype is clearly much more relevant. It would be misleading, however, to expect any close adherence to religious allegory. For any allusions to the Madonna-Christ relation have more to do with a conception of spirituality than with the outlines of the myth (i.e., the nativity story).

In the same interview quoted above, Thompson says:

> God is a newborn baby. Truly. You can really see God in a newborn baby. And it stays with them for a long time. God is in every person—that's really hard to remember sometimes. I do believe that God is in every one of my characters showing me herself. At little moments. That's as scary as it is beautiful. God is the innocence of a newborn baby; when people show that part of themselves, that eternal flame that's guarded; when they show that that's a moment of pure beauty, when they let you see it. Some people's flame seems to have gone right out.... Spontaneity—that's what we look for on stage. Bring on a dog or a baby and everyone's blown away. The search for that spontaneity is religious. (Interview 96)

Thus, Velveteen's declaration that her "baby is going to be god" is more than mere whimsy. Indeed, the concept Thompson is delineating has an important place in Catholic mysticism. The most important of all the medieval mystics, Meister Eckhardt, spoke of giving birth to God's Son within the soul, thus making explicit a chief symbolic undercurrent of Judaeo-Christian mythology: the idea that spiritual redemption begins with a figurative conception of the Godhead within the human soul much like the literal conception of new life within a womb. (Indeed, almost all the sexist residuum in the Christian church is rooted in a regrettably literal-minded interpretation of the symbolism of spiritual conception.)

In this light the significance of the yearnings of several of the characters in *Tornado* may be reinterpreted. To give birth to God is, in Eckhardt's conception, to experience grace and attain redemption. The idea attaches to the pregnant Velveteen, although for her the notion of redemption is cast partly in terms of a retrieval of inherent social dignity. She claims that her Polish ancestors were aristocrats, and she feels that she is living in a kind of spiritual exile from her rightful ancestral destiny. Where the Judaic conception of spiritual exile from ancestral destiny is apprehended as a geographic and political displacement from an idealized Jerusalem, Velveteen's sense of alienation springs from having been exiled to the other side of a class barrier. As she explains to Red, the prospect of having a child with Dexter promises a means of transcending the class barrier and recovering a sense of spiritual home:

> I always thought that since my family crossed over worlds we could never get back... to that, right? Never get back through the glass, but with Dexter, I'm back, I feel back. And I think he's my only chance. He talks gentle. (50)

Dexter in turn finds with Velveteen refuge from his life, but while his passion for having a child looks genuine enough, any spiritual element in his yearning seems to have been displaced on to sexual fantasy. His lust for Velveteen is an example of the eroticization of transgression documented by Stallybrass and White, in which the "lower" elements of a cultural and psychological hierarchy are fetishized. (Another such example of the eroticization of transgression is Red's use of a maid's outfit for her striptease routine.)

Yet, by the same token, Velveteen's own routine demonstrates that transgression of a different kind is possible by confounding the spiritual and the erotic. In a scene Thompson would reuse in *Sled*, Velveteen performs a striptease while costumed as a Mother Superior. When she ends up with her "black torn filmy slip," she "shows off her five month pregnant belly," while Dexter and the other men watch "entranced" (49). The image could be said, from one perspective, merely to trade upon the cliché of the Madonna-whore oxymoron as the quintessential object of male sexual desire. But in the context of the other religious allusions in *Tornado*, more significant is the idea that Velveteen evokes and embraces both spiritual aspiration and sexual desire through her dance. Moreover, it is appropriate to consider this combination of spirituality and sexuality as not merely an affective evocation—i.e., an experience produced in the minds of the onlookers—but as an expression of Velveteen's own uplifted state of eroticism and faith.

While the redemptive aspect of childbirth as it applied to Rose was made more explicit in the radio version of *Tornado*, in the stage version it remains apparent that in some way Rose's motherhood is a deliverance from the evil and a transcendence of the chaos into which she is regularly plunged by her seizures. Something very similar goes on in Viola's mind. What begins as a desperate attempt to hold on to her husband's love through the conception of children soon reaches well beyond the simple wish to hold on to Dexter. Viola's progressively more irrational actions evince the desperation of a woman who feels herself becoming a spiritual outcast: her lack of children has become for her a denial of grace. Hence, while Viola's kidnapping of Rose's baby, however impractical, has a modicum of rational motivation, the deeper significance of her actions becomes manifest in her totally irrational attempt to identify herself with Rose as mother, maker of life.

Significantly, Viola's identification extends not only to Rose's motherhood but to her sufferings as well. As innumerable cultural references attest, there is a natural imaginative connection between the notion of martyrdom, which involves suffering through to a triumphant state of purity, and the experience of childbirth, in which the mother's suffering begets and thus renews human innocence. Thompson further connects this pattern with the idea of the achievement of grace, a theme that as Ric Knowles has remarked, "consistently" appears in her work ("Achievement" 36). In *The Crackwalker*, for example, the theme is hinted at in subtle ways, as when Alan and Therese talk about getting married at the Church of the Good Thief (a real church just down the street from the Kingston Federal Penitentiary and the Prison for Women). The church name invokes the resilient possibility of salvation held out in Luke 23:43, where Jesus saves one of the two thieves crucified alongside him—clearly a notion pertinent to the vaguely criminal underworld of *The Crackwalker*. More obviously, there are the several occasions Therese is identified with the Madonna. That association also hints at a potentially redemptive way of regarding the death of her child (as occurs in the development of Sandy's humanitarian compassion).

A similar possibility of retrieving grace from morbidity inheres in *White Biting Dog*. At the end of the play Glidden & Pony are dead; Pascal has perhaps suffered a spiritual death; and, if we count Queenie and the Dachshunds as well, we have here a slaughter approaching *Hamlet* proportions. But Thompson has specifically argued that Pony's suicide, at any rate, signifies not a defeat but an achievement of grace:

> Pony achieves Grace because she understands when she falls in "love" that something has possessed her, taken her over, and that that something can wipe out all her moral character [...] Anyhow, Pony had the strength to conquer that radical evil [...] The old man [i.e., Glidden] in *White Biting Dog* also achieves Grace, also at the expense of his own happiness. Lomia and Cape, on the other hand, are amoral human beings who didn't even take the first step. You have to work and work and pray. (Interview 103)

The kind of work Thompson has in mind involves not merely humility but an endurance of suffering until self-awareness is attained and a childlike innocence becomes retrievable: hence the connection with childbirth, an idea dramatized in the penultimate scene of *I Am Yours*. Dee moves into the nursery at the hospital, where she believes her child is sleeping, and the stage directions tell us that "She feels purified—through birth—and also through understanding her self-hatred, her guilt about her mother—she is now able to love after having grappled with her 'shadow' or 'animal'" (176).

At any rate, the notion. of "suffering through" to a state of grace is certainly the relevant spiritual model at the end of *Tornado*. As the police and the other characters close in upon Viola at the edge of the Scarborough bluffs, the scene takes on a magic-realist tone that foregrounds the religious themes. Jake (who, despite being older than in the radio version, retains something of his status as an "angel," as Rose called him) forgoes retribution for mercy as his mother reminds him of the principle of Christian forbearance. Viola's red-handedness is an emblem of her guilt; thus, to cut off her hands would be appropriate and even just, not only in terms of what is loosely referred to as "Old Testament justice" but in the gruesome, fantastic manner of some of the Grimms' *Tales* (see the red-hot iron slippers used to punish the wicked Queen at the end of "Snow White"—though not in the expurgated Disney version). Instead, the Christian notion of suffering through to grace is embraced, so all the terror and rage within Viola erupt in a "sympathetic" epileptic seizure, a journey through the chthonian, which, once she has emerged, may enable her to retrieve control of her soul.

UNHEIMLICH MANOEUVRES

Apart from reworking *Tornado* for the theatre, Judith Thompson did not produce a new full-length stage play in the almost seven years from *Lion in the Streets*, in May 1990, until January 1997, when *Sled* had its premiere. In the interim she wrote several scripts for film (most of which were commissioned but are as yet unproduced projects), a number of radio plays, one adaptation (*Hedda Gabler*, for the Shaw Festival in 1991), and some shorter original works for the theatre. Among the works from these years that have been published are two radio plays and two very short stage plays.

Thompson's interest in reaching past the conscious defences of her audiences to create a dreamlike state in the theatre is also served by radio drama, which she treats as if it were an inner voice for the listener:

> I like this idea of voices in the dark, whispering; schizophrenics hear voices in the dark, it affects them deeply. The voice and you—I just love that, no distractions. It's a pure experience [...] I think radio is about poetry, because poetry is about rhythm, word choice. It's something that actually carves into you, the poetry and the word choice. That's what radio should do, carve into you, make those big holes like in the wheat, the circles. (*White Sand* 5)

That concept of being helplessly, profoundly penetrated by a mesmerizing voice is bound up with the themes of the two published radio plays, both of which deal with a foreboding sense of destiny.

The radio play *White Sand* (1991) carefully orchestrates the alternating voices of Velma, a Caribbean immigrant to Canada; Eleanor, her young white ward; Carl, a white supremacist skinhead; and Kimberly, Carl's girlfriend, at age eighteen—when the main events are occurring—and at thirty-one, when she is in prison. The play moves towards the murder of Velma with a dreadful inevitability, the audience knowing that all these separate sectors of voices must inevitably collide. What is surprising, however, is that it is the relatively benign Kimberly who commits the decisive violent act, for no better reason than her anxiety to make herself "worthy" of Carl's love. But, having murdered Velma, Kimberly feels the expression in Velma's eyes wearing her down like water wears rock down to white sand (27). The hard, solid rock of a soul wedded to white supremacism is, through conscience, becoming something pure and malleable, related to the Caribbean beaches Velma came from. The sense of destiny leading to Velma's murder, then, is juxtaposed with another destiny that will eventually bring Kimberly to humanism through the workings of her conscience.

In *Stop Talking Like That* (1995) the sense of destiny is given a more supernatural resonance. Joanne, an anorexic Canadian teenager, goes on a trip to Australia to visit her paternal grandfather, Fergus, with her family.[1] She feels there is something supernatural in Australia, lying beyond the material landscape and calling to her, a feeling she shares with her grandfather, Fergus. The dreadful foreboding haunting the play is offset by the implication that Joanne and Fergus are in some way yearning for death's oblivion. It would release them from their sense of not fully belonging on earth, where they feel life to be in some way *unheimlich*—a German word translating literally as "unhomelike," used to describe an uncanny or eerily alien experience. Joanne's anorexia thus suggests something symbolic, for while in some ways she remains a relatively ordinary teenager, Joanne is so preoccupied with the afterlife and the noumenal world that her insistence on annihilating her material self through starvation evokes the asceticism of the medieval mystics, those who practised self-abnegation to extremity because they believed that the soul's passage to its true and eternal home was obstructed by any fleshly indulgences whatsoever.

In such a spirit, then, she ventures with Fergus into the outback on a walkabout, a sort of quest for her own Dreaming-track—the path that the Australian aboriginals believe was laid out by their spiritual ancestors, and which are ideationally related to the migratory paths of birds, fish, and animals (see Chatwin). Fergus eventually leaves Joanne behind to pursue death and his afterlife as a bird, his totemic creature. Joanne chooses instead to return to life, but as she leaves the Rock she is picked up by a stranger in a car, who rapes and kills her, telling her: "I'm ice and I'm snow, snow inside your sweetness you ripened for me all your life little passionfruit" (165). A further way of reading Joanne's anorexia is thereby introduced: an unconscious attempt to keep herself from ripening into readiness for this brutal destiny. As the surviving members of Joanne's family search for her, only Lily, Joanne's sister, stricken with profound remorse for her betrayal of her Joanne, hears amidst the birds the strains of a church choir.

The themes of a young woman who feels she doesn't belong in her world and the haunted conscience of a woman who betrays her appear in a very different way in one of the most impressive, though certainly the shortest, of Thompson's published works from this period, the monologue *Perfect Pie* (1993). Patsy, a woman in her late thirties, living in Marmora, a small town north of Belleville in southeastern Ontario, is tape-recording a message for an old friend she has seen on television, while at the same time she makes a meat pie from scratch for a local pie-baking competition. Gradually, however, we discover that Marie died many years ago, when she and Patsy were still teenagers. In a reversal of the Father Hayes and David scene in *Lion in the Streets* Patsy has imagined a continued parallel life for the long-dead Marie.

The play is supported by a subtle repetition of imagery associated with bodily organs. These references, metaphoric and literal, to the internal secrets and the vaguely threatening (to Patsy) mysteries of life and death, would remain discrete images, perhaps, were it not that Patsy is all the while occupied with tucking animal organs into her meat pie, enfolding the "secrets" neatly within the smooth white dough before sealing and baking the result into a "perfect pie." The meat pie, in turn, is linked with the central incident around which the monologue revolves. Marie had persuaded Patsy to commit suicide with her on the railway tracks. Patsy accompanied Marie until the consuming thought of her mother's meat pie burning in the oven, the pie she had promised to look after, tore her away from Marie's side, and she abandoned her friend to a solitary death. Thus, Patsy's pie-making is a sort of cross between a therapeutic activity and a hellish punishment similar to that inflicted on Tantalus; she speaks of being blanketed beneath falling snow as she makes her pies—like the characters in James Joyce's "The Dead." Condemned to remember, Patsy compulsively, figuratively, puts the contents of a recollected inner life into her pies, never quite able to achieve perfection using the messy ingredients of the past.

Several years later Thompson expanded the *Perfect Pie* monologue into a full-length play for four characters (Patsy and Marie as adults and as children), directing it herself for the Tarragon in early 2000. The full-length version begins as did the monologue, with Patsy recording a message to her long-lost friend as she prepares a pie, though here the filling is a rather more innocuous rhubarb. The more striking difference is that as Patsy continues to speak, the adult Marie, who has changed her name to Francesca, begins to answer and moves to join Patsy in her kitchen.

The dramatic construction of the scene is echoed by that of the play as a whole. The conversation of the adult women is interspersed with scenes of them as children, and both plots, past and present, lead inexorably to the same point: the moment in which the two stood together on the tracks before the oncoming train (represented in Sue LePage's design for the premiere production by the foreboding presence of a distorted railway track). The poetic effect of this construction demands figurative comprehension of some sort. For example, one might feel that the psyches of the two women, and of their younger and older selves, were sliding towards one another like binocular lenses coming into joint focus on one subject; or that interleafed stories were combining to form a single tale. However, the most compelling metaphor by which to comprehend the structure is provided by Thompson in the stage directions. The theatrical device by which Francesca appears before Patsy at the play's opening could be a figurative rendering of a real visit, but because Patsy continues to make her pie throughout this section, a feeling persists that Patsy has invoked Francesca's presence as she kneads and rolls and cuts the pastry dough. The entities in the play divide, fold, conjoin, and interpenetrate in a dramatic process that parallels Patsy's preparation of her pie.

The scenes depicting the development of Patsy and Marie's friendship as children recall Rodney's description of his boyhood friendship with Michael in *Lion in the Streets*. Again a peculiar child, a despised social outcast, is desperately grateful for the friendship of a "normal child." Again too there is a public betrayal of the outsider's trust by someone who is horrified to have befriended a "loser," though in *Perfect Pie* the betrayal comes not from Marie's best friend but from her date for a school dance; Patsy (to that point at any rate) remains faithful. In the case of Rodney and Michael the recapitulation of the relationship and its betrayal emanated from the mind of Rodney, the outcast, the loser. In the case of Patsy and Marie the recollection is initiated by Patsy, and the scenes from the past adumbrate the nature of Patsy's fascination with Marie, a fascination that she is unable to explain when asked (52-3). The source seems to be the exotic and vulnerable qualities, the *unheimlich* or chthonic features of Marie Begg's character that, for Patsy, speak compellingly of "a world out there, an unimaginable world" (82). However, to the boys who assault her after the dance, they are chiefly threatening, however sexually arousing—another example of the eroticization of transgression. The boys try to prove to themselves that the force Marie represents is not indomitable by raping and then urinating on her. Patsy, by contrast, decides to embrace all that Marie represents by accompanying her to the tracks to await the oncoming train.

That the chthonic forces the others see in Marie, however terrifying, may be an omnipresent element of life is suggested by several allusions. Patsy's father, who is described by Francesca as a lovely man, is also remembered as slicing open the stomachs of cows that are bloated with gas—an act that is none the less horrific for Patsy's insistence that it is necessary (12-13). Worse still is Patsy's defensive account of her father shooting the family dog, Belle, then leaving its corpse tied to a tree to rot (62). So we see at least that the sort of brutality Marie experiences at the hands of the boys after the dance is endemic to this farming community. But in Marie there are glimpses of something more primal than mere human brutality, something uncanny that is related to the phobia that Patsy's mother has about lightning. Here, as in *Tornado*, this terrifying power is encountered most intensely through the grand mal seizures of epilepsy, which Thompson represents vividly with the image of a menacing stalker "with his knife and his dirty long fingernails," the spectre of death (50-1).

In childhood it is Marie who is epileptic; in adulthood it is Patsy. The transference of the disease from one to the other is given a material (if implausible) explanation: Patsy injured her head in the incident at the train tracks; Marie's father stopped striking her on the head when she left Marmora. The deeper truth, however, has to do with the intensity of Patsy's identification with Marie. From the time of the incident at the train tracks, Patsy has suffered from epilepsy because she made a profound identification with Marie and in doing so acquired her friend's access to that cthonic power, a power represented on that occasion by the instrument of their impending deaths, the oncoming train (see 61).

Now, the account we are given of the train incident in this full-length version of the play has it that Patsy, though she was tempted to flee as the smell of her mother's burning pies beckoned her back to home and safety changed her mind and decided to remain on the tracks to be killed: apparently—and here is where the account becomes suggestively vague—Marie pulled Patsy from the tracks at the last moment. "Are you saying that I… saved *your* life?" asks Francesca. "You saved my life… but you always had… saved my life," responds Patsy (85). Shortly afterwards Francesca leaves to attend a gala that may or may not be real, and Patsy is left alone to remark: "We aren't going to see each other ever again. It's going to be like you were never here. Like you were a dream" (87). So, if we have not been inclined to ask them before, a series of questions are suddenly forced upon us at the play's end: Has the visit of Francesca been a dream conjured up by Patsy as she made her pies? Is Patsy's relationship to Marie more than a memory; is it a dark place of awful power hidden within herself that she revisits privately to reacquaint herself with the thrilling, terrifying experience of being open to the "unimaginable world"? It is not merely our knowledge of the original monologue that might lead us to believe that Patsy actually abandoned her friend to die alone on the train tracks, that she chose instead a parochial life of safety, familiarity, and perfect pies, using denial and self-deception to buttress her outer self against the threat of self-doubt, but haunted within by that recurring image of the stalker.

Off the 401 (1995), a short play first produced as part of a larger multi-author work called *Stolen Lands*, takes place not very far from Marmora geographically, at and near a roadside restaurant somewhere east of Kingston along the 401 (the largest multilane highway in Canada). The setting also has a similar figurative significance, functioning as a metaphor for the characters' forcible confrontation of horrific aspects of life existing just outside their mainstream, fast-paced lives. The play chiefly depicts an ethical chasm opening up between Val and John, a middle-class couple, in a manner reminiscent of Raymond Carver's "So Much Water So Far from Home." The two see a man and an Amerindian boy sitting together in the restaurant. Val suspects—correctly, as it turns out—that the man is exploiting the boy sexually. Val insistently demands that they take action, but John refuses, and when he offers her the option of walking back along the highway the "half a mile or so" (68) to the restaurant by herself, she says that she is "too tired. It's too cold, and I've got the wrong shoes" (69). The core of selfishness, complacency, and classism hinted at in their earlier conversation and persisting immovably beneath their ethical postures has been exposed. Disillusioned and demoralized, but otherwise unchanged, they move on down the highway.

Life in bewilderingly rapid motion also provides the eponymous image of Thompson's largest play to date, *Sled* (1997). Whereas all her previous work had been under two hours' duration, Thompson remarked that seeing Robert Lepage and Ex Machina's *Seven Streams of the River Ota*, a seven-hour production, prompted her decision that her new play should be "as long as it needs to be, not as long as it conventionally should be" (Duchesne and Fletcher 34). The larger scale allowed Thompson to revisit a number of the themes of her earlier work and draw them into a unifying pattern. Unfortunately, some critics complained that the effect of combining all the different strands in one play was unwieldy and incoherent. Be that as it may, it is impossible not to admire Thompson's magnificent ambitions, and while there is no telling what the ultimate fate of *Sled* will be, the play contains so many deeply fascinating and troubling elements that it would be a grave error to dismiss it lightly.

Sled depends upon the inevitable collision of action arising from two antithetical locations, the wilderness of northern Ontario and a residential neighbourhood in downtown Toronto. At a lodge in northern Ontario, Annie, an unusual lounge singer, is insulted by Kevin and Mike. Annie's husband, Jack, a policeman known for his violent temper, forces the two to apologize. That night Kevin kills Annie in reprisal when, encountering her in the woods, he pretends to mistake her for a moose. When Mike wants to inform the police, Kevin kills him as well, then steals Annie's red dress. Meanwhile, on Jack and Annie's street in Toronto we meet Joe, who carries all the history of his multi-cultural neighbourhood in his memory. One neighbour, Evangeline, desperately longs for the return of her little brother, who was kidnapped from the house many years before. The brother is Kevin, and when he returns to his childhood home on the run from the police, he bullies Evangeline into incest and into a job as a stripper. Though Annie's ghost continues to haunt him, Jack becomes romantically involved with Evangeline, not recognizing Kevin from the lodge. When he sees Annie's dress in Kevin's room, however, the two begin a fight, which Evangeline ends by killing Jack. Kevin then kills Joe for his money and urges Evangeline to escape with him. Instructed by Annie's ghost, Evangeline takes Kevin back into the northern wilderness, where, after having a baby she names Annie, she ends by indefatigably carrying the exhausted and dying Kevin while singing a Cree hymn and awaiting acceptance into the spirit world.

The sense of inevitable doom arising from the alternation between the two main settings of *Sled* is closely related to the effect of *White Sand*, where the fatal collision proceeds from the alternating sectors in a similarly ineluctable dialectic. The original concept governing the dialectic of *Sled* seems to have been the idea of Canada itself. That fact may not be so readily apparent from the script as it now exists. But, because of the publicly and academically supported workshops that eventually produced *Sled*, the genesis and development of the play is well documented; and records of the earlier drafts helpfully deepen our understanding of the final script.

During the workshop process, the scene in the original script to which Thompson is said to have given more attention than any other, and that which she most often offered for public consumption—choosing it to be recorded for radio, for example—was what she called "the Barbecue Dream scene." The scene was finally cut from the play late in the workshop process and so does not appear in the published version of *Sled*, for two reasons that Thompson explained in a post-workshop interview: "First, it is better to show rather than to tell; and second, there is so much vulnerability to failure [i.e., on the part of directors and actors] in that scene" ("Last Things" 39). Yet Thompson continued to emphasize the importance of the scene. In the interview she asserted that "the Barbecue Dream scene is the politics of the play. In a sense it is the springboard of the play for me intellectually" (39). Even after cutting the scene, Thompson continued to append it to the copies of *Sled* she sent out because, she explained, "it's my way of summarizing what the play is about" (40). Fortunately, the scene has been published in its original form in *Canadian Theatre Review* so the intellectual "springboard" remains available for consultation (Knowles, "Great" 12-16).

In the scene, Jack, after Annie's murder, is asleep on his couch in front of the television. He dreams of a barbecue at which Annie and other characters in the play appear, greeted by a home-made sign: "Welcome Neighbours." The conversation turns towards the multicultural nature of Canadian society, and the characters, of various ethnic backgrounds—Cree, Irish, Austrian Jewish, French Canadian, Portuguese, Italian, Norwegian—discuss the "balkanization" of Canada and the threat of separatism. They all begin to revert to their ancestral languages, yearning for a sense of home, angrily laying blame for the unfortunate aspects of their histories. Meanwhile, amidst the discussion, Kevin, masked in a black balaclava, interjects allusions to his violent murder of Annie. Though he is not at first acknowledged, we feel him poisoning the atmosphere of the party—a catalyst of discord and disaster like the mythical Ate, whose uninvited appearance at a wedding set off the Trojan War, or the wicked thirteenth Wise Woman of "Sleeping Beauty" who curses the heroine at her christening. At last the anxiety and hostility reach a crescendo. Jack tries to remove Kevin's mask, but he is easily overcome, and awakes screaming Annie's name.

Taking Thompson at her word about the scene representing "the politics of the play," we may say that *Sled* uses the Canadian political context to explore the disintegration of social goodwill into the kinds of xenophobic hostility and violent self-protectiveness that destroy the possibilities of peaceful civilization. The topic is clearly enormous in its complexity and scope of possible reference. Accounts of the workshop indicate that much time was spent whittling down a vast range of allusions and plot elements into an efficient dramatic shape. The explicit references to any particular Canadian political dilemma, for example, are gone entirely from the final script. Instead, the field of concern has moved to something more internal, more to do with essential human nature.

The notion of heritage as an aspect of identity is present in *Sled*, but the chief emphasis is on its spiritual aspect. Annie's deep feeling of affinity towards her Irish heritage, or Evangeline's discovery that her previously unknown Cree heritage resonates within her own soul, recall the treatment of the theme in *Tornado*, where for Velveteen, her Polish-Catholic ancestry represents her authentic place in the world of human spirit, a sort of personal Jerusalem. Thompson even dispensed with some of the rudimentary elements of realism that would root the theme of heritage in a material setting. In an earlier draft, for example, Evangeline learned Cree in prison, from a fellow Cree prisoner. In the final version of *Sled* she adopts the Cree language and culture almost as instantly and fluently as the characters in Jack's dream had done.

What remains very strongly of the Canadian cultural theme is in the shape of a path traced from the savage and mystical Canadian wilderness to the confusing multicultural reality of Canadian urban life. The record of violence that lingers in the memories and consciences of the city-dwellers (for instance, Joe's memory of the death of his father, Jack's shame about the youth he terrorized as "Diablo" while on police duty, or Evangeline's memory of her brother's kidnapping) lurks just outside normal civilized life, as the indomitably lawless wilderness awaits just beyond the boundaries of civilization. At the same time an identification is made between the vaguely atavistic aspirations of the characters and the mystic, primordial power inherent in the wilderness. In other words, the wilderness is a figure in which both the violence and the spiritualism of the inner life finds a counterpart in the horrors and serenity beyond civilization—truly a desperate wilderness.

Robert Nunn has argued that much of the complex symbolism of *Sled* may be understood in terms of Freud's theory of the uncanny, or *unheimlich* ("Strangers"). While many of the specific references he cites (such as the parade in honour of Saint Catherine, torn apart by wild beasts or the recurrent fox and wolf imagery) have been excised from the final version of the play, the principal tenet of his argument remains applicable. He suggests that the symbolism draws on two opposing realms of meaning, which he calls the "demonic" and the "totemic," identifying them respectively with Catholic and native spirituality. The appropriateness of the terms of opposition is arguable, given that within native spirituality there can still be a kind of demonic significance attached to some animals' behaviour, and within Catholicism animals are often represented benevolently, as in the imagery of the dove, the lamb, and so on. Still, there is no doubt that the pattern of imagery in *Sled* does evince such a double feeling towards the wilderness, taking the ambivalent totemic symbolism of *Stop Talking Like That* several steps further.

It would be possible to treat the ambivalence as a version of the "garrison mentality" described by Frye—the split personality of the depiction of the Canadian wilderness as both a threat against which civilized communities provide protection and a source of mystic identification for the repressed elements of the inner self. Yet Nunn's use of Freud's theory of the uncanny is perhaps a more promising interpretive model, given the affinities between Thompson's work and Freud's theories already delineated. Freud's discussion of the uncanny centres on the idea that what is deeply rooted in the self can be hidden, only to appear suddenly as something dangerous and threatening. The uncanny is therefore attached to a sense of the familiar and un-familiar at the same time, and arises where the incommensurable perspectives of the conscious and the unconscious are suddenly made to focus upon the same object. One place we experience the uncanny, then, is where an external act of violence corresponds to an inner suppressed thought, or when those whom we thought of as close neighbours reveal a side corresponding to our deepest fears.

Thus we might say that in *Sled* Thompson offers another variation on the Freudian theme of how the repressed continues to leak out on to the tidy surface of civilized life. Moreover, as Nunn points out, Freud argues that the uncanny is especially wont to appear "in relation to death and dead bodies, to the return of the dead, and to spirits and ghosts" (Freud, "Uncanny" 241, cited in Nunn, "Strangers" 39), because the older superstitions about death persist beneath the surface of modern rationality. This takes us much further into the heart of the discussion, for as Nunn says, *Sled* is above all "a play about the interpenetration of the worlds of the living and the dead, [a] motif that can be traced through Judith Thompson's work" (31).

With *Sled*, however, Thompson had set out to address this theme more directly than in any previous work. Her original title for the play was *The Last Things*, a reference to the four last things comprised by eschatological thought: death, judgment, heaven, and hell. Thompson moves the eschatological theme away from a purely biblical context, using elements of indigenous myth. In a note placed in the program for the Tarragon premiere (reproduced in the published play) she quotes *Aurora* by Candace Savage:

> The Iroquois people... imagined the aurora as the entry point into the Land of Souls, where the sky rose and fell to let spirits into the world beyond.... The lights were seen as the actual spirits of dead ancestors. Sometimes their progress across the sky was interpreted as a torchlight procession or a joyful dance. According to the circumpolar tradition, the northern lights are the souls of those who have died through loss of blood, whether in childbirth, by suicide or through murder. Inuit shamans have been visiting the moon for millennia. Often the journey began at night, under a full moon, when the shaman was standing at a blowhole, staring into the black, swirling water and waiting for a seal to rise. Suddenly, he would notice a sled descending out of the sky. It would land nearby, and the shaman would climb on board. Once he reached the land of the moon, he might meet dead relatives or watch spirits playing ball in the northern lights.

The *Sled* image, then, suggests a headlong plunge into the life to come, including the promised four last things. At the same time Thompson shows that a powerful element of human aspiration reaches back, not forward, attempting to retrieve memory and ancestral heritage to complete personal identity. The sense of destiny thrusts us forward blindly, even while we struggle to make sense first of where we have already been and who we are.

In short, the tremendous task to which *Sled* is addressed is the articulation of that eschatology that Norman O. Brown argued was the only hope of escaping the vicious, neurotic circle that psychoanalysis had revealed within the history of civilization. Thompson provides a glimpse of how the difficult project of maintaining social kinship with other human beings, represented here through the model multicultural neighbourhood over which Joe watchfully presides, is related to how we face the four last things awaiting the individual soul. If, as Freud suggests, all images of the hereafter are intimately related to our unconscious lives, then death, judgement, heaven, and hell do not necessarily await us only at the end of the sled ride. The confrontation of these last things occurs within each of us as we go, through an encounter with the inner life. And to transcend the barrier between our conscious selves and these four last things hidden deep within marks the first step towards transcending the barriers between us and our fellow human beings.

(2001)

Note

1 Thompson's maternal grandfather, William Ford, was at one time prime minister of Australia.

Works Cited

Brown, Norman O. *Life Against Death: The Psychoanalytic Meaning of History*. 1959. 2nd ed. Middletown, Conn: Wesleyan UP, 1985.

Chatwin, Bruce. *The Songlines*. Markham, ON: Penguin, 1987

Duchesne, Scott and Jennifer Fletcher. "*Sled*: A Workshop Diary." *Canadian Theatre Review* 89 (Winter 1996): 33-8.

Freud, Sigmund. "The Uncanny." *The Standard Edition of the Complete Psychological Works of Sigmund Freud*. Vol. 17. Ed. James Strachey. London: Hogarth, 1955. 217-56.

Knowles, Richard Paul. "The Achievement of Grace." *Brick* 41 (Summer 1991): 33-36.

———. "Great Lines are a Dime a Dozen: Judith Thompson's Greatest Cuts." *Canadian Theatre Review* 89 (Winter 1996): 8-18.

Nunn, Robert. "Strangers to Ourselves: Judith Thompson's *Sled*." *Canadian Theatre Review* 89 (Winter 1996): 29-32.

Thompson, Judith. "A Conversation with Judith Thompson." Interview by Cynthia Zimmerman. *Canadian Drama/L'Art dramatique canadien* 16.2 (1990): 184-94.

———. *The Crackwalker*. Toronto: Playwrights Canada, 1981.

———. *I Am Yours. The Other Side of the Dark: Four Plays by Judith Thompson*. Toronto: Coach House, 1989: 115-76.

———. Interview. *Fair Play: 12 Women Speak (Conversations with Canadian Playwrights)*. Ed. Judith Rudakoff and Rita Much. Toronto: Simon & Pierre, 1990. 87-104.

———. "The Last Things in the *Sled*: An Interview with Judith Thompson." By Jennifer Fletcher. *Canadian Theatre Review* 89 (Winter 1996): 39-41.

———. *Lion in the Streets*. Toronto: Playwrights Canada, 1992.

———. *Off the 401* [from *Stolen Lands*]. *Canadian Theatre Review* 89 (Winter 1996): 65-69.

———. *The Other Side of the Dark: Four Plays by Judith Thompson*. Toronto: Coach House, 1989.

———. *Perfect Pie* [first version]. *Solo*. Ed. Jason Sherman. Toronto: Coach House, 1994. 161-71.

———. *Perfect Pie* [full-length version]. Toronto: Playwrights Canada, 2000.

———. *Sled*. Toronto: Playwrights Canada, 1997.

———. *Stop Talking Like That. Airplay: An Anthology of CBC Radio Drama.* Ed. Dave Carley. Scirocco Drama. Winnipeg: Shillingford, 1996. 119-68.

———. *Tornado* [radio version]. *The Other Side of the Dark: Four Plays by Judith Thompson.* Toronto: Coach House, 1989: 79-114.

———. *Tornado* [stage version]. *Canadian Theatre Review* 89 (Winter 1996): 46-64.

———. *White Biting Dog.* Toronto: Playwrights Canada, 1984.

———. *White Sand. Airborne: Radio Plays by Women.* Ed. Ann Jansen.Winnipeg: Blizzard, 1991. 1-28.

Judith Thompson's Ghosts: The Revenants That Haunt the Plays

by Claudia Barnett

Death wears many guises in Judith Thompson's plays. In *The Crackwalker* (1980), one character tells another, "[B]ein dead ain't no different from livin [...]. It's just like movin to Brockville or Oshawa or something. It ain't that different." The second character disagrees, "I know it's different" (45), but by the end of the play, the characters have reversed their positions: the second kills his own infant son and fails even to register the death, merely saying, "It's okay it's not crying anymore" (65), while the first remarks, "I think it's better off dead" (70), thus implying that being dead must be different. Life and death form a complex dialectic in this play and throughout Thompson's writing. Being dead may or may not be different from living—and it also may or may not be worse. In her early plays, mysterious forces such as a talking dog, an "animal" behind a wall, and even the darkness of an epileptic seizure, compel the characters to act; because they occur off-stage, they may be real or imagined. In Thompson's more recent plays, these forces are personified, taking on physical presence witnessed by characters and audience alike. These forces are corporeal ghosts who look and act just like human beings, only better. Unlike the early shadows, these corporeal ghosts lack ambiguity and are often well-intentioned. Thompson's dead characters try to improve the lives of the living—not only the living characters within the plays, but also the live audiences who observe them. For instance, Isobel, the dead girl who haunts *Lion in the Streets* (1992), concludes the play by addressing the audience: "I want you to have your life" (63). By breaking the fourth wall with this imperative appeal, Thompson transforms the dialectic between life and death into a dialectic between life and theatre.

By creating characters who are ghosts, Thompson aligns herself with tradition while posing the same questions as contemporary feminist theory. "Theatre... has had a long romance with ghosts," writes Peggy Phelan, who names the ghost of Hamlet's father as the birth of Western theatre's "sustained conversation with the incorporeal" (*Mourning* 2). Thompson recognizes her own plays as part of this tradition, recalling classical tropes while subverting them. Hamlet fears that his father's ghost may be an agent of the devil and therefore he flounders in doubt. The characters in Thompson's *Perfect Pie* voice the same apprehension: "And I believe in God again," says one, while the other remarks, "Oh to me that's just the devil playin' with you" (18). In spite of Thompson's humorous touch (her characters are talking about the stomach flu), such concerns are the serious subject matter of her plays; she poses them as essential dialectics: god and the devil, self and other, life and death, and she creates corporeal ghosts to embody such contradictions. Elizabeth Grosz defines the human body in terms of binary pairs that destabilize it: "The body is neither—while also being both—the private or the public, self or other, natural or cultural, psychical or social, instinctive or learned…" (23). With her creation of ghosts, Thompson comments on the meaning of the body, aligning herself with Grosz and other feminist theorists: the body is a mass of contradictions, necessarily physical yet fundamentally abstract, the key element and also the essential challenge of theatre and performance.

Within Judith Butler's assertion that gender is performative lies the assumption that the body itself is a performance site—possibly even a performance. According to Butler's argument in *Bodies that Matter*, "matter" is "not a site or surface, but… a process of materialization that stabilizes over time to produce the effect of boundary, fixity, and surface" (*Bodies* 9); the body itself becomes part of that process, a continuous performance of repeated acts, ultimately "a projected phenomenon" (*Bodies* 17). The repeated acts of a subject create that subject's identity. For instance, when *Lion in the Streets* begins, Isobel "does not know she is a ghost, but she knows that something is terribly wrong" (15). She does not know how much time has passed or that she is dead; in fact, no one seems to register this fact, thereby confirming *The Crackwalker*'s suggestion that death is no different from life. Other children tease Isobel and physically attack her, and she throws rocks at them until an adult, Sue, intervenes. The scene seems ordinary until Isobel's father appears and Sue speaks to him. He goes inside, "slamming the door," Sue leaves, and then Isobel tells the audience: "My father is dead. Yes, was killed by a subway many many years; it is breathed very hard push push over my father; push over to God. Hi, my father" (18). Isobel slowly begins to realize the source of her confusion, and with this recognition she starts to behave like a conventional, invisible ghost.

Until Isobel acts like a ghost, she is not a ghost but simply an angry, confused child. Her identity is established not by her death but by a moment of recognition that leads to acts of repetition. After Isobel's conflict with the neighbourhood children, for most of Act One, she silently watches others (18, 19, 25, 32), and in doing so, she starts to become a ghost. Her repeated act is, in fact, inaction. At first, thinking she is lost, she wants someone to take her home; then, realizing she is dead, she wants someone to take her to heaven. Throughout Act Two, however, Isobel becomes less passive. She first watches the community in hopes that someone will become her "helper"; later, she becomes that helper herself, to those who need her most. After the incident with the children, the only people who see Isobel are Sue, whose husband publicly humiliates her, a battered woman named Sherry, and Ben, the man who murdered Isobel seventeen years earlier. Otherwise, Isobel remains invisible (or at least ignored). The characters who see Isobel are damaged and desperate, and that perhaps explains their unique vision. Or perhaps, given their marginalized positions in society, they do not recognize its rules: they do not understand the signs that indicate Isobel's eschatological status—signs that, ironically, signify invisibility.

Isobel eventually understands that, as a ghost, she has a certain kind of power. While outside forces have made her what she is, she also has an inner force. In *The Psychic Life of Power* Butler explains that one becomes a subject through a process both external and internal: "Power not only acts on a subject but... enacts a subject into being" (13). Isobel's ghostliness is initiated by her murder, but becoming a subject involves a further step:

> Power is both external to the subject and the very venue of the subject. This apparent contradiction makes sense when we understand that no subject comes into being without power, but that coming into being involves the dissimulation of power, a metaleptic reversal in which the subject produced by power becomes heralded as the subject who founds power. (16)

Isobel's murderer, whom she remembers as a lion (36), represents the horrors she observes, and she warns other characters against him: "The lion is here, in your streets. He is trying to kill you, to kill all of your children. He really really is" (44). She begins to wield power by helping others. At the end of the play, she meets Ben and begs, "I want back my life. Give me back my life!" but she finds him unable to help her, hence the "dissimulation of power." Integral to this reversal is Isobel's Christ-like forgiveness of Ben ("I love you") and final words to the audience: "I take my life. I want you all to take your life. I want you all to have your life" (63). She may be dead, but she has come to terms with, and in fact created, a viable identity, and as a result, she ascends to heaven, "heralded as the subject" (Butler, *Psychic Life* 16) as the players perform a ritual dance and place a veil on her head. Being alive has less to do with breathing than with embracing and enacting identity. Isobel may be a ghost, but she has more "matter" and more power than the live characters in the play.

Like Butler, Peggy Phelan theorizes identity and power, but she focuses specifically on issues of absence and loss. She remembers childhood drives in the family station wagon with "six brothers and sisters, two parents, [and] the ghost of my dead sister" (*Unmarked* 11). Her ghost is a memory:

> There were nine of us in that car, but it was the one who was not with us that we worried about, thought about, remembered. In the clarity of her absence, we redefined ourselves. The real was the absence of her; we were representations of that loss. (*Unmarked* 12)

The sister, in her absence, acquires more presence than the living beings, who find themselves defined by her. Throughout *Unmarked*, Phelan delineates the power of invisibility. While Thompson's ghosts are not always invisible, they choose when they want to be seen, thereby achieving the dominance Phelan describes. Thompson explores such issues in *Sled* (1997) with Annie Delaney, a nightclub singer killed early in Act One who, after her death, establishes a stronger presence than she had in life. Like Isobel, Annie experiences a power reversal and thereby achieves an identity. The difference is that Isobel begins as a dead, confused child in need of help, but Annie begins as a live adult with a family and a career—and yet she becomes a subject only by becoming a ghost.

As Annie dies, she utters her regret: "I have made such a faint impression in the world a bird alighting on a branch" (40). In an early scene of *Sled*, Annie and Jack are dining at a lodge where she sings when two young men, Kevin and Mike, insult Annie, and Jack, irate, demands an apology: "You are going to apologize to my wife and to every other diner in this establishment, or I will make you sorry" (25). Later that night, the men go hunting and see Annie out walking. Kevin, pretending she is a moose, shoots her. Ann Wilson writes that, frozen in the headlights, Annie becomes dehumanized: "She is without voice, without mobility, without agency" (126). This moment is not unique for Annie but is characteristic of her marriage to Jack, as Wilson explains:

> [Jack] asks not simply for an apology [from Kevin and Mike], but for a demonstration of his power by the two young men.... And, the apology is not to Annie, but to "my wife." Jack erases Annie by appropriating whatever humiliation she might have felt to demonstrate his power: he demands an apology because *his* wife has been offended. He wants the two young men to submit to his will. Annie simply serves as the currency in this exchange.... (125-26)

Annie is not subject but object, a fact she recognizes with her dying words. She has long lamented her lack of identity and therefore longs to visit Ireland, her ancestral home. In an odd scene late in the play, a combination of memory and ghostly visitation, Annie tries to explain the reason for this trip. When Jack forbids her to go, she explodes:

> You are just like the pathetic husband in the story of the selkie, the half-woman half-seal, terrified his beautiful wife he stole from the sea would find her seal skin, her true skin because he knows if she finds it then nothing, not children, not love, not any amount of pleading, will keep her from the sea. YOU WANT TO KEEP ME FROM THE SEA. (89)

Such imagery captures Annie's objectified state throughout life, and her words here, uttered with an eerie combination of foresight and hindsight (because she is both memory and ghost), promise the self-realization she ultimately achieves through death.

Annie knew her neighbour Evangeline only superficially when she was alive, yet Evangeline senses Annie's death immediately and is the first person Annie's ghost visits. According to the stage direction, Annie "sees the horror Evangeline faces, and she reaches for her to give her strength on her journey" (60); she becomes her shadow. Like Annie, Evangeline needs to find her roots: she begins to study her heritage when she is told that her father was Indian. And like Annie, Evangeline ultimately overcomes objectification. Her brother Kevin controls her with guilt and threats, but by the end of the play, their roles reverse and Evangeline leads him on his long walk to death. Evangeline owes her empowerment to Annie, who advises her: "It happens in Canada all the time, a disappearing woman, nobody minds. Just walk. Disappear" (105). Annie thus endows

Evangeline with invisibility, a power Phelan sees as typically reserved for men. These women become subjects by entering this male domain. While Annie and Evangeline barely knew each other in life, they affect each other deeply and irrevocably in death. "One always locates one's own image in an image of the other and, one always locates the other in one's own image," writes Phelan (*Unmarked* 18). Annie and Evangeline locate their own identities in each other.

Many of the characters in *Sled* are crippled by personal loss; these characters have dedicated their lives to memory rather than to the present. The themes of the play centre around loss: lost relatives, lost heritage, lost language. Some of the characters try to reclaim the past, while others strive to escape it. The profound sense of loss in this play serves as a metaphor for the theatre, which is itself defined by loss. A present-tense genre, theatre takes place only at the moment of performance and thereafter exists only as a memory or ghost. "Performance and theatre are instances of enactments predicated on their own disappearance," writes Phelan (*Mourning* 2). Theatre, like life, cannot be preserved. Yet it may live on in the memory as powerfully as Joe's mother, the neighbour's ghost who chastises him for every childhood mistake, or as Annie, who comes home to help. Joe's mother is a negative ghost who keeps Joe fixated on the unfixable, whereas Annie is positive. With her creation of ghosts, Thompson comments on the potential of the theatre/audience to transcend the past and affect the future. Annie's ghost moves on, even blesses Jack's love affair with Evangeline, singing so that they can dance. She remains with them metaphorically, but she pushes them forward without her. The body itself forms an important part of this equation. While integral to theatre, the body is also defined by the moment, by life. "The enactment of invocation and disappearance undertaken by performance and theatre is precisely the drama of corporeality itself" (Phelan, *Mourning* 4). Thompson emphasizes this fact by reversing the roles of the ghosts and the living: in her plays, the ghosts are the most alive—and the audience is reminded to go home and live.

While Thompson's plays are often life affirming, they also present a world full of horror. Jen Harvie writes that Thompson's

> combination of the apparently real and the real... deconstructs our ideas of reality, problematizing the objectivity with which we may think we can perceive what seems 'obvious,' and positioning reality not as essential, homogenous, and therefore static, but as provisional, heterogeneous, and changeable. (83)

Thompson's ghosts personify this combination as they destabilize reality, raising a slew of unanswered and unanswerable questions—among them whether or not life is different from death. This question reappears in *Perfect Pie* (1999) with various permutations: how are life and death different, to whom, and why does it matter? *Perfect Pie* begins with Patsy reciting a letter to her old friend Marie who, on at least one level, she knows is dead: "I know you did not survive. I know in my heart you did not survive, Marie" (4). Nonetheless, Marie, now named Francesca, visits Patsy in response to that letter, and together they relive their most pleasurable memories as well as the trauma that caused their separation. At the end of their visit, Patsy raises the point that troubles the audience throughout the play: "It's going to be like you were never here. Like you were a dream. I'll be sitting here six months from now and making my pastry and the snow will be falling and this afternoon will all seem... unreal" (91). Ultimately Thompson positions reality as "provisional, heterogeneous, and changeable," challenging her audience to reconsider the strict divisions between reality and fantasy, to consider why/if it matters if Francesca objectively exists.

As Patsy recalls their final childhood moment together, a train racing toward them and her body planted firmly on the track, Francesca finally realizes what happened when it crashed: "Are you saying I... saved your life? Patsy?" (89). All these years, Francesca has lived—*if* she has lived—with the guilt that Patsy had saved her. Now she finds that the opposite is true. If Marie really died, as she most likely did, then Patsy's imagination is the stage for this encounter. She remembers herself as victim rather than hero, and by presenting this piece of information to the ghost character at the end of their afternoon, she positions it as a major confession—and then she apologizes. She apologizes for living. She empowers Francesca by erasing her guilt, and in doing so, she paradoxically erases her own guilt. Her life will necessarily be better for this encounter, real or imagined, memory or ghost, and Francesca's identity will be irrelevant. Patsy thinks of the future, after Francesca's departure:

> And I'll be looking at that snow and I will feel the pastry dough in my hands and I will knead it and knead it until my hands they are aching and I think I'm making you. I like... form you; right in front of my eyes, right here at my kitchen table into flesh. Lookin' at me, talking soft. (91)

In this prediction, Patsy grants the ghost a body, as she has throughout the play. She makes Francesca a subject and ascribes power to her—and then she appropriates that power for herself. Thus Patsy has learned the lesson taught by all of Thompson's ghosts: she takes her life.

(2003)

Works Cited

Butler, Judith. *Bodies that Matter: On the Discursive Limits of "Sex."* New York: Routledge, 1993.

———. *The Psychic Life of Power: Theories in Subjection.* Stanford, CA: Stanford UP, 1997.

Grosz, Elizabeth. *Volatile Bodies: Toward a Corporeal Feminism.* Bloomington, IA: Indiana UP, 1994.

Harvie Jennifer. "Constructing Fictions of an Essential Reality or 'This Pickshur Is Niiiice': Judith Thompson's *Lion in the Streets.*" *Theatre Research in Canada/ Recherches théâtrales au Canada* 13.1 (1992): 81-93.

Phelan, Peggy. *Mourning Sex: Performing Public Memories.* New York: Routledge, 1997.

———. *Unmarked: The Politics of Performance.* New York: Routledge, 1993.

Thompson, Judith. *The Crackwalker. The Other Side of the Dark: Four Plays by Judith Thompson.* Toronto: Coach House, 1989. 15-71.

———. *Lion in the Streets.* Toronto: Playwrights Canada, 1992.

———. *Perfect Pie.* Toronto: Playwrights Canada, 1999.

———. "Revisions of Probability." Interview with Sandra Tomc. *Canadian Theatre Review* 59 (1989): 18-23.

———. *Sled.* Toronto: Playwrights Canada, 1997.

Wilson, Ann. "'Crowding Round Her': Violence and Female Subjectivity." Afterword. *Sled.* By Judith Thompson. Toronto: Playwrights Canada, 1997. 125-30.

Monstrous History: Judith Thompson's *Sled*

by Penny Farfan

In *Lion in the Streets* (pr. 1990; pub. 1992), Judith Thompson used the device of a relay plot structure to suggest that the brutal killer of a young girl is not simply a criminal aberration but an extreme incarnation of the underlying spirit that pervades the community, manifesting itself in a range of violent acts perpetrated by a spectrum of seemingly less murderous citizens over the course of the play. As Thompson has explained, "The lion is the cruelty that is in all of us, the seed that is in everyone" (qtd. in Zimmerman, 203). In her 1997 play *Sled*, Thompson extends this earlier exploration of the monstrous wilderness within the urban heart to an epic vision of contemporary Canada and the history that has shaped it.

Sled centres on the psychopathic murderer Kevin and the consequences of his crimes for various members of a Toronto neighbourhood, but this main plotline is intersected with meditations on the multicultural histories of the citizens who comprise the neighbourhood and each one of these histories is marked by some form of violence that has been integral to Canada's past. In "Theses on the Philosophy of History," Walter Benjamin wrote that "[t]here is no document of civilization which is not at the same time a document of barbarism" (256), yet while the city as represented in *Sled* functions as a primary document of the barbarism of civilization, Thompson has also stated that "history is in the body" (Hampson R3). Indeed, in *Sled*, these two views of history coincide, so that while the city functions as a microcosmic archaeological document of the larger "civilized" nation of Canada, the individual figure of Kevin functions as a monstrous avatar of Canada's history as a settler-invader nation premised on violence from the earliest moment of European contact with the "new world" and haunted by its violent past through to the present day.

Thompson's familiarity with psychoanalytic theory is well known,[1] and it is therefore worth noting that in *Moses and Monotheism*, Freud speculated that "there probably exists in the mental life of the individual not only what he has experienced himself, but also what he brought with him at birth, fragments of phylogenetic origin, an archaic heritage" (125). This "inheritance of memory," Freud suggested, consists of "traces of what our forefathers experienced, quite independently of direct communication and of the influence of education by example" (127). Indeed, in Freud's view, the development of history was motivated by the experience of a trauma that was repressed only to return again after a period of latency, so "that the mental residue of those primeval times has become a heritage which, with each new generation, needs only to be awakened, not to be re-acquired" (170). By way of analogy, Freud notes that

> [i]t may happen that someone gets away, apparently unharmed, from the spot where he has suffered a shocking accident, for instance a train collision. In the course of the following weeks, however, he develops a series of grave psychical and motor symptoms, which can be ascribed only to his shock or whatever else happened at the time of the accident. (84)

While Freud was concerned in *Moses and Monotheism* with the history of the Jews, which he believed to have been premised on the repression of the murder of Moses, his theories have recently been extended to a more general consideration of the relation between trauma, latency, the return of the repressed, and history (Caruth) and are useful to an understanding of Thompson's representation of Canadian history in *Sled*.

Thompson has repeatedly asserted her belief in the existence of a "collective unconscious" (Rudakoff 89; Wachtel 38; Zimmerman, "Conversation" 186), and although Freud questioned the value of this term, his idea of an archaic memory of trauma imprinted upon the mind is suggested in the final moment of Act I of *Sled* when Kevin speaks Norse as he murders Annie: "*Ek skal skjota ther huortu i gegnum.* [...] Let's shoot her man. Right through the heart" (33). Kevin later provides a plausible explanation for his ability to speak Norse—an English teacher taught him: "Said I woulda been Norse, like a thousand years ago" (50)—but his uncanny use of an archaic language as he murders Annie, whose dress he then takes as a trophy, is suggestive of the first contact of Europeans with what is now Canada and casts that first contact as a barbarous moment of brutal conquest.

Freud associated the experience of "the uncanny" with moments wherein that which has been repressed manifests itself in everyday objects so that what is known, familiar, comfortable, and "homely" ("*heimlich*") becomes at once unknown, strange, frightening, and "unhomely" ("*unheimlich*") (Freud, "Uncanny" 219-56). According to Freud, then, the category of the uncanny is reserved for those "instances of frightening things [...] in which the frightening element can be shown to be something repressed which *recurs*," so that the "uncanny is in reality nothing new or alien, but something which is familiar and old-established in the mind and which has become alienated from it only through the process of repression" (241). Thus, Freud notes, the uncanny may be understood "as something which ought to remain hidden but which has come to light," and therefore "[m]any people experience the feeling in the highest degree in relation to death and dead bodies, to the return of the dead, and to spirits and ghosts" (241). Freud concludes that "an uncanny experience occurs either when infantile complexes which have been repressed are once more revived by some impression, or when primitive beliefs which have been surmounted seem once more to be confirmed" (249).

Robert Nunn has applied Freud's concept of the uncanny to a consideration of the significance of the animal imagery, ghosts, and northern lights in *Sled*, but this notion of the uncanny can also illuminate Kevin's function in the play, in which his use of Norse at the moment of Annie's murder is accounted for in the familiar "homely" terms of psychological realism but at the same time signals the character's "unhomely" status as the embodied return of the repressed pre-history that is, in Thompson's epic vision, the foundational "wound [...] upon the mind" (Caruth 3) that continues to haunt present-day multicultural Canada. Similarly, while exposition regarding Kevin's traumatic childhood experience as a kidnap victim (56-57) is provided in passing as a realistic explanation for his psychopathic adult behaviour, his earlier use of Norse suggests that this adult behaviour in fact exceeds the realistic narrative causality that is provided to account for it. Thus, Kevin is again both familiar, in the sense of being an individual character who is explicable in realistic terms, and strange, in the sense of exceeding those realistic terms to serve a larger and less literal dramaturgical function as an incarnation of the violent history of the nation that Thompson is concerned with in the play. Considered in terms of this uncanny double function, Kevin's forcible wrenching from his birth mother by his kidnapper might be seen as analogous to the violent displacements that have constituted Canada's history of conquest, colonization, immigration, and assimilation as Thompson represents it in *Sled*. Kevin's catastrophic return to the city that was the site of his childhood trauma of violent separation from his mother thus signals the inevitable return of the repressed pre-history that set the stage for the subsequent wrenchings from mother countries and suppressions of mother tongues and cultures that have defined Canada's development as a settler-invader nation and that continue to haunt its postcolonial present.

Thompson has used the expression "soul murders" to describe violations that kill the spirit rather than the physical body and that constitute the link between "normal" people and the psychopathic child-killer in *Lion in the Streets* ("Conversation" 191). In *Sled*, Kevin's crimes are literal murders, but the histories that the other characters in the play recount are all at some level concerned with "soul murders" related to the process of "civilizing" the "new world": Annie's vision of her great-great-grandmother's immigration to Canada on a disease-plagued death-ship in the early nineteenth century (30); Joe's recollection of his boyhood humiliation when his impoverished Italian immigrant mother, widowed and bereft in a new country, forced him to wear her shoes to school (72-73); Jack's shame-driven rejection of his native French language and of the French Canadian foods his mother prepared for him in childhood (42); and the deliberate withholding from Evangeline of the truth of her First Nations heritage (68-69). As Ann Wilson has stated, in *Sled*, "violence is incorporated into the weave of a community's history [...]. The bold, and perhaps unpalatable, suggestion is that violence doesn't shatter a community, but is incorporated into its identity" (130). In this way, the "soul murders" in *Sled* resonate with Kevin's physical murders, their psychic violence as closely associated with the history of Canada as the brutality of the first moment of European contact with the "new world" that is suggested by Kevin's use of Norse as he kills Annie. History is thus present not only in the uncanny figure of Kevin but "in the bodies" of the other characters as well, and this latent presence of past trauma is manifested in various ways throughout the play, from the indirect association of "diablo" Jack's rage with his violent rejection of his French Canadian roots (41-42); to Annie's statement that she herself is the Irish girl of her vision (30); to Evangeline's ability to sing "a Cree song of lamentation" (102), as if the Cree language had been there within her all along, waiting for her to discover it along with the truth of her identity; to the various ghosts—Annie, Evangeline's mother, Joe's mother—that appear on stage to haunt the living. In Ann Wilson's words, "All the dead in *Sled* continue to be presences—albeit ghostly ones—within the community" (130).

In Scene 2, Joe reveals that the street where he, Annie and Jack, and Evangeline all live was once a cow path leading to a slaughterhouse that is still in operation (15); and this earlier life as a path to slaughter is made present again when a steer escapes from the slaughterhouse and runs along the street until it is shot down (85-86). The escaped steer that instinctually knows the archaeology of the city and the association of the multicultural neighbourhood with a slaughterhouse together clarify how the past is archived not only within the individual bodies of the people who populate the city, but within the structure of the city itself. The steer thus signals Thompson's interest in the social archaeology or subtext of the city as historical document founded upon the physical and psychic murders inherent in the intersected processes of conquest, colonization, immigration, and assimilation.

Sherrill Grace has argued that *Sled* is premised upon a binary relationship between a metaphoric "North" and the metonymic "South" that has mythologized it (155), but as Grace herself points out, the wilderness setting where the play begins is in fact not very far north at all, but, rather, no further north than Algonquin Park (157). It would seem, then, that in *Sled*, Thompson is less concerned with the dichotomy of north and south than with the relationship between city and wilderness. In a stage direction, Thompson specifies that the city houses "look as though they are in the middle of a forest" (15), which Grace reads as evidence of the importance of the mythic construct of "North" in the urban characters' (and Thompson's) imaginations, particularly as a place of refuge "when the violence and degradation of urban life threaten to overwhelm us" (154). This stage direction might instead be read as another expression of Thompson's historical vision, however, calling attention both to the superimposition of the city upon the wilderness and to how the "civilization" of the Canadian "wilderness" over the course of history has created a wilderness that is other than geographic and that is embodied in the individuals who populate the city. Thus, the rapacious wild beast that Thompson imported from abroad to serve as the governing metaphor of *Lion in the Streets* has been transformed in *Sled* into an indigenous red fox that lurks in the heart of the Canadian city (17, 19, 71). In Thompson's postcolonial history play, the Canadian wilderness is not the land itself but the traumatized psyches of the people who occupy a landscape marked by a violent history of conquest, displacement, rupture, and loss.

Thompson has stated that she believes that "[w]e're living in a pathological state of denial, as a society, as a culture, and we have to stop it right now" ("An Interview" 38), and that "[o]ur whole society is founded on denial. Denial of murdering the Native people, denial of oppressing women. Everything we do"

("Offending" 34). As a consequence, she understands her job as a playwright as being to enable audiences to see "what is invisible and covered up with piles of everydayness and everyday life" ("An Interview" 37) and "to experience the painful thing of looking in the mirror": "[...] I think that awakening, slipping out of our comas, is what it's all about. Otherwise, we do not live—it's the unexamined life. The coma lifting, then, becomes political. Art is political, should be political, but only in this really essential way (Thompson, "Conversation" 193). In bringing to the stage the repressed past traumas that continue to shape present experience within a settler-invader nation such as Canada, Thompson contributes to the ongoing postcolonial project of challenging hegemonic representations of history.

Yet as Helen Gilbert and Joanne Tompkins have noted, postcolonial drama revisits history in order to regenerate the colonized (11-12), and in light of this objective, it is worth considering the ending of *Sled*, which focuses on the three characters who have been most interested in reconnecting with their lost heritages—Kevin, Evangeline, and Annie, who is now a ghost. Returning Kevin and Evangeline to the wilderness where Annie was murdered at the start of the play, Thompson in effect replays the moment of first contact not as brutal conquest but as a life-producing encounter between half-siblings of different races and, in doing so, she suggests the possibility of a new beginning through a revision of history. Children in drama often represent the future, and at the end of *Sled*, Evangeline is pregnant by her half-brother Kevin, the name of her unborn child—Annie Northstar—suggesting both a fusion of indigenous and settler cultures and the possibility of renavigating the history that led to the child's conception, which Evangeline describes as an out-of-control ride on a "runaway sled" (84).

As Kevin lies dying in Evangeline's arms under the northern lights that illuminated his murder of his friend Mike earlier in the play but are now represented as benevolent "dancing spirits" who have come for him and his half-sister (109),[2] Annie's ghost, now in a sense a specter from the future, reprises the song that she sang at the beginning of the play, "Oh heavenly time of day." Whereas the first version of the song focused on nighttime and "the sky full of stars/who are people who died" (13), however, the final version describes a movement toward clarity and the play ends on an open note as to the nature of the vision that this new clarity enables.

> Oh heavenly time of day...
> the fog and the quiet.The mist, no sun. I move out of my dream and into this day as
> the fog it clears so slowly away to reveal... to
> reveal...
> *The Snowy Owl hoots.*
> *The End.* (109; ellipses in original)

(2004)

Notes

1 Thompson has stated, "I am a devoted Freudian in some ways. I've read all his work. I went through all of it in about a year and a half and audited a course on him when I was on a Canada Council B-Grant" ("Judith Thompson Interview" 99).

2 The published version of *Sled* includes the following epigraph from Candace Savage's book *Aurora*:

> The Iroquois people... imagined the aurora as the entry point into the Land of Souls, where the sky rose and fell into the world beyond.... The lights were seen as the actual spirits of dead ancestors. Sometimes their progress across the sky was interpreted as a torchlight procession or a joyful dance. According to a circumpolar tradition, the northern lights are the souls of those who have died through the loss of blood, whether in childbirth, by suicide or through murder. Inuit shamans have been visiting the moon for millennia. Often the journey begins at night, under a full moon, when the shaman was standing at a blowhole, staring into the black, swirling water and waiting for seal to rise. Suddenly, he would notice a sled descending out of the sky. It would land nearby, and the shaman would climb on board. Once he reached the land of the moon, he might meet dead relatives or watch spirits playing ball in the northern lights. (10; ellipsis in Thompson)

According to an account of the first workshop of *Sled*, however, it would seem that this passage was brought to Thompson's attention after she had actually written the play (Duchesne and Fletcher 34).

Works Cited

Benjamin, Walter. "Theses on the Philosophy of History." *Illuminations*. Ed. Hannah Arendt. Trans. Harry Zohn. New York: Schocken Books, 1969. 253-64.

Caruth, Cathy. *Unclaimed Experience: Trauma, Narrative, and History*. Baltimore: Johns Hopkins UP, 1996.

Duchesne, Scott, and Jennifer Fletcher. "*Sled*: A Workshop Diary." *Canadian Theatre Review* 89 (Winter 1996): 33-38.

Freud, Sigmund. *Moses and Monotheism*. Trans. Katherine Jones. New York: Vintage, 1939.

———. "The 'Uncanny.'" *The Standard Edition of the Complete Psychological Works of Sigmund Freud*. Vol. 17. Ed. and trans. James Strachey. London: Hogarth, 1955. 217-56.

Gilbert, Helen, and Joanne Tompkins. *Post-Colonial Drama: Theory, Practice, Politics*. London: Routledge, 1996.

Grace, Sherrill. "Going North on Judith Thompson's *Sled*." *Essays in Theatre/Études théâtrales* 16.2 (May 1998): 153-64.

Hampson, Sarah. "Bright Lights, Dark Corners." *The Globe and Mail* 8 September 2001: R3.

Nunn, Robert. "Strangers to Ourselves: Judith Thompson's *Sled*." *Canadian Theatre Review* 89 (Winter 1996): 29-32.

"Offending your Audience: A Panel Discussion." *Theatrum* 29 (June/July/August 1992): 33-4.

Thompson, Judith. "A Conversation with Judith Thompson." By Cynthia Zimmerman. *Canadian Drama/L'Art dramatique canadien* 16.2 (1990): 184-94.

———. "An Interview with Judith Thompson." by Eleanor Wachtel. *Brick* 41 (Summer 1991): 37-41.

———. "Judith Thompson Interview." by Judith Rudakoff. *Fair Play: 12 Women Speak (Conversations with Canadian Playwrights)*. Ed. Judith Rudakoff and Rita Much. Toronto: Simon & Pierre, 1990. 88-104.

———. *Sled*. Toronto: Playwrights Canada, 1997.

Wilson, Ann. "'Crowding Round Her': Violence and Female Subjectivity" [afterword]. *Sled*, by Judith Thompson. 125-30.

Zimmerman, Cynthia. *Playwriting Women: Female Voices in English Canada*. Toronto: Simon & Pierre, 1994.

Staging the Post-Colonial Monster in Judith Thompson's *Capture Me*

by Dalbir Singh

> America's purpose is more than to follow a process—it is to achieve a result: the end of terrible threats to the civilized world. All free nations have a stake in preventing sudden and catastrophic attack. We are asking them to join us, and many are doing so. Yet the course of this nation does not depend on the decisions of others. Whatever action is required, whenever action is necessary, I will defend the freedom and security of the American people. Different threats require different strategies. (Bush)

Capture Me, a play written and directed by Judith Thompson, premiered at the Tarragon Theatre in December 2004. I had the opportunity to work on the play (as a Draft Archivist) as part of my Master's thesis at the University of Guelph. Akin to my MA project, this article will attempt to locate Thompson's latest play within Post-Colonial discourse insofar as it relates to notions of the monster/monstrous.

Capture Me invites examination of Western conceptions of "the other," and urges subversion of these concepts. I will be looking at how "otherness" is figured by concentrating primarily on the construction of the play's two male characters. Aziz Dawood is a Muslim refugee seeking asylum status and Dodge Kingston is an educator who lectures to juvenile delinquents. The men are both attracted to the principal female character, Jerry Joy Lee. The nature of this triangular relationship is established by Thompson's counter-discourse, which ultimately presents Dodge as "the other." His self-proclaimed status as a "monster" is defined by his actions, the symbolism attached to his character, and his representation as a "colonizing force." The figuring of Aziz as an empathetic character sharply contrasts the demonization of Dodge. However, Aziz's relationship to his "home" environments abroad and in Toronto reflects a deep-seated anxiety and ambivalence that is rooted in both locales being simultaneously nurturing and exploitative. By the close of the play, Aziz Dawood's character will have become integrally implicit in Thompson's deconstruction of "othering" in its various manifestations.

Capture Me both challenges and addresses issues of race and nationhood by questioning how we view "otherness" in an environment of geo-political unrest. As a result, I am locating the play within its socio-political context. Chief among the influences omnipresent in the media during the writing of the play was the racist rhetoric governing George W. Bush's "Crusade Against Evil." Indeed my epigraph, by the present American President, is highly instructive when discussing the process of "othering." Bush (like Margaret Thatcher in early 1980's England) employs an "us/them" dichotomy that frequently positions "us" as white subjects and "them" as non-white. American popular culture and the news media in the post-9/11 climate have generally rallied alongside Bush in upholding preconceived notions concerning Muslim peoples. The use of binary codes in demonstrating the recurrent "us/them" theme also plays an integral role in imperialist ideology. The us/them binary could easily be replaced with a civilized/primitive or leader/follower dichotomy. The US's current imperial incursion into Iraq is also centred in this binarism that seeks to reaffirm its superiority. Judith Thompson's *Capture Me* counters this strategy by detailing "the evil within us" (Interview). She posits this evil (or "terror," in Bush terminology) as being something internal as opposed to external (the "war on terror" and its colonialist applications); as she states, "the play is telling us what we think of as 'other' (rage, murder, etc.) is not only right next to us [...]. It is our own men who are to be feared. In other words, it is not those faraway places that breed terror. We breed it right here" (Interview). This re-circumscribing of "terrorism" becomes directly mapped onto the straight white male's body. Dodge effectively undercuts the concept of externalized "terror" by relating himself and his male students to monstrosity:

> What happens when we commit an act of violence? When we commit an act of violence, we lose our human shape, don't we? We transmogrify. Yes, we become monsters [...]. Your hands grew gigantic and your muscles burst out of your skin and your snout grew and your eyes became red and you grew teeth and claws and became wolf-monsters. It's a rush unlike any other, isn't it guys? (2.7.2-10) [1]

The monster, in this respect, is not only internal but is also manifested through an animalisation of the body. A Caucasian male professor depicted as "savage" or "animalistic" subverts the European colonialist model that characterized the colonized in such terms. Thompson effectively represents Aziz as an individual escaping the horrors of persecution while simultaneously addressing his oppression as a refugee in Canada. His immigration is part of Canada's own historicity. Thompson's original intention was to "say [that] Aziz is our future *and* our past. Most of our grandparents were refugees escaping genocide" (Interview). The play advances a blatant re-evaluation of citizenry and nationhood through the contrasts between Aziz and Dodge. Even though Aziz wasn't born on Canadian soil, he is figured as more representative of the country's populace than Dodge, who is figured as the "monstrous other." However, Thompson creates an alienation effect that ostracizes Aziz from the other Caucasian actors on stage. This effect is not utilized in order to "other" him. Rather, this alienation is reflective of the characters' ignorance (whether intentional or not) in their perceived attitudes toward his culture. For instance, Jerry's curiosity is indicative of her naïveté: "Well! You'll have to come in and talk to the kids about your country" (1.11.17). Minkle describes her own misconceptions about Aziz's motives that are based partly on racial stereotyping: "But do you ever think, like just for an uneasy minute, that he's makin' up the whole refugee thing?

And he's like a hustler from Lahore who wants the good life, the wide screen TV and the jumbo shrimp and the sweet pussy with a steady job?" (2.4.18-21). Dodge casts Aziz in terms of a "foreignness" that is laden with distinctly negative connotations. His supposed "truth" about Aziz's patriarchal culture ("You know that he has nothing but contempt for you; in his culture loose women like you are nothing but prostitutes"[1.18.18-20]) is masked by his feelings of insecurity and irrational rage toward Jerry's newfound, "foreign lover." Dodge's perceived ownership over his former wife is threatened by Aziz's presence, but a concerted effort is made to challenge these misinformed perceptions of Aziz's cultural background. Aziz's blistering monologue detailing a massacre in his native village undermines any attempt at reading his "true" motives in obtaining asylum status. Minkle also tries to understand or at least acknowledge how political "terrorism" is rooted in extreme repression: "In my experience, justice doesn't usually happen. If I were him, I'd want revenge [...] Jerry. Tell me. Tell me you wouldn't want revenge" (2.9.17-20).

In this regard, demonizing political figures such as Saddam Hussein ("the Butcher of Baghdad") and Osama Bin Laden not only obscures terrorism committed by Western leaders but the act of demonizing also neglects the complexities of networks branded terrorist and the immense suffering and political repression (either U.S.-backed or supported) that the citizenry of oppressive regimes have endured. *Capture Me* questions tropes concerning exclusivity and nation in Canadian society, and, in doing so, advances this interrogation of the us/them and good/evil binary.

Sharzia, Aziz's young daughter, is terrified of the national anthem; an immigration officer who asks seemingly inane questions interrogates Aziz. Both of these situations evoke the questionable nature of governmental leadership that is hegemonic in nature. The use of control depicted through the patrolling of the nation's borders is also marked by corporatism. Aziz remarks that he "would like true tea. I need true tea. But here there is only Red Rose" (2.8.17-18). The commodification of "true tea" follows a pattern of indicting corporate interests. Dodge's "monstrosity" becomes replicated by Sharzia's fellow classmate who

> turns [the] class into her very own torture chamber [...] She has a nose for the more fragile children [...] the children who come to school with bruises, or faces swollen with tears. She goes right for the throat with those kids, has lots of fun turning everyone else against them too. [She] is a psychopath [...] she is going to go through her life destroying everything in her sweet little path. (1.12.4-12)

Minkle then describes to Jerry another child who assumes special privilege due to his father being the Vice-President of Scotia Bank. The politics of primary school may be transplanted onto conflicts arising between the characterizations of Aziz and Dodge. This may also be reflective of the dominance of corporate powers over the third world and specifically of Dodge's representation as a "colonizing force."

The set itself is emblematic of this rift between the colonizer and the colonized and how it becomes spatially mapped. In several scenes, Dodge is repeatedly relegated to the periphery of the stage while Aziz is often located at its centre. During a rehearsal of the play's final sequence in the Tarragon production, a circle was created centre-stage that involved all of the characters except Dodge, who watched the action from down left. His strategic placement effectively positioned him as the Other, ostracized and isolated from the centrality of the characters. Also, the dominant set piece consisted of a large rippled disc that resembled an ocean. The ocean is a literal representation of the play's biblical framing narrative, as both Aziz and Sharzia repeat the following passage, "What has the fine pearl to do with the world of dust? […]. Like the moths of the sea, we come from the ocean, the ocean of the soul" (1.1.1-3). In this production, the fluidity of water was aesthetically linked to the impermanence of owning land or space by the construction of levels that resembled ripples in the set's blue oval disc. The ocean also became associated with a volcano that appeared as a pulsating red light through the slits in the disc. The volcano was both racialized and feminized. Not only was the volcanic lava flow figured as menstrual blood—

> I was a really late bloomer […] so I thought I was finally going to menstruate […] but then I was in geography class giving a little talk on volcanoes […]. Mr. Hale the typing teacher with the goatee and the white shoes, he noticed that blood was dripping onto the floor below me, "Oh no, that's just lava, said I." (2.20.51-82)—

but the volcano also connoted the burned bodies in Aziz's village who, "[…] seemed to come to life while burning" (2.8.67).

Dodge is often symbolically and literally represented in the play as a perpetrator of violent acts directed not only against Aziz, but against Jerry as well. His association with cannibalism is seen in his initial scene with Jerry. He reminds her of how he "loved that dish [she] used to make, the artichoke hearts smothered in…" (1.3.54-55). He doesn't finish this thought and concludes the scene by placing a hand on her heart while saying, "Great to see you again! And I know it's great for you I can hear your heart beating" (1.3.101-02). The sound of a heartbeat is then juxtaposed against the image of his hand on her heart. Near the close of the play, he lights a cigarette while towering over Jerry's murdered body. His depiction as a murderer is fully realized in this scene with the cigarette. The images of flame from his lighter and smoke emanating from his mouth are contrasted with the figurative volcano that has engulfed both Aziz and Jerry in its wake. By figuring Dodge within such tropes, Thompson indicts him within a system of Western patriarchal violence that re-envisions concepts of "the monster" and of "savagery." Thompson achieves this political statement by "othering" him while simultaneously depicting him as a repressive force. In *Capture Me*, both terrorist and avenging warrior are the same figure, and Judith Thompson reveals this doubling in her characterizations and stage design. She presents her audience with a more complex definition of the colonizer-colonized binary than is heard in the easy rhetoric of war: indeed, "Different threats [do] require different strategies."

(2004)

Note

[1] All quotations are from the 23 Nov. 2003 draft according to act, scene, and line number.

Works Cited

Bush, George. W. "2003 State of the Union Address." *The Washington Post.* 28 Jan. 2003. n. pag. Online. Internet. 24 Mar. 2004. http://www.washingtonpost.com/wp-srv/onpolitics/transcripts/bustext_012803.

Capture Me. By Judith Thompson. Dir. Judith Thompson. Perf: Randi Helmers, Tom McCamus, Nancy Palk, Maurice Dean Wint and Chick Reid. Sound: John Gzowski. Set/Costumes: Sue LePage. Lighting: Andrea Lundy. Tarragon Theatre. 30 Dec. – 8 Feb. 2004.

Thompson, Judith. *Capture Me.* Draft ms. 25 Nov. 2003.

———. Personal Interview. 29 April 2004.

Who is the Stranger?: The Role of the Monstrous in Judith Thompson's *Capture Me*

by Robyn Read

"I felt like a pawn—a helpless, passive victim—caught up in a ghastly game in which some men ran around trying to kill women, and others went around trying to save them" (Brison 90). This statement was made by philosophy professor Susan J. Brison in her book *Aftermath: Violence and the Remaking of a Self*, a "personal narrative of recovery and a philosophical exploration of trauma," written ten years after she went on a morning walk while in the south of France and was "attacked from behind, severely beaten, sexually assaulted, strangled to unconsciousness, and left for dead" (back cover). When her lawyer met with her while she was still in the hospital recovering, he gave her this advice: "[D]on't think of your assailant as a human being. Think of him as a wild animal, a beast, a lion" (Brison 86).

By encouraging Brison to imagine a "wild animal" or "beast," her lawyer was associating her assailant with the "so-called monstrous races" (Shildrick 15). Margrit Shildrick, in *Embodying the Monster: Encounters with the Vulnerable Self*, examines early records of "monsters, marvels and meanings" in Western history (8). In these instances, the boundaries dividing the different categories of monster are fluid. In the sixteenth century, for example, Stephen Bateman grouped "fabulous creatures of mythology" together with "hybrid human forms" and "strange animals of land and sea" in the "medieval tradition of bestiaries" (Shildrick 15, citing Bateman). However, Brison's lawyer makes one distinction: he identifies a specific species of monstrous animal, the "lion,"—a creature that appears in the plays of Judith Thompson.

Susan Brison's aftermath philosophy and Margrit Shildrick's postmodern study of the monster motivated and facilitated my study of Judith Thompson's latest play, *Capture Me*. Thompson creates characters who struggle to reconcile their separate selves, "to bridge [the] persistent gulf between the self that speaks and the self represented in the discourse as the subject, the 'I'" (Knowles 8). After her attack, Brison struggled to remake her self and also make sense of her surroundings. She felt that she had "ventured outside the human community, landed beyond the moral universe, beyond the realm of predictable events and comprehensible actions" (x). I wish to examine *Capture Me* as a bridge between two communities: one which is real and one that can only be imagined. There is a society where violence has come to be expected, and an unknown domain where a kind of trauma exists that cannot be anticipated. Thompson's choices as a playwright, and the ways in which *Capture Me* deconstructs and reconstructs the boundaries surrounding, and separating, the self and the monster, reveal how and where the monstrous may be present within contemporary Western culture.

Capture Me is the sixth play by Judith Thompson to premiere at the Tarragon Theatre in Toronto. It is the story of Jerry Joy Lee (played by Randi Helmers in the Toronto production), a kindergarten teacher who is stalked by her ex-husband Dodge Kingston (Tom McCamus). A former university professor, Dodge reforms troubled youths at the local jail. By giving seminars on violence, he attempts to rehabilitate children while philosophizing about, and fighting against, his own evil instincts.

Jerry has an obsession of her own; after many attempted phone calls where she is unable to speak, she at last makes contact with her biological mother, Dr. Delphine Moth (Nancy Palk). However, Jerry is a woman both pursued and abandoned; her mother refuses to form a relationship with her daughter. The responsibility of restoring Jerry's faith is left in the hands of her sharp-mouthed friend and fellow teacher Minkle (Chick Reid), and the father of one of her students, Aziz Dawood (Maurice Dean Wint), with whom she falls in love. Aziz has fled an unidentified Arabic nation after witnessing the massacre of his entire family except for his daughter Sharzia, who has come with him. He does not speak of his past.

Before discussing Judith Thompson and *Capture Me*, it is necessary to establish how the terms "monster" and "monstrous" are defined and utilized within the context of this essay. Shildrick states, "[M]onsters of course show themselves in many different and culturally specific ways [...] what is monstrous about them is most often the form of their embodiment" (9). Traditionally, it is the monster's body that places it in opposition to that which is intact, human, and "natural." Over time, the image associated with the monster has become a composite, an accumulation of the many shapes and forms it has taken both historically and currently in popular culture. The inability to associate just one figure or sign with the monster perpetuates its instability. However, when concerns are extended beyond solely the corporeality of the monster, when the monstrous is interpreted as a *concept* rather than a *thing*, one can start to analyze how it functions within philosophical and theatrical discourse. The contributors to Jeffrey Jerome Cohen's anthology *Monster Theory: Reading Culture*, whose essays on monsters range from Frankenstein's creation to the raptors of *Jurassic Park*, are united by this "insistence that the monster is a *problem* for cultural studies [as] a code or a pattern or a presence or an absence that unsettles what has been constructed to be received as natural, as human" (ix, emphasis in original).

Part of the puzzle is that, when studied as a theoretical concept rather than an image, the monster's deformities may not be as visible, or as tangible, as once thought. The paradox is that a monster is recognized as a being that has features that are unrecognizable. Jacques Derrida states that the future is "necessarily" monstrous because it is unrecognizable: "[T]he figure of the future, that is, that which can only be surprising, that for which we are not prepared, you see, is heralded by a species of monsters" (qtd. in Weber 386-87). The performance of the monstrous in *Capture Me* is unpredictable; it is not always obvious which characters will give into their rage and lose their human shape. Thompson was inspired to explore the theme of becoming monstrous after questioning whether rage might "simmer just under the surface of all people, especially here, in our sheltered world" ("Inspiration"). Dodge muses how, "Evil is like a riptide.... Like a current you can't fight," that it is like "being pulled out to the middle of a dark sea" (Thompson, *Capture Me* 11). *Capture Me* shows the process of becoming monstrous, instead of presenting an already established monster, in an effort to understand how transmogrification functions and why it happens.

In Thompson's earlier work, the monster was buried within the psyche of her characters. The beast was within, but hidden. *Lion in the Streets* shows just "glimpses of the lions of anger and fear, repression and denial that lie in wait not just in the streets but in the abysses of the human heart" (Wasserman 259). In *I Am Yours,* the lion torments the imagination of the character Dee, but according to the stage directions, she wills the animal to "stay behind the wall, and not enter her being" (*I Am Yours* 119). This animal is imagined to be unnatural and uncivilized. The pertinent question that Dee's sister Mercy asks her is, "Aren't you afraid of what your ANIMAL might do?" (*I Am Yours* 144). But where the creatures in *I Am Yours* and *Lion in the Streets* haunt those plays from the edges, the monster in *Capture Me* does not keep a distance. According to Jerry Wasserman, Thompson's characters have "an obsessive need to reconcile the innate violence of their unconscious life—the animal, the dark side, or whatever other metaphors she uses for the Freudian id—with their equally profound pull toward some unnameable, transcendent pole of experience" (257). *Capture Me* is a play about "becoming what we most fear" (Nestruck 2), as well as that "profound pull" towards an unknown experience: an encounter with the monstrous.

When Dodge asks, "Who here in this room believes in EVIL?," it is a rhetorical question (11). One of the play's themes is the prevalence of violence in Western society, something that is seen on the news every day (51). Therefore it is crucial to acknowledge not just that the monster is seen in *Capture Me*, but *where* the monster is presented, within human characters rather than on the periphery as an animal or a lion. Dodge philosophizes, "Radical Evil is within US. It is us. Within you and me and every human being on this earth in fact EVIL is what MAKES us human" (Thompson, *Capture Me* 11). This reflects Shildrick's statement that "monsters" or "strangers in general [...] may not be outside at all" (4). The monster is no longer kept outside in *Capture Me*, as Julie Adam writes of Thompson's previous plays, "hovering around the periphery of civilization" (23). Instead, the monster manifests itself within the human characters on stage.

Considering that *Capture Me* deconstructs the binary between what is human and what is monster, it is interesting to consider the transformation that Thompson herself goes through for her profession:

> To write, I have to become, basically, a child who is a wild animal. The rest of the time, I am an ordinary, rather slow-witted but good-humoured woman, the kind of mother who falls asleep in front of CBC documentaries at ten fifteen every night, and does two loads of laundry before waking the kids at eight in the morning. ("I Will Tear" 27)

Thompson has said, "I am written in my plays, whether I want to be or not. My breath is their breath" (Turcott viii). In an interview with Judith Rudakoff, she stated that sometimes the only way for her to write characters is to act the parts out: "For instance, in *I Am Yours* there was a male character I was having trouble with and I thought, 'Well, why not inhabit him for a while?' And then I realized, suddenly, how everything should be" ("Judith Thompson" 92). However, when I asked Thompson if she had to inhabit Dodge in order to understand the type of monster that he could become, she responded, "I only inhabited the good part of him. I inhabited him during his talks [his seminars on violence] because I learned a little about Kant and radical evil and I thought, what would I like to say to these boys if I really wanted to help them and help make the world better?" ("Witnessing" 97). It was as a creative artist that Thompson found a means to cross the threshold into a monstrous state of mind:

> I've been in states where I've been irrational or unreasonable. You get in an argument with someone, even a friend, and that friend asks you to just stop, you know, let's go for a walk or something, but you're in that mode where you can't stop. It's this weird altered state you get into when arguing, and it's like you have to almost break a spell to get out of it. And I think that's what [Dodge is] in. ("Witnessing" 97)

A "spell" is a device that Thompson uses to write about the monstrous. In order to write about transmogrification, seen as a problem in literary studies because it is a pattern with certain unrecognizable elements, she allows her creative thought process to not only incorporate, but be determined by irrational instincts. Thompson saw Dodge's experience of becoming a monster as similar to losing a battle with alcoholism. After establishing a foundation for Dodge—his historical determination, his past fueled by his hatred for women—Thompson developed his character by allowing herself to think in a "spell," an altered state. She thought about the forces of dependency and addiction, and how they would determine Dodge's mood and actions.

For those attempting to fight addiction, as well as those trying to overcome trauma, the benefit of group therapy is the presence of active listeners. Susan Brison believes that in order for survivors to recover from the aftermath of violence they require an audience to listen to what they have endured. However, after her own attack, Brison discovered that although people listened to her they were unable to consistently remember what had happened to her. She came to realize that this was not a result of "ignorance or indifference, but [...] an active fear of identifying with those whose terrifying fate forces us to acknowledge that we are not in control of our own" (x). In rehearsals for *Capture Me*, the traumatic scenes were heavily workshopped in order to "articulate [the] ideas clearly, balance the play, refine and cut the 'music' of each scene" ("Witnessing" 98). The scenes in *Capture Me* are composed like music, a mnemonic method for presenting the monstrous. As Ric Knowles argues, Thompson's work is not "conventionally naturalistic" (8). The traumatic events are recreated and reconstructed in a way that may be "fragmented and discontinuous" (Knowles 8), but which is memorable. The monstrous is presented in a way that begs to be acknowledged and analyzed, and neither simplifies nor denies its mysterious chemistry.

Judith Thompson's inspiration for *Capture Me* is discussed in her article "'I Will Tear You to Pieces': The Classroom as Theatre." It started with a storytelling session in one of her classes. A student decided to share a story about bullying another adolescent to drastic measures, giving graphic and violent details in an attempt to entertain, or perhaps merely provoke a reaction from, his colleagues. Thompson sensed, "He was proud of what he had done. There was not a hint of any kind of regret," and her response to this student was, "That was an excellent story; it tells us a lot about our culture" ("I Will Tear" 31-32). Professor and therapist Gregory K. Moffatt discusses not just violent acts in Western society, but also the language of violence in *Violent Heart: Understanding Aggressive Individuals.* This is a language that may show itself in the form of "tantrums, foul language, sexual harassment, vandalism, throwing of objects, abuse of children or spouses, aggressive driving," but also, he suggests, "perhaps merely in aggressive thinking" (viii).

When this student played the title role in a scene from *Othello* that they were rehearsing, Thompson recalls:

> He scared the student playing Iago, and he scared me. It was as if there was lightning coursing through his body; his eyes were those of an attacking animal; his voice was like an exploding building. At one point in the scene, he, who had never broken the "fourth wall," looked out at me, the only other person in the room, and said his line: "I will tear her to pieces." ("I Will Tear" 33)

It is possible that this student was unaware of the implications of breaking the fourth wall. It is possible that this student thought if he scared Thompson, the only other person in the room and therefore his entire audience, he would be demonstrating his capability as an actor. The result was that Thompson felt like an "outsider" rather than an "authority" in her own classroom ("I Will Tear" 32). There was something about the element of the monstrous that resided inside him, which became visible to spectators when he was dramatizing or retelling acts of violence, that alarmed Thompson. When the student was telling the story of breaking another boy's jaw, he became, according to Thompson, "excited by the blood" ("I Will Tear" 31). This student left such a strong impact on Thompson that she integrated this scene from *Othello* into *Capture Me.* When Dodge encounters Jerry on her walk home from school, he describes to her how Othello "explodes with this most wonderful phrase, full of real muscular intention, 'I will tear her all to pieces.' So simple" (Thompson, *Capture Me* 23).

Lee Strasberg, in his article "The Actor and Himself," discusses how an actor can accomplish a great performance while insisting, "I don't know how I do it" (623). However, Strasberg contends, an actor must find control, a balance between what is planned and what is instinctual. Strasberg refers to Jacques

Copeau's theory that an actor's challenge has to do with "his blood." In order to learn her characters' thoughts, natures, and human limits, Thompson "*inhabits* her characters—or, as she herself has said, she stands in their blood" (Kareda 11). Thompson uses blood as a trope for one's personality. The "battle with the blood of the actor" is a struggle between who the actor really is and the character he or she is portraying, an attempt to perform actions that he or she normally would not with a certain "ease and warmth" (Strasberg 624). Copeau brings to Strasberg's attention a quote from *Hamlet* that connects acting with the idea of the monstrous: "Is it not monstrous that this player here,/But in a fiction, in a dream of passion,/Could force his soul so to his own conceit"? (2.2.551-53). Hamlet further questions, "What would he do/Had he the motive and cue for passion/ That I have?" (2.2.560-62). Is acting the ability to be excited by the thought of another's blood, a struggle of instincts, or a monstrous thing?

Strasberg's theory, that there are both unconscious and subconscious elements to the art of acting, suggests that theatre is a forum that has the ability to inform spectators about the monstrous. Thompson's student addressed her with aggression, in a veiled manner, and his projects and presentations in class were always spontaneous, unprepared, and thus unpredictable. However, what she maintains is that his work "was theatre at its best. It was simply brilliant and ready for any professional stage" ("I Will Tear" 32). The monster, as a theatrical concept or project with both recognizable and unrecognizable elements, is compelling.

The relationship between Thompson and her student displaced her from the position of authority and upset the roles of teacher and student. When we have lost control to another, Thompson states, "we hate for our future to be in their hands" ("I Will Tear" 31)—a future that is, as previously noted, unpredictable, "heralded by a species of monsters" (Weber 387). This disturbing dynamic is part of "the perplexing relationships between parents and children" that "remain a central organizing principle in the deployment of [Thompson's] characters" (Kareda 9). *Capture Me* is both a dramatization of the monstrous and a story of quests for parental figures gone unfulfilled. After seven years of separation, Dodge returns to Jerry with a renewed desire for her to love him, unconditionally, and care for him even though he is at his worst. Once Dodge has given in to his rage, he cannot accept a life without Jerry. But it seems that his need for a woman in his life is connected to childhood. At one point Dodge addresses his students:

> I look at you and I see the perfect little boys that you once were. Perfectly sweet to your mothers, your sisters; see, the trouble is, we need them. We NEED the fair sex, not just because we need sex, but because they civilize us, don't they? They make us better people... but we NEED them and that pisses us off, and so we are sometimes unfair to the women in our lives we are sometimes even... brutal. (29)

Dodge feels that he is physically dependent on Jerry, and that he needs Jerry in order to function as a human being. His desire for her to "civilize" him seems to be a yearning for discipline; Dodge wants Jerry to mother him.

Although Delphine says that she "would not be human if [she] did not respond in some way" (59) to Minkle's request for her to meet with her daughter, she tells Jerry "I cannot bring you, fold you into my life like egg yolks into sugar, it just would not be possible" (60). Delphine asserts that she is not responsible for Jerry. She cannot anticipate how close Jerry is to danger and leaves her alone in the dark. As Shildrick states, "at the very simplest level, the monster is something beyond the normative, that stands against the values associated with what we choose to call normality [...]." This is a cause of cultural anxiety, and "mothers, as a highly discursive category, have often represented both the best hopes and the worst fears of societies faced with an intuitive sense of their own instabilities and vulnerabilities" (29-30). However, the reason that Delphine is subverting the fundamental assumptions of what it is to be a mother is that she herself is transmogrifying.

A monster, in the form of cancerous cells, enters Delphine's body and leaves her mutilated, one-breasted. This monster has taken over parts of Delphine; the "rust has spread to the brain" (Thompson, *Capture Me* 52). When she refuses to accept her role as Jerry's mother, that refusal is accompanied by the thought, "don't think for a minute you're going to tell her you're dying of Cancer to get yourself a long lost loving daughter to smear Vaseline on your lips when they are cracked to to change the bed pan... to to sit by the bed through the night as you struggle to breathe" (52). She sees her body, itself, as monstrous. When Jerry breaks down, knows she is in danger, and screams her rage, she calls for "Mother," the only person present and capable of saving her (62). But Dodge is able to come and take Jerry's life because the monstrous is not only manifested in him, as a recognizable evil, but is in Delphine as well.

Although Jerry is abandoned by her biological mother, Aziz is a character in *Capture Me* who also has the potential to rescue her from her history of being an adopted child and her cycle of loneliness. He communicates his affection by telling Jerry, "I would die for you. Without question" (41), just as a parent would protect his or her young. He also scolds and lectures her in the same section of dialogue, telling Jerry to stop behaving like a child. It is established early on that theirs is not a sexual relationship; Aziz is not filling the void left by the absence of a husband, but by the absence of a mother, for whom Jerry had an "overwhelming yearning" (9). Aziz becomes glorified in Jerry's eyes. However, the destinies of both Aziz and Delphine are defined by monologues about catastrophe. Though each finds shelter in a tree (Aziz and his daughter escape the war zone by climbing an actual tree and Delphine experiences a moment of peace reading a poem about a tree), the feeling of security is temporary, the branches are breaking.

From the very first introduction of Aziz, his difference is established: he comes from a place full of extreme violence; unlike most of the other parents of Jerry's students, he works three jobs; and, he has left his country to come "knocking on the door of [Jerry's] country" (13). To Jerry, he is the "handsomest man [she has] ever seen in her life" (16), and he is presented to the audience as a loving parent. It is Dodge who attempts to manipulate Jerry's perception of Aziz. When Aziz leaves her, Jerry assumes it is to "find the murderers [of his family] and bring them to justice" (45). It is Dodge who makes Aziz out to be a monster: "What do you wanna bet he got the call and he's going to go and blow himself up. You'll see it on the news any day Jerry. You'll see he is NOT the SAINT you think he is" (51). Shildrick suggests:

> [Once the Other] begins to resemble those of us who lay claim to the primary term of identity, or to reflect back aspects of ourselves that are repressed, then its indeterminate status—neither wholly self nor wholly other—becomes deeply disturbing. In short, what's at stake is not simply the status of those bodies which might be termed monstrous, but the being in the body of us all. (3)

The monstrous is like a disease, and the human cannot be seen in opposition to the monster: the two bodies are not distinct. Whether it is a mental affliction or a physical illness, the monstrous is both a mutation and a mutiny, within and against the bodies and minds of Delphine, Aziz, and Dodge. When Jerry lets Dodge back into her bed one night, after Aziz has left her, it blurs the corporeal border that separates human and monstrous body; Dodge assumes that he and Jerry can blend together, like "cream and coffee," although she tells Dodge it was "a terrible fall" (54).

Capture Me stages the monstrous first by showing transmogrification, and then ultimately by showing that what opposes the monstrous is not humanness, but forgiveness—specifically, *pure forgiveness*. Derrida defines "pure forgiveness" as follows: "One can only truly forgive that which is unforgivable. If one forgives what is easily forgiven, one does not really forgive. One must forgive what is unforgivable, and so do the impossible" (*Derrida*). To distinguish who is the monster, to dramatize where the monstrous resides, Thompson does not establish poles of good and evil, but rather emphasizes who is capable of pure forgiveness.

Jerry tells Minkle, "What Aziz and I have is pure. It's all about [his daughter] Sharzia and poetry and here and now" (25). Although Aziz shies away from Jerry's touch, his faith allows him to see the beauty inside her: "I don't care about the outside. That is Western Corruption, Illusion. You have a pure and a beautiful soul" (40). Aziz's faith continuously ties him to his home country, and yet segregates him from Western culture. Faith is the rationale behind everything Aziz does, but the moment that his "purity" establishes his difference is when Aziz is not able to forgive the unforgivable; Aziz is not able to feel "pure forgiveness." If connections are to be drawn between Dodge and Aziz, it should be acknowledged that the men are not capable of the same kind of violence. The rage that fuels Aziz is of a religious and a righteous nature; he suggests he is planning to avenge his family's deaths, not gain revenge against a previous spouse. However, unable to rest until he does "what he must do" (49), Aziz is inextricably linked to the act of revenge which ultimately connects him to Dodge. It is Jerry, not Aziz, who attempts to forgive the unforgivable, and who reaches out to the man who is about to kill her, insisting that she is able to love him as her friend.

In the Tarragon production of *Capture Me*, the other characters were separated from Jerry by a scrim at the back of the stage as the monster approached her.

They existed as figments of Jerry's dream or imagination, shouting to her in poetic, fragmented dialogue. Minkle begs Jerry to "tear [Dodge's] fucking throat out or die trying" (65). Instead, Jerry attempts to save Dodge; she tells him that she loves him, as her friend, and she offers him her hand. Forgiveness has appeared in the final scenes of previous plays by Thompson. In *I Am Yours*, "Toilane and Dee search and beg for forgiveness in the final scenes [...] and are rewarded with transfiguration" (Kareda 13). Similarly, at the end of *Lion in the Streets*, Isobel forgives Ben and "ascends, in her mind, to heaven" (Thompson, *Lion* 288). Like Jerry, who demonstrates that she is capable of both rage and compassion, Isobel ultimately "resolves the battle between 'the forces of vengeance and forgiveness warring inside her'" by offering love to her aggressor (Wasserman 259). In *Capture Me*, Jerry forgives Dodge at the very moment that he is about to kill her and therefore before he is able to commit the unforgivable act. She is still able to see him as human: "You are not the devil there is no devil there is you" (65). Thompson explains:

> If you force yourself to see the monster within the human, then the theory is [he] becomes human, like in a fairy tale. Like kissing the frog. But the trouble is, that's what we wish could happen, but that's not the immediate reality. Now, we can talk about dead bodies on stage, but this is a redemptive moment, because in a way it's our only hope for the world. If we can all see each other as human. ("Witnessing" 99)

After Jerry's death, the play ends with a scene in which Jerry and Minkle are in a car, driving away. Jerry speculates to Minkle, "maybe I am dead. And that this is the dream, like a dream right before I putrefy" (67). *Capture Me* is a dramatization of this moment, right before the body transforms, becomes or transmogrifies. It is a play that problematizes the standard definition of monster by revealing the disadvantages of a society that is conditioned to believe that we can see, or recognize, a boundary that protects the self from the monster. When Thompson deconstructs the categories of victim and perpetrator, she shows that both good and evil can exist, and perhaps do exist, in everyone. In an interview with Eleanor Wachtel Thompson says, "I think each character in my play is a sort of microcosm for the whole culture, because there is evil and good warring in the culture at all times. And I do think it's in every human being" ("An Interview" 39). As well, as Cynthia Zimmerman states, the work of Judith Thompson presents "what our unconscious already knows: that much of what there is to be afraid of resides in our own human nature" (190). When she is writing, Thompson may turn into a wild animal, but she is also a mother and a teacher who questions how to keep calm and order, and she is also a theatre practitioner striving to produce the most dramatic outcome. *Capture Me* communicates the monstrous by staging transformation. According to Susan Brison: "[B]earing witness to traumatic events not only transforms traumatic memories into narratives that can then be integrated into the survivor's sense of self and view of the world, but it also reintegrates the survivor into a community, re-establishing bonds of trust and faith in others" (Brison xi).

Capture Me explores whether stopping transmogrification is as simple as maintaining one's human shape, not becoming like "playdoh" when in the hold of an emotion (57). Dodge says to his young male students, "You poor guys, you are nothing but pawns; your violence is so over-determined you didn't have a chance" (45). But in the "ghastly game" in which Brison found herself, "in which some men ran around trying to kill women, and others went around trying to save them," it was she, the victim, who felt like a pawn (Brison 90). Her body sustained multiple head injuries and a fractured trachea, the visible symptoms of a much deeper and lasting shattering of the self. What Shildrick claims one can learn from the study of the monstrous is "not a matter of denying that the medium of the body has reality, but of affirming that there is no essential corpus upon which meaning is inscribed" (120). Brison's body would heal, but she had to remake her sense of identity in the aftermath of trauma. *Capture Me* theatricalizes, in a series of seminars, spells, and confrontations, the language and practice of the monstrous, transmogrification rather than an established monster. If the reality, as Dodge puts it, is that, "every person in this world has become a monster at one time or another" (45), then the perpetrator and the victim, the human and the monster, the separate pieces of the "ghastly game" in which Brison found herself, are not in opposition. As in the very earliest records of monsters and their meanings, the boundaries are blurred, the lines on the game board are not definitive. The monstrous is a problem to which the philosopher, the scholar, and the playwright can only respond with more questions, rather than definitive solutions. One question, rather than who should be captured, is what to counsel within ourselves, in order to end the game.

(2005)

Works Cited

Adam, Julie. "The Implicated Audience: Judith Thompson's Anti-Naturalism in *The Crackwalker, White Biting Dog, I Am Yours* and *Lion in the Streets.*" *Women On the Canadian Stage: The Legacy of Hrotsvit.* Ed. Rita Much. Winnipeg: Blizzard Publishing, 1992. 21-29.

Bateman, Stephen. *The Doome Warning All Men to the Iudgemente: Wherein are contayned for the moste parte all the straunge Prodigies hapned in the Worlde.* London: Ralph Nubery, 1581.

Brison, Susan J. *Aftermath: Violence and the Remaking of a Self.* Princeton: Princeton UP, 2002.

Canada.com News. 5 January 2004. <http://www.canada.com/components.html>

Cohen, Jeffrey Jerome, ed. *Monster Theory: Reading Culture.* Minneapolis: U of Minnesota P, 1996.

"Derrida". By Kirby Dick and Amy Ziering Kofman. VHS, Zeitgeist Film Ltd., 2002.

Kareda, Urjo. Introduction. *The Other Side of the Dark: Four Plays by Judith Thompson.* Toronto: Coach House, 1989. 9-13.

Knowles, Ric. Introduction. "The Fractured Subject of Judith Thompson." *Lion in the Streets.* By Judith Thompson. Toronto: Playwrights Canada, 1992. 7-10.

Moffatt, Gregory K. *A Violent Heart: Understanding Aggressive Individuals.* Westport, Connecticut: Praeger, 2002.

Nestruck, J. Kelly. "Dark lady: Judith Thompson's plays take on the flip side of sweetness and light." *The National Post* 3 January 2004.

Shakespeare, William. *Hamlet. The Arden Shakespeare Complete Works.* Ed. Richard Proudfoot, Ann Thompson and David Scott Kastan. London: Thomson Learning, 2001. 291-332.

Shildrick, Margrit. *Embodying the Monster: Encounters with the Vulnerable Self.* London: SAGE Publications, 2002.

Strasberg, Lee. "The Actor and Himself." *Actors on Acting.* New York: Crown Publishers, 1970. 623-28.

Thompson, Judith. *Capture Me.* Dir. Judith Thompson. Perf: Randi Helmers, Tom McCamus, Nancy Palk, Chick Reid and Maurice Dean Wint. Tarragon Theatre, Toronto, ON. 30 December to 8 February 2004.

———. *Capture Me.* Tarragon Theatre, Toronto, ON. Unpublished Script. 10 January 2004.

———. "'I Will Tear You To Pieces': The Classroom as Theatre." *How Theatre Educates: Convergences and Counterpoints.* Ed. Kathleen Gallagher and David Booth. Toronto: U of Toronto P, 2003.

———. "Inspiration for *Capture Me.*" E-mail to Robyn Read. 22 Oct. 2003.

———. "Judith Thompson Interview." By Judith Rudakoff. *Fair Play: 12 Women Speak (Conversations with Canadian Playwrights).* Ed. Judith Rudakoff and Rita Much. Toronto: Simon & Pierre, 1990. 87-104.

———. "An Interview with Judith Thompson." By Eleanor Wachtel. *Brick: A Literary Journal* 41 (Summer 1991): 37-41.

———. "I Am Yours." *The Other Side of the Dark: Four Plays by Judith Thompson.* Toronto: Coach House, 1989. 115-76.

———. "Lion in the Streets." *Modern Canadian Plays Volume Two.* 4th Ed. Ed. Jerry Wasserman. Vancouver: Talonbooks, 2001. 261-88.

———. Personal Interview. 24 March 2004. University of Guelph, Guelph, ON.

———. "Witnessing the Workshop Process of Judith Thompson's *Capture Me*: Mothers, Masks and Monsters: A Conversation Between Teacher and Student." By Robyn Read. *Canadian Theatre Review* 120 (Fall 2004): 96-100.

Turcott, Iris. Introduction. *Habitat.* By Judith Thompson. Toronto: Playwrights Canada, 2001. viii.

Wasserman, Jerry. "Judith Thompson." *Modern Canadian Plays Volume Two.* 4th Ed. Vancouver: Talonbooks, 2001. 257-60.

Weber, Elizabeth, ed. *Points... : interviews, 1974-1994. Jacques Derrida.* Stanford: Stanford UP, 1995.

Zimmerman, Cynthia. "Judith Thompson: Voices in the Dark." *Playwriting Women: Female Voices in English Canada.* Toronto: Simon & Pierre, 1994. 176-209.

Environmental Affinities: Naturalism and the Porous Body

by Laura Levin

Many students shudder when they hear the term: "Naturalism." It is the dirty word uttered at the beginning of modern drama courses, stirring up feelings of boredom and resistance. These knee-jerk reactions stem from a contemporary North American bias, promoted by academics and artists, which aligns naturalism with the static, the unthinking, and the un-dialectic. When approached from this critical perspective, naturalism often fails to make the cut-off for membership in the twentieth-century avant-garde. In fact, the very idea of an "avant-garde" comes into being through a repudiation of naturalism and its reactionary conventions. Presented as the antecedent to a century of modernist and postmodernist innovation, naturalism has become the scapegoat for the standard dramatic literature syllabus. It is the foil needed to understand Brecht, or the topic that must be suffered through before getting to the "good stuff"—to the plays that invite artistic, political, and philo-sophical transformation.

Since its inception in the nineteenth century, playwrights have experimented vigorously with the forms and conventions of naturalism. A number of stylistic variants immediately come to mind: the super-naturalism of Eugene O'Neill, the feminist and symbolist naturalism of Susan Glaspell, and the absurdist naturalism of Sam Shepard. While extraordinarily diverse in form, these works often unsettle common assumptions about the meaning of naturalism and its intrinsic conservatism. Judith Thompson's plays offer some of the most striking examples of this kind of theatrical innovation. In this essay, I will suggest several ways in which Thompson radicalizes the naturalist aesthetic, exposing the experimental and politically enabling aspects of the genre. Specifically, through her use of space and visual form, she draws out disavowed affinities between the naturalist project and that of the early surrealist avant-garde. I hope to illuminate the feminist implications of locating Thompson's work within this twinned lineage, marking the ways in which she genders key spatial concepts in surrealist art. Instead of viewing her plays as yet another departure from naturalism, I will explore the theoretical advantages of positioning them within the naturalist rubric. When read from this perspective, not only do Thompson's plays expand our understanding of the naturalist project, but they also serve as powerful attempts to draw out naturalism's unrecognized possibilities. Naturalism emerges as a dramatic form with significant ethical potential, one capable of reimagining traditional self-environment relations.

There is already a large body of work that offers a range of rich perspectives on Thompson's plays. Critics tend to begin by situating Thompson's plays in relation to naturalist traditions. Few critics, however, are content to define her work as simply naturalist. For some, this definition falls short since Thompson continually puts reality in quotations. Julie Adam calls her work anti-naturalist, pointing to Thompson's persistent use of anti-illusionist and Brechtian devices. Thompson's anti-naturalism brushes up against "the ostensible subject matter of her plays—human suffering, both physical and psychological, especially of the so-called underprivileged" (22). This subject matter, Adam argues, leads spectators to mistake her plays for "slice of life studies" (22). Critics like Robert Nunn and Jennifer Harvie define Thompson's work less in terms of an artistic break than as an expressive form of naturalism. This style opens the texture of realism to surrealism, and to the realm of fantasy and dream. Ric Knowles uses the term "poetic" naturalism to define Thompson's technique, pointing to the lyrical style that she has cultivated in residence at Toronto's Tarragon Theatre (7). Thompson privileges this latter frame, describing her style in similar terms as an "emotional naturalism" (Thompson, "Last Things" 39). The word "emotional" gestures toward the outpouring of psychic and bodily contents in the typical Thompson play. Approaching the terrain of expressionism, emotional naturalism suggests a blurring of internal and external reality staged across the sensate body.

In many readings of Thompson's work, especially those offered by critics that call her plays anti-naturalist, the "real" serves as the most prominent index of the naturalist aesthetic. These interpretations rely, in other words, on the widely popularized definition of naturalism as an artistic method of truthfully reproducing reality. This definition is influenced by the traditional alliance of naturalism with nineteenth century methods of scientific empiricism. In his essay on the form, Raymond Williams argues that the dominant usage of the word naturalism—as the "accurate or lifelike reproduction of character, action, or scene" (205)—is both limited and limiting. He contends that it has allowed artists "to claim that they have abandoned, 'gone beyond', naturalism, when it is clear [...] that many 'non-naturalist' plays are evidently based on naturalist philosophy" (222). This enduring naturalist tendency might be better understood if we attend to what Williams sees as the less elaborated sense of naturalism—a profound interaction between character and environment. The presence of an environment that forcefully influences character goes well beyond the definition of naturalism as the presentation of "'permanent' human characteristics in an accurately reproduced natural or social 'setting'" (205). Describing the symptomatic relationship between human and environment in high naturalism, he writes:

> It is a question of a way of perceiving physical and social environment, not as setting or background through which, by other conventions, of providence, goodwill, freedom from prejudice, the characters may find their own ways. In high naturalism the lives of the characters have *soaked* into their environment. Its detailed presentation, production, is thus an additional dramatic dimension,

> often a common dimension within which they are to an important extent defined. Moreover, the environment has *soaked* into the lives. The relations between men and things are at a deep level interactive, because what is there physically, as a space or a means for living, is a whole shaped and shaping social history. (217; emphasis added)

In this passage, Williams offers a particularly suggestive reading of the environmental processes that are often at work in naturalist drama. These processes are too easily overlooked when critics move to dismiss naturalism as an inherently conservative genre. Williams presents us with a naturalism that undermines the traditional boundaries of the individual—the bourgeois figure that dominates this genre. Character is imagined as a decidedly porous entity, making the individual's claims of personal distinction a significant problem.

Williams' articulation provides another way into the naturalist world of Thompson's plays. If her work approaches the style of naturalism, it does so most evocatively through its presentation of environment. As in many conventional naturalist dramas, Thompson's presents the meeting of individual and environment as a site of complex entanglement. In fact, Thompson takes Williams' definition one step further by literalizing his idea of a "soaked" naturalism, presenting us with characters that become linguistically and physically oversaturated in their environments. Her plays extend the naturalist project by showing us that the separation between human and environment, figure and ground, cannot be perceptually sustained.

So what does this over-saturation look like, and what alternate interpretive lenses does it offer? Thompson's plays usually specify particular Canadian environments as their settings. These sites range from the urban slums in Kingston to small towns like Marmora to posh neighborhoods in Toronto. Guided by the first sense of naturalism—naturalism as objectivist verisimilitude—we might read these environments as reproductions of everyday locales familiar to Canadian spectators. Read this way, the environment remains merely a recognizable setting in which the action takes place. There is nothing here that is remotely destabilizing to the spectator's habits of perception. But Thompson's plays seem somehow closer to Williams' definition, with the environment refusing to stay in the background. It aggressively seeps into the lives of the characters, disallowing the expected delineation of human from surroundings.

This over-saturation is figured through Thompson's exorbitant references to local detail. Revealing what Williams calls a deep interactivity between people and things, her characters constantly engage with the minutiae of Ontario consumer culture: "Horny Tim's" or Tim Horton's donut shops, Timbits (miniature round donuts made from donut "holes"), Coffee Time stores, Export A cigarettes, the Eaton's Centre, Mapleview Lanes (a fusion of Ontario's shopping malls Mapleview Centre and Hazelton Lanes). In this landscape of commodities, the consumption of brands is conflated with the gratification of physical needs. Making a connection between Williams' "saturation" and bodily satiation, the local is literally consumed, or taken into the body. Characters engage in excessive bouts of donut eating at local stores (Theresa in *The Crackwalker*, Rhonda in *Lion in the Streets*) and, even more tellingly, satisfy other appetites at the same franchises (Joe in *Crackwalker*: "we'd... pick up some juicy pie down at Lino's or Horny Tim's, drive it out to middle road, fuck it blind, and have em home by one o'clock," [36]). Commodities become stand-ins for individual characters, casting doubt on their singularity and the originality of their desires.

References to the geographic particular perform a *hyper-locality* that disrupts the conventional separation of figure and ground. According to Rem Koolhaas, the "hyper-local" manifests itself in overly literalized depictions of local culture. Koolhaas sites the hyper-local in places like airports, where encounters with "a drastic perfume demonstration, photomurals, vegetation, [and] local costumes give a first concen-trated blast of local identity" (1251). Thompson presents us with a similarly concentrated blast of the local through obsessive and repetitive descriptions of environment that linguistically produce setting as a field of unmitigated excess. This technique structures *Habitat*, Thompson's recent play about the opening of a group home for troubled adolescents in the wealthy neighborhood of Mapleview Lanes. Consider, for example, this exchange between two of the home's new residents, Sparkle and Raine, which offers a superabundance of environmental detail:

> SPARKLE. What's the name of this street anyway? It's like something out of fucking Pleasantville.
> RAINE. Mapleview Lanes...
> SPARKLE. (*laughs hysterically*) That's hilarious! MAPLEVIEW LANES!! AGHHHH! I love it. I just LOVE those NAMES of any development built from the sixties on? Like ahhh 'Fairfield Estates' or Winchester Woods or or Birchmeadow Crescent All EXCLUSIVE LIFESTYLE LIVING ExCLUDING the likes of US, right? (37)

Sparkle's rant moves in and out of capitalization, in and out of punctuation, mirroring the negotiations of self in relation to the environmental field. As in Koolhaas' hyper-local airport displays, references to "Pleasantville" and to cookie-cutter housing developments for the elite point to the simulacral realm of consumer culture. To rephrase Williams' claim slightly, the environment becomes an entity that humans consume and in which they are consumed. More importantly, we are not presented with an authentic reproduction of an upper class Toronto neighborhood. Just as the costumes displayed in Koolhaas' airport rarely resemble those worn by city locals, Sparkle's description yields no "true" picture of Toronto. The setting is rather like Pleasantville, a site of mimetic and capitalist excess.

In *Habitat*, as in other Thompson plays, the hyper-local is often produced through textual form. It surfaces in overdrawn and redundant lists of names and adjectives, which enmesh the speaker in illuminated context and present the setting as more than background. This technique appears in the first speech delivered to Mapleview residents by Lewis Chance, the director of the group home. Providing more context than is needed (or desired) by his audience, Lewis refers to Mapleview Lanes as "exclusive," as "fantastically beautiful [and] tree-lined," and, more emphatically, as "one of the finest neighborhoods in Etobicoke, a neighborhood of accomplished and distinguished and really well-dressed, well shod people" (10). This uncanny use of repetition and over-saturation in environmental detail is profoundly unsettling to the stable form of reference through which we try to comprehend the play. When watching conventional naturalistic dramas, we turn to the context to gain a sense of narrative coherence. Here, however, the context seems somehow *too contextual*, denying us stable grounding in relation to it.

Thompson's approach, which replays the naturalist orientation in excess, recalls a similar set of operations at work in the aesthetics of surrealism. This movement, unlike naturalism, is still considered experimental and avant-garde. Thompson's spatial techniques remind us of those surrealists who attempted to break down perceptual boundaries between self and environment, between the ego and external objects. To achieve this end, they created numerous images in which bodies merge with their natural or built environments. Some famous examples of this motif can be found in the work of surrealist photographer, Man Ray. In Man Ray's *The Return to Reason* (1923) we are presented with a female torso that is formally drawn into its setting. A series of shadows, emanating from furnishings in the room, are cast onto the woman's body. In another image, *The Primacy of Matter over Thought* (1929), a reclining nude recedes into the floor, her physical extremities melting into a thick liquid.

The negotiation between body and environment is especially pronounced in works created by women affiliated with the surrealist movement. In her self-portrait *Roots* (1943) Frida Kahlo presents her body as an extension of the earth, her arteries affixed to the roots in the ground. In this reciprocal exchange, the environment becomes a character in its own right, assuming human-like traits. Lenora Carrington's *Self-Portrait* (1938) provides another example of this phenomenon. In this image, the artist mimics the forms of her furnishings and the furnishings mimic her in turn. As Helaine Posner explains, Carrington shows us "a curiously anthropomorphic chair [which] sprouts the delicate hands and booted feet of its striking artist-occupant" (158). Later surrealist artists, including Francesca Woodman, continue in this tradition, experimenting with visual processes that disperse the subject within an environmental field. In her photograph *House #3* (1975-76), Woodman uses a long exposure to generate a blurry image of her body that creates the impression that she is dissolving into her domestic surroundings.

Like Thompson's plays, these images can be read in relation to surrealist theories of space. They recall, first of all, the writings of Roger Caillois, who explored the processes by which organisms blend into their natural environments. Through camouflage, he explained, an insect mimics the forms of its physical setting. Responding excorporatively to the formal patterns of its background, this being can no longer claim to be "the origin of [its] coordinates, but one point among others" (Caillois 28). Rosalind Krauss notes the effects of this spatial mimicry on human and animal subjects: "The life of any organism depends on the possibility of its maintaining its own distinctness, a boundary within which it is contained, the terms of what we would call self-possession. Mimicry, Caillois argues, is the loss of this possession, because the animal that merges with its setting becomes dispossessed, derealized" ("Corpus" 74).

Caillois' theory of spatial mimicry points to a fundamental concept of surrealism: the notion of the *informe*, usually translated as the "formless" or the "un-formed." Coined by Georges Bataille, the *informe* resists the circumscription of matter within a definite form. "All of philosophy has no other goal," Bataille writes, "it is a matter of fitting what is there into a formal coat, a mathematical overcoat" (qtd. in Hollier 16). The *informe*, however, cannot be understood as the opposite of form. As Hal Foster argues, the *informe* is a set of operations, a process through which "significant form dissolves because the fundamental distinction between figure and ground, self and other, is lost" (112). In this sense, the *informe* is posed as a challenge to dualistic Cartesian thinking, which positions man as a delineated figure standing over and against his environment in a relation of disembodied and vertical mastery.

By reading Williams' account back through surrealist conceptions of space, a different picture of Thompson emerges, one that resists the simplistic alliance of surrealism with anti-naturalism. Thompson's play *I Am Yours* provides the clearest example of the surrealist approach to environment. The *informe* is represented scenically through the dissolution of physical and psychic boundaries. A series of architectural borders are erected to keep the human subject separate from external entities that threaten self-disaggregation. The central character, Dee, senses that there is an animal hiding behind the wall, which periodically breaks free and inhabits her body. As Robert Nunn points out, the divisions that Dee establishes between internal and external worlds, between self and desire (the animal), were built into the designs for the Tarragon productions (1984, 1987). As in other stagings of Thompson's plays, these sets were "multileveled," calling attention to "vertical and horizontal dimensions and to walls and partitions between one part of the set and another" (4). Like the surrealists, Thompson reveals these divisions to be illusory. Dee can no more restrict her desires than she can control which elements from the outside world filter into her body. She makes this clear when confiding in her sister: "It's like [the animal] got out of the wall. Like a shark banging at a shark cage and sliding out. Out of the wall and inside me. I feel something taking over" (140).

Thompson presents character as a porous scrim, one which is not only, as others suggest, open to the forces of desire, but is also open to the nonhuman environment. This porosity makes sense in *I Am Yours*. It is arguably Thompson's most overtly surrealist play, its action wavering in and out of dream. But a porous dramaturgy also emerges in plays that seem more naturalist, reminding us that the co-saturation of self and world is a shared preoccupation of these stylistic approaches. *Sled*, one of Thompson's "grittiest" plays, immediately comes to mind. In *Sled*, the deep snow of the Canadian North appears to consume the characters. The snow has not only soaked into the characters' lives; the characters are actually sinking into the landscape.

In the first scene, Annie is immersed in the wilderness of northern Ontario. The stage directions describe this spatial enmeshment: "*White birches, snow, a Great Snowy owl, and a trail, with a hill, running around behind or through the audience. ANNIE appears walking fast and hard, out of breath through deep snow and birches*" (19). Unlike Dee, Annie seeks out a connection between her body and the landscape, even to the point of courting her own erasure. "Oh heavenly time of day," she sings, "the snow and the quiet/the birch/white pine/so high and so high/Shall I sink in the snow and just lie there for hours/alone there for hours/till dark night erases me?" (19). As part of her bond with the external world, Annie develops strong relationships with non-human entities. Recalling Kahlo's famous image in which she presents herself as part woman and part deer (*The Little Deer*, 1946), Annie identifies with the animals that she encounters. In her performance at the lodge, she tells a story of exchanging knowing glances with a fox. At a formal level, her body sympathizes with this animal. Her "*beautiful red dress with long red velvet gloves*" (23) mirrors the fox's luxurious and velvety red coat.

The interconnectedness of human and environment is almost always registered in ethical terms. In *Sled*, Annie's openness to the physical world is opposed to the brutalization and objectification of women, animals, and nature. Conversely, qualities of goodness and affect are metaphorized through unions of the human and the nonhuman. In *Habitat*, Lewis compares his devotion to the group home residents with the loving actions of a maple tree. Reminding us of Khalo's *Roots*, he tells Raine that his house is the tree trunk: "strong and firm holdin' all of you, my family, my girls and boys, all of you up, and the roots? The roots they go deep deep into the ground, right? And they spread far and wide and they drink of the groundwater the groundwater is the love we all have for each other, eh?" (27). Of course, as is characteristic of Thompson's writing, which works to undo philosophical binaries, her plays track contradictions and anxieties produced by this ethical position. The collapse of human-nature distinctions is attended by a range of potential dangers that she does not attempt to explain away. Annie, for example, is killed when two men are hunting for moose. At first, they are unable to distinguish Annie from the landscape. The stage directions read: "*The snowmobile's light beams on her. There are birches between her and the snowmobile. There is a stand of birches blocking their view of her*" (37). Even when a clear view of Annie emerges, Kevin chooses to see her as a "she-moose," and shoots her down (a possible act of revenge for his humiliation by her husband). Indeed, violence is often the result of behaviors that threaten to do away with self-other distinctions altogether. Lewis' attempt to shelter his children flips over into a stubborn authoritarianism when confronted with the unruly actions of individual residents or, more specifically, when his idyllic image of the group home fails to cohere. In such cases, the words used in his maple tree analogy—"strong and firm holdin' all of you"—accrue a disturbing double meaning.

As human figures become enmeshed in complex ways with their environments, the background insistently takes on a life of its own. Here we might say, following Williams, that Thompson's environments do not appear as "illustrative settings" (217), but rather as "integral parts of the dramatic action, indeed, in a true sense, [as] themselves actors and agencies" (205). This is most apparent in *The Crackwalker*, in which the menacing urban environment encroaches upon the domestic space. Alone in her apartment, Sandy stays up nights in terrible fear listening to the sounds of the street (cats screaming, the thud of footsteps). At times the background is transformed into a figure: Charlie Manson, the monster she calls the Crackwalker, and the "Indian Man" roaming the streets. Vomiting and bleeding, this aboriginal character literalizes—not unproblematically—the condition of the *informe* and embodies the landscape of desperation in the play. In effect, he becomes synonymous with the environmental ground itself. The stage directions call for the Man to sit in a grounded position; he is situated on the "*warm air vent*" that is a central feature of the street space (68). Adam reports that in the 1990 Tarragon staging, the Man "sprawled diagonally" on the set, and remained in this position "for some time after one of his encounters with Alan" (20). Physically tied to the material properties and horizontal axis of the street, the Man is presented as a morphological extension of the urban space.

Yet the formal treatment of this raced and emphatically feminized figure points towards a more complex strategy in Thompson's works, one that has not adequately been accounted for. As I have suggested, Thompson presents the interpolation of self into setting as politically and ethically enabling. In this respect, the process of backgrounding serves to undermine the individual subject's will to mastery and claims of self-possession. However, Thompson complicates this process by illuminating the ways in which women and other feminized persons have historically been obliterated as background or have been made synonymous with space itself. As Shannon Jackson argues, female characters are all too often represented as "the place" and men as "the people." In such cases, women become the "providers of 'ground' on which male self-figuration occurs" (700). Jackson explains: "To perform 'ground' in [a] theatrical scenario is to engage in a repetitive and circumscribed network of motions (in kitchens, in station wagons, in gardens) that are essential to the cultivation of spatial comfort" (700). While "performing ground" may be a feminized act, it is not particular to women. As Thompson illustrates in her formal treatment of the Man in *The Crackwalker*, non-white, queer, and lower class characters frequently stand in as background as well.

In Thompson's plays, acts of performing ground take place along vertical and horizontal axes, reminding us of the spatial operations of the *informe*. Rosalind Krauss contends that the *informe* counters the logic of the vertical—the gravitational pull of figure away from ground or the moment when man stands up and separates himself from the brute materiality of nature. In a Lacanian sense, the vertical plane has been associated with "the hanging together or coherence of form [...] the very drive of vision to formulate form, to project coherence in a mirroring of the body's own shape" ("Cindy" 130). The *informe*, however, envisions a different organizational and bodily schema. Its figures are perpetually "falling from the vertical into the horizontal" (*Optical* 156), from self-cohesion into self-dissolution.

Thompson uses this vertical/horizontal axis as the basis for her environmental imagining. Unlike Krauss, however, she draws out its gendered and classed implications. In *Crackwalker*, for example, Sandy is tied to the horizontal space of her apartment. Laboring to fit the role of the traditional housewife, Sandy is obsessed with the cleanliness and orderliness of the domestic space. She is in contact with the ground when we first meet her, "*scrubbing the floor furiously*" (20). Later on, we find that Sandy is still preoccupied with the ground. A stage direction tells us: "*She picks something up off the floor and starts to take it into the kitchen*" (30). Almost immediately afterwards, she finds herself falling back into the horizontal. The next direction reads: "*JOE* [her abusive husband] *grabs her as she tries to pass him and throws her to the floor*" (30). Standing over her, he screams: "You CUNT" (30). As in other Thompson scenes, falling into the horizontal is tied explicitly to violence against women (often to rape) and the phallocentric definition of woman-as-body.

This visual scheme, which sutures feminine and feminized bodies to the horizontal floor space, is a central dramatic element of *Habitat*. Janet, one of the wealthy residents of Mapleview Lanes, fears that her widowed mother is slowly being consumed by the mounds of dirt piling up in her house. She warns her mother that her body will disappear into the ground: "MUM. Really. Just... I mean... look around you. Please. These floors—you have not swept the floors since he died. Have you? I mean... what is this white dust? That is you, your skin, all over the floor, as if you were, I don't know, ROTTING in here, and one day, I'll come in and you will be just dust" (15). Since Janet is a called a feminist, we might read this statement as a plea directed towards her mother, and to women in general, to move from the position of ground to figure. But Thompson complicates this solution by showing us how this move would only leave the figure/ground binary intact. It does little to register the ways in which all scenes are structured through infinitely receding backgrounds. In *Habitat*, that other "ground" is the working class. Janet counsels her mother to liberate herself from the home while, at the same time, consigning other women to the status of ground: "you need, you DESERVE a cleaning lady, Mum. Listen, Peggy Creese does wonderful work for me—she gets down on her hands and knees... and scrubs till you can see your face in the FLOOR" (14).

By showing us the hidden ground-work of maintenance, Thompson draws out and politicizes another aspect of naturalism. As August Strindberg once wrote, "the true naturalism [...] seeks out those points in life where the great conflicts occur, [and] rejoices in seeing what cannot be seen every day" (288-89). Thompson reveals what might be called the environmental unconscious, showing the lower classes to be the invisible constitutive ground that props up the affluent of Mapleview Lanes. Margaret and Janet turn a blind eye to this ground as they engage in a legal battle to have their underprivileged neighbors removed from their community. These adolescents are treated as mere extensions of the amorphous and non-figural class that maintains the property value of Mapleview Lanes and provides the conditions for "spatial comfort" (Jackson 700). In Sparkle's words, the group home teens are "the writhing seething k-mart masses, who mow your lawns and clean your floors and do your hair and your nails and sew your hems" (68). Once again, an obsessive list of domestic details appears, making clear what is so deeply troubling about this form of contextuality. As Naomi Schor reminds us, the "most threatening [thing] about the detail" is "its tendency to subvert an internal hierarchic ordering of the work of art which clearly subordinates the periphery to the center, the accessory to the principal, the foreground to the background" (20).

This hierarchical reordering was visualized in the set created for The Canadian Stage Company's production of *Habitat*, which featured a large area of grass, with Margaret's living room located in one corner and Lewis' group home at another (Hoile). By situating Lewis and Margaret's homes on the shared grass area (an element of the set which itself had few spatial demarcations), the design signaled the artifi-ciality of classed boundaries and established a visual connection between the geographies of their respective social spheres. The set thus withheld those visual cues that would, in a traditional naturalist (or bourgeois) set, demarcate the margins from the centre and the private from the public. In a more general sense, I want to suggest that the formal openness of this kind of design can allow for a use of space in naturalist theatre that foregrounds the complex entanglements of self and other, figure and ground, that I have been trying to trace. Not only are these categories shown to be formally interdependent, but their separation also appears socially contingent, predicated upon a range of gendered, classed, and raced fictions.

Ultimately, it is this intrinsic spatial dependency that serves as a basis for the radical ethics opened up by Thompson's work. This environmental relation is not predicated upon individualistic self-delineation and Cartesian self-possession. Rather, following the explorations of naturalist and surrealist artists, it embraces the possibilities of breaking down divisions between body and external world. The notion of "world" that operates in Thompson's plays is necessarily expansive; it encompasses all of those environments—natural, commercial, social—in which we are implicated and to which we are ethically responsible. Using a dramatic form that often pits the individual in antagonistic relation to its environment, Thompson re-figures the naturalist character as a being that is sensuously linked to the bodies of its neighbors. The failure of self/environment distinctions is signaled throughout her plays in the deliquescence of physical forms and boundaries. We hear of amniotic fluid trickling, honey pouring, snow falling, and stone walls breaking apart. This imagery of oozing, of liquid emission and spatial collapse, hints at an inescapable porosity of self to world. Unlike Posner, who reads the porous as an example of the surrealist impulse to "dissolve difference" (158), Thompson shows this formalist maneuver to be untenable and undesirable, reminding us that social differences are in fact the precondition for an ethical encounter with the other. In her porous approach to character, Thompson respects alterity by permitting us to imagine self-world relations as an incessant transference between separate yet indistinct entities.

Porosity, of course, does not come without dangers. Openness to the other can lead to asphyxiation, penetration, and even engulfment. This is intimated in the German poem found in *I Am Yours*: "You are locked in my heart/The key is lost/You will always have to stay inside it.../For always" (157). Yet, as the play's title makes clear, this position is reversible. The words *I Am Yours* signal both the threat of captive possession and a productive relinquishing of self-mastery. Even more poignantly, it points to the risks and promise inherent in the naturalist project. The naturalist model of environment has, after all, operated in a similarly possessive mode, claiming the subject within a deterministic schema that squashes the prospect of social change. Yet, as Thompson's plays make clear, the co-saturation of subject and setting need not always be understood in deterministic terms. In applying this reading, we frequently misrecognize as determinism moments in a text that might otherwise be seen as a fruitful interconnection of human and environment. By experimenting with the formal parameters of naturalism, Thompson allows a more productive self-world relation to come into view, one which counters the traditional exclusion of the subject from the material world. Thompson's work, finally, asks us to locate ourselves inside naturalism and vigilantly embrace our enmeshment in a matrix of worlds that we can make and of which we are made.

(2005)

Works Cited

Adam, Julie. "The Implicated Audience: Judith Thompson's Anti-Naturalism in *The Crackwalker, White Biting Dog, I Am Yours,* and *Lion in the Streets.*" *Women on the Canadian Stage: The Legacy of Hrotsvit.* Ed. Rita Much. Winnipeg: Blizzard, 1992. 21-29.

Caillois, Roger. "Mimicry and Legendary Psychasthenia." Trans. by John Shepley. *October* 31 (1984): 17-32.

Foster, Hal. "Obscene, Abject, Traumatic." *October* 78 (Fall 1996): 107-24.

Harvie, Jennifer. "(Im)Possibility: Fantasy and Judith Thompson's Drama." *Onstage and Off-stage: English Canadian Drama in Discourse.* Ed. Albert-Reiner Glaap and Rolf Althof. St. John's Newfoundland: Breakwater Books, 1996. 240-56.

Hoile, Christopher. "Habitat is a Shambles." *Stage Door.* 2001. <http://www.stage-door.org/reviews/misc2001g.htm>

Hollier, Denis. *Against Architecture: The Writings of Georges Bataille.* Cambridge: MIT Press, 1989.

Jackson, Shannon. "Partial Publicities and Gendered Remembering." *Cultural Studies* (Fall 2003): 692-712.

Knowles, Richard Paul. "Introduction: The Fractured Subject of Judith Thompson." *Lion in the Streets.* Toronto: Playwrights Canada, 1992. 7-10.

Koolhaas, Rem. *S,M,L,XL.* Designed by Bruce Mau. New York: The Moncelli Press, 1998.

Krauss, Rosalind. "Cindy Sherman: Untitled." *Cindy Sherman: 1975-1993.* New York: Rizzoli International, 1993. 101-59.

———. "Corpus Delicti." *L'Amour fou: Photography and Surrealism.* Ed. Rosalind Krauss and Jane Livingston. New York: Abbeville Press, 1985. 55-112.

———. *The Optical Unconscious.* Cambridge and London: The MIT Press, 1998.

Nunn, Robert. "Spatial Metaphor in the Plays of Judith Thompson." *Theatre History in Canada* 10. 1 (Spring 1989): 3-29.

Posner, Helaine. "The Self and the Word: Negotiating Boundaries in the Art of Yayoi Kusama, Ana Mendieta, and Francesca Woodman." *Mirror Images: Women, Surrealism, and Self-Representation.* Ed. Whitney Chadwick. Cambridge, MASS and London: The MIT Press, 1998. 157-71.

Schor, Naomi. *Reading in Detail: Aesthetics and the Feminine.* New York and London: Methuen, 1987.

Strindberg, August. "On Modern Drama and Modern Theatre (1889)." *Samlade Skrifter.* XVII. Stockholm: Bonniers, 1912-19.

Thompson, Judith. *The Crackwalker. The Other Side of the Dark: Four Plays by Judith Thompson.* Toronto: Coach House, 1989. 15-72.

———. *Habitat.* Toronto: Playwrights Canada, 2001.

———. *I Am Yours. The Other Side of the Dark: Four Plays by Judith Thompson.* Toronto: Coach House, 1989. 115-76.

———. "The Last Things in the *Sled*: An Interview with Judith Thompson." By Jennifer Fletcher. *Canadian Theatre Review* 189 (Winter 1996): 39-41.

———. *Sled.* Toronto: Playwrights Canada, 1997.

Williams, Raymond. "Social Environment and Theatrical Environment: The Case of English Naturalism." *English Drama: Forms and Development.* Cambridge: Cambridge University Press, 1977. 203-23.

Building an Ethical Architecture: Judith Thompson's *Habitat* and the Shape of Radical Humanism

by Kim Solga

> [E]thics is not about finding solutions, but about creating openings in and through the uncertainty of strange encounters. (Shildrick 7)

> [W]hat am I supposed to be feeling here? Is there something I'm supposed to be feeling? (*Habitat* 5)

Habitat first drew me in with its title. I was moved by the contours of the word: on the surface clinical and precise, it nevertheless echoes an activism motivated by a deep compassion for the shared living spaces of our world. Then, after visiting and revisiting the play, I was struck by something else: characters in *Habitat* never use the word "habitat," though it hangs over their story. It ghosts their choices and haunts the action, spectral yet central to their dilemma, and to our experience of it as readers and viewers. The word is, for those of us on the outside, a lens but also a question mark. What is a "habitat," to you and me? Better yet: what *could* it be?

For those of us in the developed West, "habitat" is a value-loaded term. I think of the fight to save the habitats of endangered species; I think of environmental concerns over the increasingly rapid degeneration of human habitats (our water, our air, our atmosphere); I think, perhaps think first, of Habitat For Humanity, the community-building program that engages volunteers from across the social spectrum to work with needy families in building those families a home of their own. Although superficially a scientific marker for dwelling-place, "habitat" is most resonant in its social iterations: it proposes dwelling to be a shared enterprise, a collective experience of vulnerability and risk (habitats, ours included, seem perennially under siege), yet one marked by a utopian potential, by the hope that, working together, we might overcome the threat and build a better life for all. Unlike a house or even a "home," both of which imply security-in-exclusivity framed by closed doors and mediated by private capital, a habitat is a profoundly inclusive, ethical architecture.

Thompson's *Habitat* is a call to ethical architecture: the play is about our need for it, about our failure, in our psychic and social solipsism, our increasing personal and political isolation, to make a place for or a priority of it, but *Habitat* is also, most critically, about the potential for and the possible shape of it. Below its rather cynical surface, the play proposes a discrete but compelling model for communal dwelling, what I will call an *intercorporeal architecture*, which gestures toward the possibility of an entirely different encounter with intersubjectivity than the one offered by either Freudian and Lacanian psychoanalysis or post-structuralist metaphysics. The play laments our failure to build such a space, yet proffers in turn a way that we may come together, may be with rather than against—or of necessity apart from—one another in the Real.[1]

At its most basic, *Habitat* is an issue-driven play, conjuring up the distasteful spectre of NIMBYism in suburban Toronto. Raine loses her mother to cancer and rejects the prospect of living in Cornwall with her father and his new wife; suddenly homeless, she ends up in a brand-new group facility run by Lewis Chance on Mapleview Lanes, a prosperous street in Etobicoke. The neighbours make good on Lewis's predictions of fear and loathing: they begin a campaign to have the facility shut down that lands them before City Council and ends in a spectacular blaze, as Raine and her fellow resident Sparkle set fire to their former home. Ultimately, however, the play is about more than a neighbourhood's ploys to protect its borders; it is about the very organization of our shared spaces, and it represents an attempt to rethink and to restructure in specifically material terms Thompson's by-now conventional interests in the spatial dynamic of the psyche, in our obsessive anxieties over the borders of body and self, and in the insistent, inevitable disruptions of our seemingly sealed interiors (see Nunn). Framed by a literal land battle—for the shape of a community, for a place for its outcasts—the play poses in real space and real time many of the questions that are latent in Thompson's earlier works: how are we supposed to come to feel, not just *for* one another but *with* one another? (How do we transform condescending sympathy into a genuine encounter with our others, recognized in their proper alterity?) Why must our personhood be defined by distance, by an obsessive guardianship over our selves and/as our spaces? If we either fetishize our isolation or let ourselves be terrorized by a pervasive fear of loneliness, what hope do we have of building what Arthur Frank has recently termed a "relation of care": "a dialogue not only of words but of touch" (27)? The "spatial metaphors" that drive our supposed experiences of subjectivity (as well as our experience of much of Thompson's own *oeuvre*, as Robert Nunn has convincingly argued) have serious ramifications in actual space, and it is therefore not enough, this play argues, for analysis to remain entrenched at the level of metaphor: we must also realize the extent to which our psychic models have in turn modeled every inch of our material world on the stultifying play of plenitude (we are complete in ourselves) and lack (we exist at a distance from all others, as from ourselves), on an agon that admits no middle ground, no shared space between where we can encounter, and honour, one another.

Before I excavate what I believe to be *Habitat*'s implied ethical architecture, I want to telescope its central social dilemma (this community isn't big enough for the both of us; there simply *isn't enough space* here to accommodate our differences) by reading its summative first scene through the recent writings of a trio of female ethicists. Luce Irigaray, Kelly Oliver and Margaret Shildrick share my dissatisfaction with conventional subject-object relations as well as *Habitat*'s dissatisfaction with the suffocating material effects of those relations: a total lack of space within a neighbourhood of plenty. Irigaray, Oliver and Shildrick each re-theorize our most pervasive current beliefs about the self/other dynamic and pose an alternative model of intersubjective experience that is, I argue, in its focus on the physicality of embodiment and in its privileging of a metaphysics of touch over a metaphysics of sight,[2] specifically architectural. These women revise subject-object relations by posing those relations in overtly spatial terms, and by arguing that more generous, more ethical relations with our others can only be imagined by rethinking our relationship with shared space through what Shildrick and Price have called "the intercorporeal" (see also Oliver 199). With these insights in hand I will go on to examine two key moments in Thompson's play where the suffocating experiences of the first scene are refocused through an intimate, empathetic, even intercorporeal encounter between two characters, an encounter which is ultimately destroyed by the intervention of apparently sympathetic human hands. The intimacy *lost* in these moments is salient: the loss to some extent explains the root of the problem on Mapleview Lanes, the deep disconnect of each group of residents from the other. Yet, critically, this loss is figured in these moments as redeemable (though not necessarily redeemed), a "Real" we can and must access: *Habitat* insists that an intimate yet respectful physical connection with others is not only possible but essential if we are to build a true habitat—a genuine community.

The Space-Between of Radical Humanism

> Air, that which brings us together and separates us. Which unites us and leaves a space for us between us. (Irigaray, *i love to you* 148)

Habitat opens without air: Cath is in hospital, in the last stages of cancer, fighting to breathe. Raine fights the image as well as the idea of her dying mother, focusing her attempt at conversation on mundane matters, asking Cath if she may go and live with her friend Crystal, if she may have money for new jeans. Cath cannot answer, except with the sounds of struggled breathing, and, for Raine, this uncanny exercise in mother-daughter communication becomes the catalyst for an entirely typical teenage response: rage against the perceived injustice of her situation, against the parent with whom she can no longer connect nor from whom yet fully separate. Raine is in limbo, so she accuses her mother of faking the severity of her illness (5), vents her rage at having to perform grief at the funeral (6), and reminds Cath that her own suffering, too, has been intense and worthy of reaction. She fights to overcome her mother's overwhelming corporeality, fights to forge a place for herself in its (her) place.

This (literally) suffocating first scene is divorced from the main action of the play, and functions both to foreshadow the troubling animosities of Mapleview Lanes and, more importantly, to contextualize them. Raine's behaviour toward her dying mother is both unforgivable and understandable; it is, as I have suggested, conventional despite its startling circumstance. We may feel inclined to ask how Raine can say such things, how a mother and daughter can be so far apart in this shared moment of intimate bodily and emotional struggle, but the better question—the question I think the play would prefer us to ask, sets the scene so atypically in order to ask—is how they can be otherwise, how any other arrangement is possible. Cath is dying; isn't that kind of pain and suffering supposed to be deeply isolating, segregating? Aren't mothers and daughters always divided, combative, cut off from one another's experience in the birth moment, never to regain the intimacy of the womb? Aren't Raine and Cath just acting out in extremis the experience of so many mothers and daughters—including that of Margaret and Janet, Mapleview owners both, later in the play? Both Cath and Raine are suffocating, both are alone, but the chasm between them, paradoxically, confirms their humanity.

Much of Luce Irigaray's work in the last decade has been dedicated to over-turning the supposed normalcy of this gulf between loved ones. In place of the chasm she theorizes a space "between" bodies (between men and women, between hierarchized interlocutors) through which she posits the emergence of a self both intimately connected to and yet separate from its others, a self that defies the creation narrative of modern Western metaphysics by neither assimilating the other to its own image, nor estranging it for failing to assimilate.[3] One of her earliest articulations of this space "between" can be found in "Belief Itself," an essay in which she links the myth of the chasm directly to the myth of normative mother-child relations, the myth that Raine need be so far away from Cath in the moment of Cath's last breath. "Belief Itself" is an extended riff on Freud's fort/da scene from *Beyond the Pleasure Principle* (12-17), and on Derrida's reading of it in *The Postcard.* Freud watches his grandson play with a reel of string and concludes that he is using the game to symbolize his mother's absences, to manage her material disappearance (she, like Cath, will die) by assimilating her into a language he can manipulate and control. Derrida, re-reading the scene, reveals that the boy's play involves not only the reel and string but also the curtain of his bed, into which he throws the string as he happily shouts "fort" (there, or gone); he concludes that the curtain must symbolize the boy's mother's hymen (308), returning her absent spectre forcefully and materially to the scene, but goes no further.

At the curtain Irigaray enters and makes the connection Derrida will not: beyond hymen (space of primal terror) to womb (seat of primal comfort). In her appropriation, the missed and dismissed curtain—or veil, as she terms it—is folded back on itself, doubled. One veil separates bodies and psychic lives, as Freud would have it; the other veil forges connections between bodies, taking its power as metaphor from the connective membrane of the womb. Irigaray's move "beyond" the veil that separates, and toward this second veil that connects, defines her renovation of the psychoanalytic Imaginary: for her, it is neither a space of undifferentiated corporeality nor a space where the empathy forged by intimate corporeal connection need be followed by cathartic rejection at the mirror. In place of the tyrannous spatial dynamic envisioned by modern psychoanalysis, in which one must settle either for no space in which to breathe (self recognizes other as a version of the Same), or for an unending abyss of air (we exist only in our distance from one another), Irigaray imagines a space where the dynamic energy that circulates between bodies maintains their separate selves, yet knits them together in a mutually beneficial dependence.

Like Irigaray, who rescues the over-mythologized space of the womb in order to return it to its proper material status as a psychic and bodily architecture, Kelly Oliver and Margrit Shildrick develop new models of ethical relations by refiguring the elided space between subjects, replacing the chasm or "empty void" (Oliver 12) of philosophical and psychoanalytic myth with a space made magical by the physical properties of air, light, and energy generated by touch. Taking issue with the distancing eye, the now-pervasive theory that identity is a product of (mis)recognition, Oliver rehabilitates vision itself as a tactile sense that has been misrecognized by theory as necessarily distancing. Vision is circulatory for Oliver, vital and communal like blood, and the space in which vision circulates is, therefore, conjoining rather than "alienating," the medium through which we both connect to our others and recognize ourselves as fundamentally connected to them (14-15). Shildrick, meanwhile, takes Irigaray's metaphysical refiguration and Oliver's social-scientific re-materialization of the space-between to another level, imagining it as a space bridged by literal touch and allowing us to see its deeper relevance to the issues Thompson raises in *Habitat*'s first scene and beyond. Shildrick argues that physical encounters with our others set our "mutual becoming" in motion because they occasion, simultaneously, a personal encounter with our own essential vulnerability (102). For Shildrick, the space between bodies is a space of personal risk we must cross in order to grow; our bodily differences imply an ethics precisely because we are all fragile (see also Frank 8-9), and our very fragility is what makes connecting with others scary or embarrassing, and therefore potentially also rewarding, a gift as well as an obligation. Raine is scared, and embarrassed, but she will not make the ethical leap for which Shildrick calls: she will not reach out and touch Cath (*Habitat* 8), will not confront her own fear of the connection such a touch would imply. For Shildrick, thinking through the work of Maurice Merleau-Ponty, the reversibility of touch,[4] of skin against skin, marks a crucial moment of crossover between bodies, when the doubleness of sensation muddles the question of precisely where I end and you begin (see also Shildrick and Price), but this "chiasmatic relation to the other does not imply a merging in which all sense of self is forfeit, but rather *a space of holding together* in which radical difference replaces pale reflection" (Shildrick 119, emphasis added). This "space of holding together" re-imagines the gap between myself and another, myself and the person I "see" myself to be, peopled not just with the bodies of others to whom I am indelibly linked and with whom I share fragments of a world, but also with aspects of myself sensed in their own alterity: we all "hold together" in a space in which I can freely sense the limits of my bodily experience, and sense also the freedom those limits engender in the very fact of my recognizing them. The space-between as a space of shared touch makes room for me to reposition my body alongside the bodies of others, and to reframe the "lack-to-be" of my subjectivity as the limit that marks the beginning of another world (Irigaray, *i love to you* 41), a world of shared vulnerability and mutual risk we build together.

Irigaray, Oliver and Shildrick argue that the narratives of possession and abjection on which contemporary theories of subjec(tiva)tion pivot both fail to capture the material, phenomenal complexity of intersubjective relations (Shildrick 103) and, as a result, compromise our ethical responsibility to our others. Reclaiming the communicative, identity-forming power of touch is central to their work, as is theorizing the physical shape of the implied tactile relation. The resulting intercorporeal architectonic, based on the image of two bodies connected in their individuality, differentiated yet touching, serves as a physical model for "being-in-the-world-with-others" (Shildrick 108). Raine, trapped in Cath's room at the moment of Cath's failing breath, cannot find a way to be with her mother as her mother's world ends because she cannot bring herself to take the risks implied by Cath's ending, by her new, monstrous corporeality. But, as the above writers would teach us, fear of touching the "strange" is not what marks us as subjects; it is precisely what prevents us from *becoming* fully-fledged, ethically motivated subjects. (Inter)corporeality is the third term Irigaray, Oliver and Shildrick insert between "subject" and "object," "self" and "other," "same" and "different": it represents the radical alterity of physical bodies in space, so easily elided by theories of identity based on visual recognition and psychic assimilation, and it positions us all in relation to a set of shared obligations that are the glue that connects us in the space-between. For these writers, as well as for others working under the banner I have here termed "radical humanism,"[5] subjectivity cannot be acquired outside the encounter with our collective physical alterity, with the material fact of our different experiences of a shared embodiment, and with the responsibility to one another that shared embodiment, our mutual yet non-identical corporeality, occasions. When Raine fails to reach for her mother, she fails fully to embody her own self—and she sets the stage for a series of catastrophic failures that will culminate in a fire, a house destroyed, a *literal* gulf ripped through the fabric of a street that had believed itself a community.

Complicating the Material

As an intervention into the failure, and the promise, of an intercorporeal ethics, *Habitat* signifies foremost in the material. This marks something of a departure for Thompson; critics, too, have up to now been reluctant to engage too deeply with the material dimension of her plays. Although a social agon is central to her work, as many have pointed out, even those committed to exploring that agon tend finally toward psychoanalytic or spiritualized readings. Jen Harvie makes a salient comment in connection with her own choice to read the early plays through the lens of psychic fantasy: her reading, she explains, will endeavor to treat the "reality" of the plays "as something more than the purely material and obvious" (252). The "material," however, is neither "obvious" nor (as Margaret Shildrick would remind us) in any way "pure," and the genius of *Habitat*, as Cath and Raine's opening two-hander aptly demonstrates, lies in its ability to pose material relations, the stakes of our "being-in-the-world-with-others," precisely as a function of the vexed relationship of the material to the psychic (the Real to the Imaginary), a relationship determined in large part by choices we make based upon beliefs we have internalized about what constitutes proper subject-object relations. Just as in the foundational Thompson works of the 1980s, characters in *Habitat* patrol their borders and organize raids on one another's—only, this time, the borders are made of wood and stone, and the raids are a contravention of private property underwritten by legal guarantees. The play deftly dramatizes how this normalized intersubjective landscape manifests itself in the annexation, the privatization, and the commercialization of communal, lived spaces, and, now that space is an actual, rather than merely a latent, character in the drama, the effects our psychical impulses have on the shape of our lived experience can be explored in depth, and alternative relations may be modeled in that very space as a shift in the physical dynamic between characters.

For every character in this play private property operates as a manifestation of private trauma. The irate owners guard their land from the encroachment of the psycho-social underclass: everyone worries that the children at Lewis's home are messed up, perhaps even criminals, but they seem most dangerous in their lack of boundary-sense. Margaret protects her home as a storehouse of memories of her late husband, Ian; when Raine barges in, she assumes Raine is a thief but appears not to fear her. Instead, she transforms Raine into a mirror of her loss, appropriating Raine's memories of Cath as a version of her memories of Ian and her beliefs about motherhood (18-19). (Raine subsequently becomes a favourite of Margaret's because Margaret sees Raine as, at bottom, middle class: Raine isn't someone she needs to get to know, to encounter as different, because she is already a child Margaret could *imagine* rearing [36-37]). Sparkle and Lewis, meanwhile, regard the private homes on Mapleview Lanes as theirs for the taking, acting out long buried slights and wrongs they have felt at the hands of the upper classes (9-11; 29). There seems to be no room between "mine" and "yours" in this play: "ours" is a choice refused at each turn.

Yet it is not a choice unimaginable, and to find its first potent trace we need to return to Cath's hospital room at the top of act one. Raine, raging against the encroaching darkness, invokes a long-ago trauma, and the realist frame of the scene is suddenly broken as Cath and Raine fall into a trance to rehearse their shared memory of Raine's infant illness, "[t]hat Sunday night when I was a baby [...] when you tried to breast feed [and] I fell off your breast!" (6). Cath "*takes RAINE in her arms*" (6) as the narrative shifts to another hospital, where Raine is promptly torn from her mother's body, against which she has been lying, "breathing with" Cath and yet "dream[ing]" she is "drowning" (7). The intimacy and protection of the intercorporeal bond of mother and child is both shaken and made more acute by Raine's fall and Cath's late recognition of her illness, but when the two reach the hospital it is completely severed, their space of common breath and tactile comfort replaced by "nurses with gowns and with masks" and "all the needles inside [Raine] for breathing" (7). This is the moment when the communicative value of Cath and Raine's shared touch is lost, when the mutual vulnerability of two female bodies engaged in the reciprocal acts of breathing and nursing morphs into literal as well as figurative isolation, into life made sustainable only by the invasion of foreign objects, gloved hands, a refusal of intimacy masquerading as a modern standard of care. The doctors and nurses will not permit Cath to hold or breastfeed Raine because she might "lose" her (7): fearing the risk of contact with another's vulnerable body they protect Raine from her mother for her "own good," thus precipitating her supposedly necessary movement out of early childhood intercorporeal embodiment and into a mature separation marked as normative, desirable, healthy.[6]

The centrality of the mother-child bond as well as its deep ambivalence in Thompson's work has recently been remarked upon by Ric Knowles; it is often read as psychically significant (Nunn), or as broadly redemptive (Nunn, Toles, Harvie), but it is rarely engaged in its materiality. This critical elision is worth remarking, because the essential disruption of the physical bond between mother and child is something we assume as axiomatic in the West, something we remark upon frequently enough but rarely engage at depth.[7] I am not arguing here for greater mother-child tactility; I am not a clinician and am not equipped to present evidence for or against such an argument. I am, however, suggesting that *Habitat* reflects, via its rough severing of Cath's physical bond with Raine at the top of the play and in the authoritative environment of a hospital, the sterile manner in which we, as a culture, choose to normalize our relations with our others and force the resulting divisions to assume prominence everywhere. The assumption that the isolation of the mirror-stage moment is either typical or inevitable is just that—an assumption. We *choose* to value isolation over connection; we are the authors of our own break with others, of the transformation of physical interdependence into something dirty, disgusting, hygienically as well as psychically unacceptable. Brecht-like, the disconnect of Cath and Raine's depressing opening exchange embeds its opposite: they perhaps cannot regain their lost intimacy, but their re-enactment suggests with telling force that the loss is by no means inevitable.

If the first scene of act one demonstrates the loss of an intimacy we can (perhaps) only dream of beyond early infancy, the final scene of act one models a radical connectivity in terms accessible to all post-natal humans. Echoing Cath and Raine, Lewis recounts the story of rushing his young brother to the hospital, carrying him miles through a winter snowstorm in his coat (46-47). He and his brother share the breath inside their fabric cocoon; his body keeps William's warm, alive, while William's warmth and breath remind Lewis that his numb legs have a purpose, an obligation. Their two bodies are quite literally conjoined, made stronger by their mutual incorporation for the duration of their difficult journey. Then, as Cath is from Raine, Lewis is severed from William when they arrive at the hospital; the nurses and doctors regard Lewis's presence as a distasteful liability and throw him out while they care for William (47). Nevertheless, it is the space of the journey—the space of shared breath and warmth forged by skin against skin, inside Lewis's coat—that gives this scene its primary dramatic force, and that is designed, I would argue, to be a model for the recognition of mutual vulnerability and the obligation to mutual care Mapleview Lanes is unable to imagine for itself in the main body of the action.

Lewis, too, must share the blame for this lack of imagination: he ultimately turns his and William's story into a fetish narrative of personal oppression that makes it impossible for him to recognize the critical differences between that early experience and the one in which he currently finds himself. The story is less his model than his mask: it distracts him from the individual needs of the children in his group home and makes it impossible for him to respect or appreciate the gestures of opening extended by Janet on behalf of the Mapleview owners at the top of act two. Acknowledging difference is an essential component of the space-between of radical humanism: only by acknowledging you in your specificity can I appreciate the nodes of connection between us; otherwise, I risk folding your experience into my own, cutting off your air.[8] For Lewis, difference is cruel and hateful, its valuation in any form heretical; his refusal to acknowledge the separate interests or individual needs of Janet, Margaret and the other owners ensures, ironically, that the home will fail, that no shared space may be forged between them, no place made for the "we" that results from the encounter with others respected in their alterity (Irigaray, *i love to you* 104).

***

> No one can hope to change the world without changing themselves. (Harvey 235)

Lewis is a deeply unsympathetic figure, not only because he may be a thief, but because he will not risk the "uncertainty" of "strange encounter" (Shildrick 7) that lies at the core of his own ethical investment in the group home. Lewis makes space for nobody; instead, he assimilates both friend and foe into his pre-existing worldview: all owners are bastards, and all his kids are a version of William. His refusal of encounter is, of course, mirrored in the similar refusal of most of the Mapleview owners, and forces us to wonder where, in (post)modern (sub)urban communities, we might generate a genuine relation of care, build a space-between that is more than a memory. The structure of middle-class residential neighbourhoods mirrors relations known to us through binary theories of subjectivity: they are "privatopias" (Harvey 239), fortresses of individualism knit together by our only reluctant acknowledgement of group interdependence. Yet, as Raine emerges to close the play, she suggests that such disconnection may be shifted by our simple willingness to make a different choice, to re-imagine our shared space under a different set of assumptions. Her final monologue recalls the electrified space of shared embodiment proposed by Shildrick, Oliver and Irigaray, as she transforms her traumatic memory of separation from her mother into the possibility of a lived, life-long, intercorporeal connection between her and her others, her past and her future. Raine dreams Cath into air, into the breath she constantly takes from and gives back to the world around her—into the element that, as Irigaray writes, both separates and connects us, makes in the flux and flow of its currents "a space for us between us" (*i love to you* 148). If *Habitat*'s first scene chronicles breath's failed exchange, foreshadowing the suffocation of its title's promise, this final scene offers its most promising argument: that the air between bodies is not a distance to be revered or to be eliminated; it is exactly what gives us life.

(2005)

Notes

1 The "Real" is Lacan's cryptic term for the inaccessible space beyond/before both Imaginary and Symbolic relations, where those conditions Symbolic relations are meant to mask—the absolute failure of our desire to achieve its object, the finitude of our lack-in-being, isolation (from our others as from ourselves) as an essential condition of subjectivity—come glaringly to light. Characterized by nostalgia as well as loss, the Real is at once a utopia and a house of human horrors. My use of the term here is determinedly ironic; as I hope will shortly become clear, while I am influenced by and often in sympathy with Lacan's teachings, I do not believe that the "reality" of our quotidian experience bears out his nightmarish vision of our founding isolation as a necessary condition of intersubjective relations. On the contrary: I believe our commitment as critics to the narrative of founding isolation is exactly what may prevent us from envisioning a new, more ethical psychical architecture.

2 Of the subject born in specular engagement with its imago, at an implied distance from itself.

3 The "space-between," although articulated through the writings of Bakhtin and in the context of his more general critique of generosity, is also central to Frank. See, for example, 114, 133, 140.

4 There is, as Shildrick herself notes, a potential problem with the lionization of touch, particularly in relation to the vulnerable self, as an alternative to the often oppressive metaphysic of sight: not all touch is benign. Touch, too, can be deeply distancing, just as, in Oliver's conception of sight, the visual becomes tactile, connective. My goal here is to draw attention to touch's potential as an alternate sensory basis on which to theorize subjective experience; for the purposes of this argument I assume a touch that is willingly reciprocal.

5 Traces of this "radical" humanism—which could also be termed "posthumanism" (Shildrick 120), or perhaps ethical humanism—can of course be found in writings concurrent with or even predating humanism itself. I use the term in part to emphasize a break from both the tenets of modern humanism (the other is, of course, a version of the self), and the tenets of its poststructural critics (the self has an irritating but more or less irrevocable tendency to recognize its other as a version of itself). In our political moment, it seems more vital than ever to theorize alterity through other possible relational models. For a compelling example from contemporary performance theory, see Dolan.

6 Arthur Frank's recent *Renewal of Generosity* offers a useful assessment of the need for a standard of care that makes room for doctors and patients to relate to one another in their shared vulnerability; his wealth of anecdotal and literary evidence suggests that modern medicine continues to fail to treat the subject

in the patient, preferring instead to objectify the ill in an attempt to maintain a safe and "professional" distance.

7 The current trend toward what the popular press has called "SUV strollers" makes an interesting example of this peculiar cultural blind spot. The strollers often come with removable seats that transfer to the car and house and, as one friend of mine remarked recently, could permit you to take your baby out for the day and back again without ever having to touch her.

8 "The power of a negative prevails between us. I recognize you goes hand in hand with: you are irreducible to me, just as I am to you. We may not be substituted for one another" (Irigaray, *i love to you* 103). Ironically, substitution is exactly what Lewis has in mind when he insists upon the children's "right" to call Mapleview Lanes "their" neighbourhood (*Habitat* 56): he prefers the possessive "their" to the inclusive "our", assuming that victory is a privileging of one group's rights over the other's, rather than the discovery of a middle ground where both might be accommodated.

Works Cited

Derrida, Jacques. *The Postcard: From Socrates to Freud and Beyond.* Trans. Alan Bass. Chicago and London: U of Chicago P, 1987.

Dolan, Jill. "'Finding Our Feet in the Shoes of (One An) Other': Multiple Character Solo Performers and Utopian Performatives." *Modern Drama* 45.4 (2002): 495-518.

———. "Performance, Utopia, and the 'Utopian Performative.'" *Theatre Journal* 53 (2001): 455-79.

Frank, Arthur W. *The Renewal of Generosity: Illness, Medicine, and How to Live.* Chicago: U of Chicago P, 2004.

Freud, Sigmund. *Beyond the Pleasure Principle.* 1920. Trans. and Ed. James Strachey. New York and London: Norton, 1961.

Harvey, David. *Spaces of Hope.* Edinburgh: Edinburgh UP, 2000.

Harvie, Jennifer. "(Im)Possibility: Fantasy and Judith Thompson's Drama." *On-Stage and Off-Stage: English Canadian Drama in Discourse.* Ed. Albert Reiner-Glaap with Rolf Althof. St. John's: Breakwater, 1996. 240-56.

Irigaray, Luce. "Belief Itself." *Sexes and Genealogies.* Trans. Gillian C. Gill. New York: Columbia UP, 1993. 23-53.

———. *i love to you: Sketch for a Felicity Within History.* Trans. Alison Martin. New York: Routledge, 1996.

Knowles, Ric. Introduction. "Reading Judith Thompson." *Judith Thompson: Late 20th Century Plays, 1980-2000.* Toronto: Playwrights Canada, 2003. iii-vi.

Nunn, Robert. "Spatial Metaphor in the Plays of Judith Thompson." *Theatre History in Canada/Histoire du théâtre au Canada* 10.1 (1989): 3-29.

Oliver, Kelly. *Witnessing: Beyond Recognition.* Minneapolis: U of Minnesota P, 2001.

Shildrick, Margrit. *Embodying the Monster: Encounters With the Vulnerable Self.* London: Sage, 2002.

Shildrick, Margrit, with Janet Price. "Thinking Through the Intercorporeal." Lecture. University College, University of Toronto. 20 Apr. 2004.

Thompson, Judith. *Habitat.* Toronto: Playwrights Canada, 2001.

Toles, George. "'Cause You're the Only One I Want': The Anatomy of Love in the Plays of Judith Thompson." *Canadian Literature* 118 (1988): 116-35.

Suggested Further Reading

Notes: A companion volume to this one including Judith Thompson's writings and interviews about her work, edited by Ric Knowles, will be published in Spring 2006 by Playwrights Canada Press. There is also a wealth of published and unpublished material available for consultation in the Judith Thompson Collection and the Tarragon Theatre collections at the Theatre Archives at the University of Guelph Library.

Published Writings by Judith Thompson on her work

"Epilepsy and the Snake: Fear in the Creative Process." *Canadian Theatre Review* 89 (Winter 1996): 4-7.

"It's My Birthday Forever Now: Urjo Kareda and Me." *Canadian Theatre Review* 113 (Winter 2003): 11-14.

"I Will Tear You to Pieces." *How Theatre Educates: Convergences and Counterpoints With Artists, Scholars and Advocates.* Ed. Kathleen Gallagher and David Booth. Toronto: U of Toronto P, 2003. 25-34.

"Mouthful of Pearls." *The Monkey and Other Stories.* Ed. Griffin Ondaatje. Toronto: Harper Collins, 1995. 209-17.

"No Soy Culpable." *Writing Away: The PEN Canada Travel Anthology.* Ed. Constance Rooke. Toronto: McClelland and Stewart, 1994. 307-16.

"One Twelfth." *Language in Her Eye: Visions on Writing Gender by Canadian Women Writing in English.* Ed. Libby Scheier Sarah Sheard, and Eleanor Wachtel. Toronto: Coach House, 1990. 263-67.

"Second Thoughts (What I'd Be If I Were Not A Playwright)." *Brick* 51 (Winter 1995): 26-29.

"Why Should a Playwright Direct Her Own Plays?" *Women on the Canadian Stage: The Legacy of Hrotsvit.* Ed. Rita Much. Winnipeg: Blizzard, 1992. 104-08.

"The World Made Flesh: Women and Theatre." *The Death of the Playwright? Modern British Drama and Literary Theory.* Ed. Adrian Page. Basingstoke: MacMillan, 1992. 24-42.

Interviews and Panels

Fletcher, Jennifer. "The Last Things in the Sled: An Interview with Judith Thompson." *Canadian Theatre Review* 89 (Winter 1996): 39-41.

Knowles, Richard Paul. "Computers Keep Your Office Tidier: An Interview with Judith Thompson." *Canadian Theatre Review* 81 (Winter 1994): 29-31.

Peerbaye, Soraya. "Look to the Lady: Re-examining Women's Theatre (Six Women in a Roundtable Discussion)." *Canadian Theatre Review* 84 (Fall 1995): 22-25.

Read, Robyn. "Witnessing the Workshop Process of Judith Thompson's *Capture Me*: Mothers, Masks and Monsters: A Conversation Between Teacher and Student." *Canadian Theatre Review* 120 (Fall 2004): 96-100.

"Revisions: Offending your Audience (Panel Discussion)." *Theatrum* 29 (June/July/August 1992): 33-34.

Rudakoff, Judith. "Judith Thompson: Interview." *Fair Play: 12 Women Speak (Conversations with Canadian Playwrights)*. Ed. Judith Rudakoff and Rita Much. Toronto: Simon & Pierre, 1990. 88-104.

"Turning an Elephant into a Microphone: A Conversation on Translation and Adaptation." *Canadian Theatre Review* 114 (Spring 2003): 47-53.

Tomc, Sandra. "Revisions of Probability: An Interview with Judith Thompson." *Canadian Theatre Review* 59 (Summer 1989): 18-23.

Wachtel, Eleanor. "An Interview with Judith Thompson." *Brick* 41 (Summer 1991): 37-41.

Zimmerman, Cynthia. "A Conversation with Judith Thompson." *Canadian Drama* 16.2 (1990): 184-94.

Secondary Sources

Bennett, Susan. "Who Speaks? Representations of Native Women in Some Canadian Plays." *Canadian Journal of Drama and Theatre* 1.2 (1991): 13-25.

Bessai, Diane. "Women Dramatists: Sharon Pollock and Judith Thompson." *Post-Colonial English Drama: Commonwealth Drama since 1960*. Ed. Bruce King. London: Macmillan, 1992. 97-117.

Campbell, Gregor. Introduction. Judith Thompson. *Perfect Pie*. Toronto: Playwrights Canada, 1999. [iii-v].

Canadian Theatre Review: Judith Thompson 89 (Winter 1996).

Cooper, Douglas. "The Soul in the Cartoon." *The Idler* 24 (July/August 1989): 61-62.

Duchesne, Scott. "Our Country's Good: The Export Market Favours Walker, Tremblay and Thompson." *Theatrum* 38 (April/May 1994): 19-23.

Duchesne, Scott and Jennifer Fletcher. "*Sled*: A Workshop Diary." *Canadian Theatre Review* 89 (Winter 1996): 33-38.

Filewod, Alan. "Critical Mass: Assigning Value and Place in Canadian Drama." *On-stage and off-stage: English Canadian Drama in Discourse.* Ed. Albert-Reiner Glaap and Rolf Althof. St. John's, Nfld: Breakwater, 1996. 32-50.

Gilbert, Helen. Afterword. *Judith Thompson: Late 20th Century Plays, 1980-2000.* Toronto: Playwrights Canada, 2002. 493-95.

Glaap, Albert Reiner. "Anguished Human Relations and the Search for Love: Plays by Canadian Writers Brad Fraser, Judith Thompson and Dianne Warren; Papers Given on the Occasion of the Sixth Annual Conference of the German Society for Contemporary Theatre and Drama in English." *Anthropological Perspectives.* Trier, Germany: Wissenschaftlicher, 1998. 109-19.

Glassman, Marc. "Judith Thompson." *Canadian Screenwriter Magazine* (Fall 2001). 4 November 2004 <http://www.writersguildofcanada.com/magazine/articles/thompson.html>

Hall, Sharon K., Ed. "Judith Thompson." *Contemporary Literary Criticism Yearbook 1985.* Detroit: Gale, 1986. 250-53.

Harvie, Jennifer. "(Im)Possibility: Fantasy and Judith Thompson's Drama." *On-stage and Off-stage: English Canadian Drama in Discourse.* Ed. Albert-Reiner Glaap and Rolf Althof. St John's, Nfld: Breakwater, 1996. 240-56.

Herst, Beth. "Clare Coulter: Notes from Underground." *American Theatre* 16 (April 1999): 43-44.

Hunt, Nigel. "In Contact with the Dark: Judith Thompson's Plays are Composed of 'Collected Images' and her Mind is 'a screen door swinging between conscious and unconscious.'" *Books in Canada* 17, 2 (March 1988): 10-12.

Jansen, Ann. Introduction. *Airborne: Radio Plays by Women.* Winnipeg: Blizzard Publishing, 1991: vi-xix.

Kareda, Urjo. Introduction. *The Other Side of the Dark: Four Plays by Judith Thompson.* Toronto: Coach House, 1989. 9-13.

Knowles, Ric[hard Paul]. "The Achievement of Grace." *Brick* 41 (Summer 1991): 33-36.

———. "The Dramaturgy of the Perverse." *Theatre Research International* 17.3 (Fall 1992): 226-35.

———. "The Fractured Subject of Judith Thompson," Introduction. Judith Thompson. *Lion in the Streets.* Toronto: Coach House, 1992. 7-10.

———. "'Great Lines are a Dime a Dozen': Judith Thompson's Greatest Cuts." *Canadian Theatre Review* 89 (Winter 1996): 8-18.

———. "Reading Judith Thompson." Introduction. *Judith Thompson: Late 20th Century Plays, 1980-2000.* Toronto: Playwrights Canada, 2002. iii-vi.

———. "The Theatre of Form and the Production of Meaning: Contemporary Canadian Dramaturgies. Part I The Dramaturgical Inheritance: Versions and Perversions." *Australasian Drama Studies* 29 (October 1996): 43-56.

———. *The Theatre of Form and the Production of Meaning: Contemporary Canadian Dramaturgies.* Toronto: ECW, 1999. 49-52.

Lane, Harry. "Redefining the Comfort Zone: Nancy Palk, on Acting Judith Thompson." *Canadian Theatre Review* 89 (Winter 1996): 19-21.

Manguel, Alberto. "Stages of Youth: Four young playwrights lead the new generation of dramatists emerging on the Toronto stage." *T.O.* (November/ December 1984): 46-49.

Maufort, Marc. "Exploring 'The Other Side of the Dark:' Judith Thompson's Magic Realism." *Union in Partition.* Belgium: L3-Liege, Language and Literature, 1997. 191-200.

———. "Poetic Realism Reinvented: Canadian Women Playwrights and the Search for a new Theatrical Idiom." *Études Canadiennes* 42 (1997): 27-38.

———. *Transgressive Itineraries.* New York: Peter Lang, 2003: 27-41.

Nunn, Robert. "Canada Incognita: Has Quebec Theatre Discovered English Canadian Plays?" *Theatrum* 24 (June/July/August 1991): 14-19.

———. "Crackwalking: Judith Thompson's Marginal Characters." *Siting the Other: Revisions of Marginality in Australian and English-Canadian Drama.* Ed. Marc Maufort. New York: Peter Lang, 2001. 311-23.

———. "Strangers to Ourselves: Judith Thompson's *Sled.*" *Canadian Theatre Review* 89 (Winter 1996): 29-32.

Rudakoff, Judith. "Under the Goddess's Cloak: recalling the Wild, Engendering the Power." *Women on the Canadian Stage: The Legacy of Hrotsvit.* Ed. Rita Much. Winnipeg: Blizzard Press, 1992: 115-30.

Sinclair, Gregory J. "Live from Off-Stage: Playwrights Walker, Walmsley and Thompson Shout from the Street." *Canadian Forum* 66 (August/September 1986): 6-11.

Swan, Susan. "A Novel's Journey into Film." *Essays on Canadian Writing* 76 (Spring 2002): 46-50.

Tompkins, Joanne. "Canadian Theatre and Memorializing." *Canadian Theatre Review* 115 (Summer 2003): 5-11.

Turcott, Iris. Introduction. *Habitat.* Judith Thompson. Toronto: Playwrights Canada, 2001. [xiii].

Vowles, Andrew. "Inside Playwright Judith Thompson: Behind the Mask." *Guelph Alumnus: The University of Guelph Magazine* (Winter 1999): 20-25.

Walker, Craig Stewart. *The Buried Astrolabe: Canadian Dramatic Imagination and Western Tradition.* Montreal: Queen's UP, 2001: 355-411.

Wasserman, Jerry. "It's the Do-Gooders Burn My Ass." *Modern Drama* (43:1) 2000: 32-47.

———. "Judith Thompson. Introduction to *Lion in the Streets.*" *Modern Canadian Plays.* 4th Ed. Ed. Jerry Wasserman. Vancouver: Talonbooks, 2000. 257-59.

Wilson, Ann. "'Crowding Round Her': Violence and Female Subjectivity." Afterword. Judith Thompson. *Sled.* Toronto: Playwrights Canada, 1997. 125-30.

———. "The Culture of Abuse in *Under the Skin, This is For You, Anna,* and *Lion in the Streets.*" *Contemporary Issues in Canadian Drama.* Ed. Per Brask. Winnipeg: Blizzard, 1995. 160-70.

———. "Canadian Grotesque." *Canadian Theatre Review* 89 (Winter 1996): 25-28.

Zimmerman, Cynthia. "Judith Thompson: Voices in the Dark." *Playwriting Women: Female Voices in English Canada.* Toronto: Simon & Pierre, 1994. 176-209.

Notes on Contributors

Julie Adam has taught Canadian drama and theatre history at the University of Toronto. She is author of *Versions of Heroism in Modern American Drama* and numerous articles in *Modern Drama, Canadian Theatre Review* and *New Theatre Quarterly*, among others. In the early 90s, she served as dramaturge for Toronto's Horizontal Eight theatre company.

Claudia Barnett teaches drama and playwriting at Middle Tennessee State University. Her essays on women playwrights have appeared in *Modern Drama, Theatre Journal, Canadian Theatre Review*, and *TDR*. She is currently writing a play set in Manhattan in 1642-43.

Penny Farfan is Associate Professor of Drama and English at the University of Calgary. She has written many articles on modern and contemporary theatre and drama, and her book *Women, Modernism, and Performance* was published by Cambridge University Press in 2004.

Sherrill Grace, Professor of English at the University of British Columbia, holds the Brenda and David Mclean Chair in Canadian Studies, 2003-05. She has published extensively on 20th century and Canadian literature, culture and theatre, and is writing a biography of Sharon Pollock.

Jen Harvie lectures in Drama at Queen Mary, University of London. Her books, *Staging the UK* (Manchester University Press) and *The Routledge Companion to Theatre and Performance* (with Paul Allain), are forthcoming in 2005.

Ric Knowles is Professor of Drama at the University of Guelph. He is author of *The Theatre of Form and the Production of Meaning, Shakespeare and Canada*, and *Reading the Material Theatre*, editor of *Theatre in Atlantic Canada*, and co-editor of *Staging Coyote's Dream: An Anthology of First Nations Drama in English* (with Monique Mojica) and *Modern Drama: Defining the Field* (with Joanne Tompkins and W.B. Worthen). He is Editor of the journals *Modern Drama* and *Canadian Theatre Review*.

Laura Levin: is a Ph.D. Candidate in Performance Studies at the University of California, Berkeley. Her research, which has been funded by a Canada-U.S. Fulbright, explores alternative imaginings of space in contemporary North American performance. She is currently co-editing a special issue of *Theatre Research in Canada* on space and subjectivity in Canadian theatre. The oral version of her essay in this volume was awarded the Robert G. Lawrence Prize from the Association for Canadian Theatre Research. She has directed a number of productions, including *Signs of Life*, *Charming and Rose*, *Never Swim Alone*, and most recently, the U.S. premiere of *Tooth and Nail*, a play by South Africa's Junction Avenue Theatre Company.

Robert Nunn was, until his retirement, a Professor in the Department of Fine Arts at Brock University. He is the author of a number of articles on Canadian drama and dramatists, two of which received the Richard Plant Essay Prize. He is on the editorial board of *Theatre Research in Canada/Recherches théâtrales au Canada* and *Essays in Theatre/Études théâtrales*. He is now editing a collection of essays on the plays of Drew Hayden Taylor for Guernica.

Robyn Read is a recent graduate of the Master's Program in English at the University of Guelph. Her work on mothers and monsters in Judith Thompson's *Capture Me* was presented at the Association of Canadian Theatre Research and published in *Canadian Theatre Review* and *Theatre Research in Canada*. Her creative writing has appeared in *Echolocation* and *Carousel* and was presented at *FemFest*.

Dalbir Singh is a recent graduate of the Master's Program in Drama at the University of Guelph. His creative work has appeared in *She Speaks*, an anthology of monologues edited by Judith Thompson published by Playwrights Canada Press, and his latest play, entitled *Your Palace in the Sky: The Bombing of Air India Flight #182*, will be produced by Buddies in Bad Times Theatre in the summer of 2005.

Kim Solga is Assistant Professor of English at the University of Western Ontario. She is currently working on a book-length project entitled "Imagined Spaces: Architectures of Feminist Performance."

George Toles is Professor of English and Chair of Film Studies at the University of Manitoba. He is the author of *A House Made of Light: Essays on the Art of Film*. He has been a frequent collaborator with film director Guy Maddin, most recently on the screenplay for *The Saddest Music in the World*. He has directed university productions of two Judith Thompson plays discussed in the essay reprinted here: *White Biting Dog* and *I Am Yours*.

Craig Walker is Professor of Drama at Queen's University and Artistic Director of Theatre Kingston. He is the author of *The Buried Astrolabe: Canadian Dramatic Imagination and Western Tradition* (McGill-Queen's, 2001) and co-editor, with Jennifer Wise, of *The Broadview Anthology of Drama* (Broadview, 2003).

CPSIA information can be obtained
at www.ICGtesting.com
Printed in the USA
LVOW08s0917010817
543329LV00014B/108/P